THE BEAST
OF REVELATION

Other books by Kenneth L. Gentry, Jr.

The Christian Case Against Abortion, 1982
The Christian and Alcoholic Beverages, 1986
The Charismatic Gift of Prophecy: A Reformed Analysis, 1986
Before Jerusalem Fell: Dating the Book of Revelation, 1989

THE BEAST
OF REVELATION

Kenneth L. Gentry, Jr.

Institute for Christian Economics
Tyler, Texas

Published by the Institute for Christian Economics

Distributed by Dominion Press, Fort Worth, Texas

Typesetting by Nhung Pham Nguyen

Printed in the United States of America

ISBN 0-930464-21-4

Dedicated to the

**Congregation of the
Reedy River Presbyterian Church**

which "endured to the end"
through the several years of studies in
Revelation that led to the writing of this book

TABLE OF CONTENTS

PUBLISHER'S PREFACE
by Gary North

I will raise them up a Prophet from among their brethren, like unto thee, and will put my words in his mouth; and he shall speak unto them all that I shall command him. And it shall come to pass, that whosoever will not hearken unto my words which he shall speak in my name, I will require it of him. But the prophet, which shall presume to speak a word in my name, which I have not commanded him to speak, or that shall speak in the name of other gods, even that prophet shall die. And if thou say in thine heart, How shall we know the word which the LORD hath not spoken? When a prophet speaketh in the name of the LORD, if the thing follow not, nor come to pass, that is the thing which the LORD hath not spoken, but the prophet hath spoken it presumptuously: thou shalt not be afraid of him (Deut. 18:18-22).

"Oh, boy! A new book on Bible prophecy!" It certainly is. But it is not a book about the future. It does not make any predictions. It is not about Christian eschatology: "the doctrine of last things."

This statement may initially confuse people. How can a book be about Bible prophecy but not be about eschatology? Easy. For example, a book on the subject of Old Testament prophecies regarding the coming of Jesus the Messiah can certainly be about prophecy yet not be about eschatology. "Yes, yes," you may be thinking, "but what about a book on New Testament prophecy? Surely it has to be about the future. There was nothing of prophetic significance that took place in between the New Testament authors and today." But there was: *the fall of Jerusalem to the Roman army in A.D. 70.* That historic event was clearly prophesied by Jesus

(Luke 21:20-24), yet it took place long ago. It took place after the New Testament writings were finished but long before you or I appeared on the scene.

The fact is, the vast majority of prophecies in the New Testament refer to this crucial event, the event which publicly identified the transition from the Old Covenant to the New Covenant, and which also marked the triumph of rabbinic Judaism over priestly Judaism, Pharisee over Sadducee,[1] and the synagogue system over the temple. So central was the destruction of the temple to the future of both Christianity and Judaism that Jesus linked it symbolically to His death and resurrection:

> Then answered the Jews and said unto him, What sign shewest thou unto us, seeing that thou doest these things? Jesus answered and said unto them, Destroy this temple, and in three days I will raise it up. Then said the Jews, Forty and six years was this temple in building, and wilt thou rear it up in three days? But he spake of the temple of his body (John 2:18-21).

Dating The Book of Revelation

"But," you may be thinking to yourself, "John wrote the Book of Revelation (the Apocalypse) in A.D. 96. Everyone agrees on

---

1. The Sadducee sect of Judaism disappeared, since it had been associated with the priests who officiated at the temple. Herbert Danby, whose English translation of the Mishnah is still considered authoritative by the scholarly world, both Jew and gentile, commented on the undisputed triumph of Pharisaism after the fall of Jerusalem (which lives on as Orthodox Judaism). "Until the destruction of the Second Temple in A.D. 70 they had counted as one only among the schools of thought which played a part in Jewish national and religious life; after the Destruction they took the position, naturally and almost immediately, of sole and undisputed leaders of such Jewish life as survived. Judaism as it has continued since is, if not their creation, at least a faith and a religious institution largely of their fashioning; and the Mishnah is the authoritative record of their labour. Thus it comes about that while Judaism and Christianity alike venerate the Old Testament as canonical Scripture, the Mishnah marks the passage to Judaism as definitely as the New Testament marks the passage to Christianity." Herbert Danby, "Introduction," *The Mishnah* (New York: Oxford University Press, [1933] 1987), p. xiii. The Mishnah is the written version of the Jews' oral tradition, while the rabbis' comments on it are called Gemara. The Talmud contains both Mishnah and Gemara. See also R. Travers Herford, *The Pharisees* (London: George Allen & Unwin, 1924).

this. Thus, John could not have been prophesying events associated with the fall of Jerusalem, an event that had taken place a quarter of a century earlier." This is the argument of Dallas Theological Seminary professor Wayne House and Pastor Tommy Ice in their theologically creative but highly precarious revision of traditional dispensationalism.[2] It is also the intellectual strategy taken by best-selling dispensational author Dave Hunt, who writes in his recent defense of Christian cultural surrender to humanism that "the Book of Revelation was written at least 20 years after A.D. 70, most likely about A.D. 96. This one fact destroys this entire theory" about the fall of Jerusalem being the prophesied event that many today call the Great Tribulation.[3] But like so much of what Dave Hunt has written,[4] this "fact" is not a fact. John did not write the Book of Revelation in A.D. 96.

When did John write the Book of Revelation? This technical academic question must be answered accurately if we are ever to make sense of New Testament prophecy. Establishing the date of John's Apocalypse and the events that followed within a few months of this revelation is what *The Beast of Revelation* is all about, as is Dr. Gentry's larger and far more detailed study, *Before Jerusalem Fell: Dating the Book of Revelation* (Institute for Christian Economics, 1989). If his thesis is correct, then the "last days" are not ahead of us; they are long behind us. And if the "last days" are behind us, then all "futurism" — dispensationalism, most contemporary non-dispensational premillennialism, and the more popular forms of amillennialism — is dead wrong. Anyone who says that "dark days are ahead of the church because the Man of Sin is surely coming" is a futurist.[5] Thus, this book is not simply an

---

2. H. Wayne House and Thomas D. Ice, *Dominion Theology: Curse or Blessing?* (Portland, Oregon: Multnomah, 1988), pp. 249-60.

3. Dave Hunt, *Whatever Happened to Heaven?* (Eugene, Oregon: Harvest House, 1988), p. 249.

4. Gary DeMar and Peter J. Leithart, *The Reduction of Christianity: A Biblical Response to Dave Hunt* (Ft. Worth, Texas: Dominion Press, 1988).

5. The other positions are idealism, the church historical approach, and preterism. The first view does not try to tie the prophecies to any particular post-New

obscure academic exercise. If futurists prove incapable of refuting it and its larger companion volume, they have surrendered their intellectual position.

Silence in the Face of Criticism Is Suicidal

It is my opinion that they will prove incapable of refuting Gentry's evidence. It is my opinion that dispensationalists will not even try; they will instead adopt the traditional academic strategy that dispensational seminary professors have used for over half a century to deal with any book that challenges their system: "Let's keep quiet and pray that nobody in our camp finds out about this, especially our brighter students."

The best example of this keep-quiet-and-hope strategy is the unwillingness of any dispensational scholar to challenge post-millennialist Oswald T. Allis' comprehensive critique of dispensationalism, *Prophecy and the Church* (1945) for two decades.[6] Charles C. Ryrie's brief, popularly written, and intellectually undistinguished attempt to refute a carefully selected handful of Allis' arguments appeared in 1965: *Dispensationalism Today.*[7] The fact that this slim volume is still the primary defense of traditional (Dallas Seminary) dispensationalism, despite the fact that it has never been revised, testifies to the head-in-the-sand approach of the dispensationalist world to its Bible-believing critics. This dearth of intellectual defenses is especially noticeable today, given the fact of Dr. Ryrie's unexpected and somewhat acrimonious departure from the Dallas Seminary faculty several years ago. Another exam-

---

Testament event. The prophecies are seen as merely principles. Church historicism teaches that the Book of Revelation describes the course of history. This was the common view of the Reformation, in which all Protestant groups identified the Papacy as the antichrist. (This was the only universally agreed-upon specifically Protestant doctrine that united all Protestant groups.) The preterists are those who believe that most Bible prophecies had been fulfilled by the time Jerusalem fell, or at least by the time the Roman Empire was Christianized. This is my view, Gentry's, and Chilton's.

6. Phillipsburg, New Jersey: Presbyterian & Reformed.

7. Chicago: Moody Press.

ple is their silence regarding William Everett Bell's 1967 New York University doctoral dissertation, "A Critical Evaluation of the Pretribulation Rapture Doctrine in Christian Eschatology," which has been reprinted by Bell. Major books deserve full-scale refutations in books, not simply brief negative book reviews in the in-house, small-circulation journal. Any philosophical, theological, or ideological system that is not defended intellectually and publicly by its academic spokesmen, decade after decade, despite a growing mountain of cogent criticisms, is close to the end of its influence. Its brighter, younger recruits will drift away or else be recruited by the critics. Eventually, the defending institutions will drift theologically, as formerly dispensational Talbot Theological Seminary did after 1986. A defensive mentality, a "form a circle with the wagons" mentality, cannot be sustained forever. If a movement does not move forward, it either stagnates or moves backward culturally. If a movement adopts a view of time which says that cultural progress in term's of the movement's worldview is unsustainable, and that only "upward" movement or "inward" movenent is truly significant, then the movement has drunk the eschatological equivalent of Jim Jones' Kool-Aid. This analytic principle applies equally well to the New Age mystic's quest for inner escape or the dispensationalist's rapture fever. This is why dispensationalism is dying.

Bible-believing Christians need an alternative.[8]

The Last Days

This book is about the last days. It is not about the end times. The last days are different from the end times. The last days are not in the present or in the future; they are in the past. Still confused? So are millions of other Christians. The confusion stems from the fact that Christians have jumped to the conclusion – a wholly erroneous conclusion – that the "last days" spoken of in the New Testament refer to the last days of the church (or to the

---

8 Gary North, *Unconditional Surrender: God's Program for Victory* (3rd ed.; Tyler, Texas: Institute for Christian Economics, 1988).

misleadingly identified "Church Age"). This conclusion is not warranted by the various biblical texts. *The last days spoken of in the New Testament were eschatological last days only for national Israel, not for the New Covenant church.* The "last days" were in fact the early days of the church of Jesus Christ.

How do we know this? How do we know that we are not now living in the last days and never will be? How do we know that the New Testament was written in the last days, which came to a close over 1,900 years ago? Because the New Testament clearly says so. The author of the Epistle to the Hebrews specifically identified his own era as the "last days." He wrote that God "Hath *in these last days* spoken unto us by his Son, whom he hath appointed heir of all things, by whom also he made the worlds" (Heb. 1:2). He was quite clear: he and his contemporaries were living in the last days.

The Destruction of the Temple

So, we need to ask this obvious question: The last days of what? The answer is clear: *the last days of the Old Covenant, including national Israel.* The New Testament writers were living in *the last days of animal sacrifices in the temple.* This is the primary message of the Epistle to the Hebrews: the coming of a better sacrifice, a once-and-for-all sacrifice, Jesus Christ. We read: "And for this cause he is the mediator of the new testament, that by means of death, for the redemption of the transgressions that were under the first testament, they which are called might receive the promise of eternal inheritance. For where a testament is, there must also of necessity be the death of the testator" (Heb. 9:15-16). The inescapable concomitant of Jesus' sacrifice at Calvary was His annulment of the Old Covenant's sacrificial system:

> And almost all things are by the law purged with blood; and without shedding of blood is no remission. It was therefore necessary that the patterns of things in the heavens should be purified with these; but the heavenly things themselves with better sacrifices than these. For Christ is not entered into the holy places made with hands, which are the figures of the true; but into heaven itself, now to appear in the presence of God for us: Nor yet that he should offer

himself often, as the high priest entereth into the holy place every year with blood of others; For then must he often have suffered since the foundation of the world: but now once *in the end of the world* hath he appeared to put away sin by the sacrifice of himself. And as it is appointed unto men once to die, but after this the judgment: So Christ was once offered to bear the sins of many; and unto them that look for him shall he appear the second time without sin unto salvation. For the law having a shadow of good things to come, and not the very image of the things, can never with those sacrifices which they offered year by year continually make the comers thereunto perfect. For then would they not have ceased to be offered? Because that the worshippers once purged should have had no more conscience of sins. But in those sacrifices there is a remembrance again made of sins every year. For it is not possible that the blood of bulls and of goats should take away sins. Wherefore when he cometh into the world, he saith, Sacrifice and offering thou wouldest not, but a body hast thou prepared me: In burnt offerings and sacrifices for sin thou hast had no pleasure (Heb. 9:22-10:7).

Notice the key phrase: "in the end of the world." In the original Greek, it reads: "completion of the ages." This phrase must be taken literally, but its literal frame of reference was the fall of Jerusalem and the annulment of the temple's sacrificial system. The author was therefore prophesying the imminent end of national Israel as God's covenant people.[9]

The leaders of national Israel had refused to believe Jesus. Subsequently, they refused to believe the message of the apostles. They did not admit to themselves the truth of what the New Testament message announced, namely, that *God has no permanent pleasure in burnt animal offerings.* This had been the message of the Old Covenant, too, and their religious predecessors had paid no

9. Romans 11 teaches that Israel as a separate corporate people will be converted to Christ at some point in the future. On this point, one denied by virtually all amillennial commentators, see the postmillennial commentaries by Robert Haldane, Charles Hodge, and John Murray. Nevertheless, the Jews will regain their status as a covenant people only through adoption into the church, just as all sinners do. They will not be treated by God differently from any other covenanted people.

attention: "For I desired mercy, and not sacrifice; and the knowledge of God more than burnt offerings" (Hos. 6:6). The New Testament authors declared that God would soon bring an end to these futile and misleading animal sacrifices, *never to be restored.*[10] They understood that they were living in the last days of the Old Covenant era, and they warned their readers of this fact. This, in fact, is the primary message of the Book of Revelation.[11]

So, the New Testament authors did write about prophecy, but most (though not all) of their prophetic messages dealt with the immediate fate and future of national Israel. Thus, when they wrote prophetically, they wrote primarily about *Israel's near-term eschatology* (last days), not the church's long-term eschatology (end times). They were writing prophetic warnings to people of their own era regarding crises that were almost upon them, not crises of Christians and Jews living at least 1,900 years later.

Let me ask an obvious question, which futurists never publicly ask: If your church were in the early stages of a life-and-death

---

10. Traditional dispensationalism teaches that the temple will be rebuilt and animal sacrifices will be restored for a thousand years, even though only as a "memorial," as C. I. Scofield says in his reference note on Ezekiel 43:19. *The Scofield Reference Bible* (New York: Oxford University Press, 1909), p. 890. The embarrassment of the *New Scofield Bible's* revision committee is apparent in the note that this prophecy of restored sacrifices can be explained either in terms of the "memorial" thesis (which they strategically refuse to identify as Scofield's original view) or as figurative — a startling suggestion from theologians who proclaim that dispensationalism's principle of interpretation is "literal whenever possible" (i.e., "literal whenever convenient"). *The New Scofield Bible* (New York: Oxford University Press, 1967), p. 888. If the temple is to be rebuilt for use during the New Testament's millennium — a dispensational doctrine which the revision committee did not dare to challenge — then for what other purpose would the temple be used except for offering animal sacrifices? As a tourist attraction? Thus, if the rebuilt temple of Ezekiel 43 is a prophecy referring to a New Testament era millennium rather than to the rebuilt temple of Nehemiah's day, itself a prophetic symbol of worship in the worldwide church — which is my view — then the re-establishment animal sacrifices cannot sensibly be regarded as figurative. But the theological implications of this re-established animal sacrifice system were too embarrassing for the Scofield revision committee to handle forthrightly. They fudged.

11. David Chilton, *The Days of Vengeance: An Exposition of the Book of Revelation* (Ft. Worth: Dominion Press, 1987).

crisis — the public execution of the church's founder — and he gave you a warning regarding problems that would face Christians two thousand years from now, would you regard his warning as timely, fully rational, and relevant to your immediate needs? Would you regard this warning as being of crucial importance to your daily walk before God or the life of the local church? No? Neither would I. *Neither would Jesus' listeners.* Therefore, I conclude that the immediacy of the disciples' concern was why Jesus warned them of the coming tribulation of national Israel: "Now learn a parable of the fig tree; When his branch is yet tender, and putteth forth leaves, ye know that summer is nigh: So likewise ye, when ye shall see all these things, know that it is near, even at the doors. Verily I say unto you, This generation shall not pass, till all these things be fulfilled" (Matt. 24:32-34).

Another question: If that hypothetical warning from the founder referred to events that will be seen by "this generation," would you instinctively conclude — as all dispensational expositors of this verse have concluded and must conclude, given their need a coherent system of interpretation — that the phrase "this generation" refers to some generation living at least 1,950 years later? No? Then why not take Jesus' words literally? "Verily I say unto you, This generation shall not pass, till all these things be fulfilled."

All of these things *were* fulfilled. In A.D. 70.

But What About the Beast?

Well, what about the beast? If my thesis is correct — that the phrase "the last days" refers to the last days of Old Covenant Israel and the destruction of the temple in A.D. 70 — then who was the beast? After all, if New Testament prophecies regarding the beast were not fulfilled during the lifetime of John, but refer to some individual still in the church's future, there would seem to be no reason to believe that the other prophecies regarding "the last days" were also fulfilled in his day. These prophecies must be taken as a unit. It is clear that the beast is a figure who is said to be alive in the last days. This is why it is imperative that we discover who the beast is or was. If he has not yet appeared, then the last days must also be ahead of us, unless we have actually entered into them. If he has already appeared, then the last days are over.

This book identifies the prophesied beast beyond any reasonable doubt. This much I will tell you now: it is not Henry Kissinger.

If all of the potential buyers of *The Beast of Revelation* were to discover in advance that it is not filled with prophecies about brain-implanted computer chips, tatoos with identification numbers, cobra helicopters, nuclear war, and New Age conspiracies, most of them would not buy it. Customers of most Christian bookstores too often prefer to be excited by the misinformation provided by a string of paperback false prophecies than to be comforted by the knowledge that the so-called Great Tribulation is long behind us, and that it was Israel's tribulation, not the church's. (For biblical proof, see David Chilton's book, *The Great Tribulation*.)[12] They want thrills and chills, not accurate Bible exposition; they want a string of "secret insights," not historical knowledge. Like legions of imaginative children sitting in front of the family radio back in the 1930's and 1940's who faithfully bought their Ovaltine, tore off the wrapper, and sent it in to receive an official "Little Orphan Annie secret decoder," fundamentalist Christians are repeatedly lured by the tempting promise that they can be "the first ones on their block" to be "on the inside" – to be the early recipients of the "inside dope." And that is just exactly what they have been sold, decade after decade.

Nine-year-old children were not totally deceived in 1938. They knew the difference between real life and make-believe. Make-believe was thrilling; it was fun; it was inexpensive; but it was not real. The decoded make-believe secrets turned out to provide only fleeting excitement, but at least they could drink the Ovaltine. Furthermore, children eventually grow up, grow tired of Ovaltine, and stop ordering secret decoders.

---

12. David Chilton, *The Great Tribulation* (Ft. Worth, Texas: Dominion Press, 1987).

When will Christians grow up? When will they grow tired of an endless stream of the paperback equivalent of secret decoders? When will they be able to say of themselves as Paul said of himself: "When I was a child, I spake as a child, I understood as a child, I thought as a child: but when I became a man, I put away childish things" (I Cor. 13:11).

False Prophecies for Fun and Profit

Those Christians who believe that we are drawing close to the last days are continually trying to identify both the beast and the antichrist. This game of "find the beast and identify the antichrist" has become the adult Christians' version of the child's game of pin the tail on the donkey. Every few years, the participants place blindfolds over their eyes, turn around six times, and march toward the wall. Sometimes they march out the door and over a cliff, as was the case with Edgar C. Whisenant, whose best-selling two-part book announced in the summer of 1988 that Jesus would surely appear to rapture His church during Rosh Hashanah week in mid-September. Half the book was called *On Borrowed Time*. The other was more aptly titled, *88 Reasons why the Rapture is in 1988*. I can think of one key argument why his book's thesis was incorrect: no rapture so far, and it is now February, 1989. So much for all 88 arguments. The anti-Christian world got another great laugh at the expense of millions of fundamentalists who had bought and read his two-part book. The story of Mr. Whisenant's book was front-page news briefly around the U.S. But Mr. Whisenant is now ancient history, one more forgotten laughingstock who brought reproach to the church of Jesus Christ while he piled up his press clippings.

This is the whole problem. The victims self-consciously forget the last self-proclaimed expert in Bible prophecy whose predictions did not come to pass. They never learn to recognize the next false prophet because they refuse to admit to themselves that they had been suckered by the last one. Thus, this sucker's game has been going on throughout the twentieth century, generation after generation, a pathetic story chronicled superbly by Dwight Wilson in his well-documented book, *Armageddon Now!*, a book that was not regularly assigned to students at Dallas Seminary, I can assure you.[13] Again and again, some prominent world political figure has been identified as either the beast or the antichrist: Lenin, Mussolini, Hitler, Stalin, and even Henry Kissinger.[14] (It was President Reagan's good fortune that he was a conservative so beloved by fundamentalists, given the remarkable structure of his name: Ronald [6] Wilson [6] Reagan [6].)

The back cover promotional copy of former best-selling author Salem Kirban's self-published book, *The Rise of Anti-Christ*, is representative of this paperback prophetic literature. Published in 1978, it boldly announced:

**We are already living in the
AGE OF ANTICHRIST!**

The world is on the threshold of catastrophe. Scientific advances are really scientific tragedies that will spell chaos, confusion and terror.

Within the next 5 years . . .
DESIGN YOUR OWN CHILD
by going to the "genetic supermarket."
YOUR MIND WILL BE PROGRAMMED
without your knowing it!

Within the next 10 years . . .
YOUR BRAIN WILL BE CONTROLLED
by outside sources!
YOUR MEMORY WILL BE TRANSFERRED
into a live embryo.

---

13. Dwight Wilson, *Armageddon Now! The Premillennial Response to Russia and Israel Since 1917* (Grand Rapids, Michigan: Baker Book House, 1977).

14. Salem Kirban, *Kissinger: Man of Peace?* (Huntington Valley, Pennsylvania: Salem Kirban Inc., 1974). As you might expect, this book is no longer in print. It sometimes appears in local library book sales for a dollar or less. If you spot it, buy it. It is a classic.

And so on. None of this has happened, of course. My favorite is this one: "HEAD TRANSPLANTS will become a reality." I wonder who will be the first two volunteers? Who will get what? This book is to Bible exposition what the *National Enquirer* is to journalism. (The trouble is, the *National Enquirer* sells 7 million copies each week; it is by far America's largest-circulation newspaper.)

If we take Mr. Kirban's words literally — as literally as he expects us to take the Bible — we are forced to conclude: "This man simply did not know what he was talking about when he wrote those predictions." But he sold a lot of books in the 1970's — 30 different titles on prophecy by 1978 alone, the back cover informs us, plus a huge study Bible, plus a comic book. By 1980, the total number of Mr. Kirban's book titles had soared to 35, according to back cover copy on *Countdown to Rapture* (published originally in 1977). He concluded on page 188 of this book:

> "Based on these observations, it is my considered opinion, that the time clock is now at
>
> **11:59**
>
> When is that Midnight hour . . . the hour of the Rapture? I do not know!"

He wisely avoided the mistake of putting a date on the rapture — a mistake that Mr. Whisenant made (assuming that the publicity and mailing list from well over four million books sold constitutes a mistake) — but his book was sufficiently explicit. Given the fact that the supposed "clock of prophecy" reached 11:56 in 1976, when the world's population passed 4 billion people (p. 45), and then reached 11:59 in only one year with the peace accord between Israel and Egypt in 1977 (p. 175), you get the general picture. Only "one minute" to go in 1977! The rapture will be soon!

Once again, however, pre-tribulational dispensationalism's notoriously unreliable "clock of prophecy" stopped without warning.[15]

---

15. Technically speaking, pretrib dispensationalism requires that the clock of prophecy not begin again until the rapture. But this kind of low-key view of prophecy

The years passed by. No beast. No antichrist. Few book sales. Scrap the topic! Try something else. Why not books on nutrition? Presto: Salem Kirban's *How Juices Restore Health Naturally* (1980). Oh, well. Better a glass of fresh carrot juice than another book on the imminent appearance of Jesus or the antichrist.

Nevertheless, a stopped "clock of prophecy" is always good news for the next wave of pop-dispensational authors: more chances to write new books about the beast, 666, and the antichrist. There are always more opportunities for a revival – a revival of book royalties. After all, a sucker is born every minute, even when the "clock of prophecy" has again ceased ticking. The next generation of false prophets can always draw another few inches along the baseline of their reprinted 1936 edition prophecy charts. They can buy some new springs for a rusted prophetic clock. These stopped clocks are a glut on the market about every ten years. Any fledgling prophecy expert can pick one up cheap. Clean it, install new springs, wind it, make a few modifications in a discarded prophecy chart, and you're in business! Example: as soon as Salem Kirban retired, Constance Cumbey appeared.

(I give little credence to the rumor that "Constance E. Cumbey" is the pen name adopted by Mr. Kirban in 1983. I also have real doubts about the rumor that the woman who claims to be Mrs. Cumbey is in fact a professional actress hired by Mr. Kirban to make occasional public appearances. Nevertheless, it is remarkable that Mr. Kirban's name appeared on no new books after 1982, the year before Mrs. Cumbey's *Hidden Dangers of the Rainbow* appeared. Could this be more than a coincidence? It is also strange that "Mrs. Cumbey" seems to have disappeared from public view ever since the second book with her name on it failed to make it into Christian bookstores. Is it possible that "Mrs. Cumbey" was fired by Mr. Kirban when the book royalties faded to a trickle and there was no further demand for her public appearances? I realize

---

sells few books. Thus, the dispensationalism known to most buyers of prophecy books is the dispensationalism of the ticking clock, however erratically it may tick.

that all this may sound a bit implausible to most people, but perhaps not to someone who has accepted the thesis of "Mrs. Cumbey's" *A Planned Deception: The Staging of a New Age "Messiah."* If a "Messiah" can be staged, so can a previously unknown lady researcher from Detroit. The "Messiah" has not yet appeared, and "Constance Cumbey" has now disappeared from public view. Messiahs apparently come and go without much warning — indeed, without ever even appearing in public; so do those who expose them, although this takes a bit longer.)

The main problem with this never-ending stream of utterly false but sensational interpretations of Bible prophecy is that sincere Christian readers are grievously misled by authors who seem to speak authoritatively in the name of the Bible. These writers write authoritatively about topics that they know little or nothing about, or who misrepresent whatever they do know about. It takes time for each prophecy fad to fade. Emotionally vulnerable Christians are warned repeatedly in the name of the Bible that inescapable cataclysmic events are imminent — "signs of the times" — yet these inevitable events never take place as predicted. This goes on decade after decade, generation after generation, although the self-appointed prophets keep changing.

Question: If the pre-tribulation rapture can come "at any moment," then how can there be any fulfilled prophecies to write about that take place in between the New Testament documents and the future rapture? How can there be any "prophetic signs of the times"? How can anyone who believes in the "any moment coming" of Jesus also believe some self-declared prophecy expert who announces that specific Bible prophecies are being fulfilled in our day? If any event is said to be a fulfilled Bible prophecy today — an event that absolutely had to take place, as all true Bible prophecies obviously must — then the rapture surely was not an "any moment rapture" prior to the fulfillment of the allegedly fulfilled prophecy. Some prophesied event therefore had to happen before the rapture could occur. This, obviously, is a denial of the doctrine of the "any moment coming" of Christ. This fact does not seem to deter any particular decade's reigning paperback prophets or their gullible disciples.

Once a particular prophecy expert's predictions begin to be perceived as being embarrassingly inaccurate, another expert appears with a new set of prophecies. Christians who become temporary followers of these false prophets become ominously similar to the misled women described by Paul: "For of this sort are they which creep into houses, and lead captive silly women laden with sins, led away with divers lusts, Ever learning, and never able to come to the knowledge of the truth" (II Tim. 3:6-7). Eventually, these frantic (or thrill-seeking) victims become unsure about what they should believe concerning the future. Everything sounds so terrifying. Christians become persuaded that personal forces beyond their control or the church's control — evil, demonic forces — are about to overwhelm all remaining traces of righteousness. How, after all, can the average Christian protect himself against mind control and memory transfer, let alone head transplants, assuming such things are both technically and culturally possible and imminent? (The fact that such things are not technically possible in the time period claimed for them never seems to occur to the buyers of paperback prophecy books.)

A steady stream of this sort of material tends to reduce the ability of Christians to reason coherently or make effective long-term decisions. Sensationalism becomes almost addictive. Sensationalism combined with culture-retreating pietism paralyzed the fundamentalist movement until, in the late 1970's, fundamentalism at last began to change. That transformation is nowhere near complete, but it surely has begun. Fundamentalists are at last beginning to rethink their eschatology. They are less subject to uncontrolled spasms produced by rapture fever. The back cover promotional copy on *Whatever Happened to Heaven?* reveals that Dave Hunt is aware of the fact that his version of pop-dispensationalism, like Hal Lindsey's, is fading rapidly. (Mr. Lindsey largely disappeared from public view about the time he married wife number three. Gone are the days of his guest appearances — and everyone else's — on "The Jim and Tammy Show." He does have a weekly radio show and a weekly satellite television show.) Hunt's promotional copy announces: "Today, a growing number of Christians are exchanging the hope for the rapture for a new hope . . . that Christians can clean up society. . . ." The promise — unfulfilled, I might add — of the back cover is that this book will show old fashioned dispensationalists "how we lost that hope [the rapture] and how it can be regained." The success of his books proves that there are still buyers of the old literature who love to be thrilled by new tales of the beast. This means, of course, that they do not want to hear about the biblical account of the beast of Revelation. They much prefer fantasy.

This Book Is About Hope

If the rapture is just around the corner, then the beast and the antichrist are in our midst already, preparing to take advantage of every opportunity to deceive, persecute, and tyrannize the world generally and Christians in particular. This would mean that all attempts by Christians to improve this world through the preaching of the gospel and obedience to God's Word are doomed. There would be insufficient time to reclaim anything from the jaws of inevitable eschatological defeat. This is precisely what dispensationalists believe, as I hope to demonstrate in this subsection.

Dave Hunt assures us that the cultural defeat of the church of Jesus Christ is inevitable. Our task is to escape this world, not change it. Those who teach otherwise, he says, "mistakenly believe that the church is in this world to eliminate evil, when in fact it is only here as God's instrument of restraint. It is not our job to transform this world but to call out of it those who will respond to the gospel."[16] In short, he views the church's work in this world in terms of his view of the church's only hope: *escape from the trials and tribulations of life.* We are to call men out of this world, spiritually speaking, so that Jesus will come back in the clouds and call

---

16. Hunt, *Whatever Happened to Heaven?*, pp. 268-69.

His church out of this world, literally speaking.[17]

His view is exactly the same as that of House and Ice, who make it plain that Christians are working the "night shift" in this world. (And we all know how far removed from the seats of influence all "night shift" people are!) They write: "The dawn is the Second Coming of Christ, which is why he is called the 'morning star' (2 Peter 1:19). Our job on the 'night shift' is clarified by Paul in Ephesians 5:1-14 when he says we are to expose evil (bring it to light), not conquer it. . . ."[18]

The Right Hand of Glory

This anti-dominion perspective conveniently ignores the "passage of passages" that dispensationalist authors do their best to avoid referring to, the Old Testament passage which is cited more times in the New Testament than any other, Psalm 110. What few church historians have recognized is that it was also the church fathers' most cited passage in the century after the fall of Jerusalem.[19] (Dispensationalists keep citing unnamed early church fathers in general for support of their thesis that the early church fathers were all premillennialists – an assertion disproved by one of their own disciples.)[20] Psalm 110 may be the dispensationalists' least favorite Bible passage, for good reason.

The LORD said unto my Lord, Sit thou at my right hand, until

---

17. For a Bible-based explanation of what "this world" means, see Greg L. Bahnsen, "The Person, Work, and Present Status of Satan," *Journal of Christian Reconstruction*, I (Winter 1974), pp. 20-30. See the extract I provide in my book, *Is the World Running Down? Crisis in the Christian Worldview* (Tyler, Texas: Institute for Christian Economics, 1988), pp. 220-22.

18. House and Ice, *Dominion Theology*, p. 172.

19. David Hay, *Glory at the Right Hand* (Nashville, Tennessee: Abingdon, 1973).

20. In a 1977 Dallas Seminary Th.M. thesis, Alan Patrick Boyd concluded that the early church fathers were both amillennial and premillennial, and he rejected then-Dallas professor Charles Ryrie's claim that the early church fathers were all premillennialists. Boyd, "A Dispensational Premillennial Analysis of the Eschatology of the Post-Apostolic Fathers (Until the Death of Justin Martyr)." Gary DeMar summarizes Boyd's findings in his book, *The Debate Over Christian Reconstruction* (Ft. Worth, Texas: Dominion Press, 1988), pp. 96-98, 180n.

I make thine enemies thy footstool. The LORD shall send the rod of thy strength out of Zion: rule thou in the midst of thine enemies (Psa. 110:1-2).

This passage makes it clear that a legitimate goal of God's people is the extension in history and on earth of God's kingdom, to rule in the midst of our spiritual enemies and opponents. But more to the point, the Lord speaks to Jesus Christ and informs Him that He will sit at God's right hand until His enemies are conquered. Obviously, God's throne is in heaven. This is where Jesus will remain until He comes again in final judgment.

This is also what is taught by the New Testament's major eschatological passage, I Corinthians 15. It provides the context of the fulfillment of Psalm 110. It speaks of the resurrection of every person's body at the last judgment. Jesus' body was resurrected first in time in order to demonstrate to the world that the bodily resurrection is real. (This is why liberals hate the doctrine of the bodily resurrection of Christ, and why they will go to such lengths in order to deny it.)[21] This passage tells us when all the rest of us will experience this bodily resurrection. What it describes has to be the final judgment.

> For as in Adam all die, even so in Christ shall all be made alive. But every man in his own order: Christ the firstfruits; afterward they that are Christ's at his coming. Then cometh the end, when he shall have delivered up the kingdom to God, even the Father; when he shall have put down all rule and all authority and power. For he must reign, till he hath put all enemies under his feet. The last enemy that shall be destroyed is death (I Cor. 15:22-26).

Jesus reigns until God the Father has put all enemies under Jesus' feet. But Jesus reigns from heaven; if this were not true, then how on earth could He be seated at the right hand of God, as Psalm 110 requires? *Any suggestion that Jesus will rule physically on earth*

---

21. A notorious example of such literature is Hugh J. Schonfield, *The Passover Plot: New Light on the History of Jesus* (New York: Bantam, [1966] 1971). It had gone through seven hardback printings and 14 paperback printings by 1971.

in history (meaning before the final judgment), away from His place at God's right hand, is also a suggestion that the right hand of glory is not all that glorious. Yet this is exactly what premillennialists say must and will happen in history. This is premillennialism's distinctive doctrine.

Representative Presence

What premillennialism inevitably denies is that Jesus Christ reigns in history through His earthly followers, and *only* through them, just as Satan rules his kingdom in history through his earthly followers, and only through them. Satan never will appear physically in history to command his troops, and neither will Jesus Christ. Satan does not have to reign from some city in order for him to exercise power; neither does Jesus Christ. Are we to believe that Satan's kingdom is not a true kingdom just because he is not present physically? Yet Dave Hunt, exposer of cults and New Age conspiracies, denouncer of satanism everywhere, nevertheless insists: "There can be no kingdom without the king being present. . . ."[22] He refuses to understand what Jesus taught from the beginning: *Jesus Christ is covenantally present with His people in their weekly worship services and especially during the Lord's Supper.*[23] Jesus exercises covenantal judgment in the midst of the congregation during the Lord's Supper, which is why *self-judgment* in advance is required.

> Wherefore whosoever shall eat this bread, and drink this cup of the Lord, unworthily, shall be guilty of the body and blood of the Lord. But let a man examine himself, and so let him eat of that bread, and drink of that cup. For he that eateth and drinketh unworthily, eateth and drinketh damnation to himself, not discerning the Lord's body. For this cause many are weak and sickly among you, and many sleep. For if we would judge ourselves, we should not be judged. But when we are judged, we are chastened

22. Hunt, *Whatever Happened to Heaven?*, p. 259.

23. Dave Hunt is quite self-conscious about his rejection of any view of the Lord's Supper that involves anything more than a memorial: *ibid*, p. 302.

of the Lord, that we should not be condemned with the world. Wherefore, my brethren, when ye come together to eat, tarry one for another (I Cor. 11:27-33).

I suspect that it is dispensationalism's lack of emphasis on the sacrament of Holy Communion that has led them to adopt the strange belief that Satan's kingdom rule is real even though he is not physically present on earth, yet Jesus' kingdom reign cannot become real until He is physically present on earth. In each case, the two supernatural rulers rule *representatively.* In neither case does the Bible teach that the supernatural ruler needs to be bodily present with his people in order for him to exercise dominion through them.

Obvious, isn't it? But when have you heard a sermon or read a book that mentions this?

No Earthly Hope

If the church is just about out of time, as dispensational authors keep insisting, decade after decade, then what legitimate hope can Christians have that they can leave the world a better place than they found it? None, says Lehman Strauss in Dallas Seminary's journal, *Bibliotheca Sacra:*

> We are witnessing in this twentieth century the collapse of civilization. It is obvious that we are advancing toward the end of the age. Science can offer no hope for the future blessing and security of humanity, but instead it has produced devastating and deadly results which threaten to lead us toward a new dark age. The frightful uprisings among races, the almost unbelievable conquests of Communism, and the growing antireligious philosophy throughout the world, all spell out the fact that doom is certain. I can see no bright prospects, through the efforts of man, for the earth and its inhabitants.[24]

This same pessimism regarding Christians' ability to improve

---

24. Lehman Strauss, "Our Only Hope," *Bibliotheca Sacra,* Vol. 120 (April/June 1963), p. 154.

society through the preaching of the gospel has been affirmed by John Walvoord, for three decades the president of Dallas Seminary: "Well, I personally object to the idea that premillennialism is pessimistic. We are simply realistic in believing that man cannot change the world. Only God can."[25] But why can't God change it through His servants, just as Moses changed the world, and as the apostles changed it? The apostles' enemies announced regarding them: "These that have turned the world upside down are come hither also" (Acts 17:6b). No one has ever announced this about dispensationalists!

This Book Is About Responsibility

This utter pessimism concerning the earthly future of the institutional church and Christian civilization is what lies behind the traditional premillennialists' lack of any systematic social theory or recommended social policies. They believe that it is a waste of their time thinking about such "theoretical" matters, since they believe that the Christians will never be in a position to implement them, even if such standards exist. The fact is, because they self-consciously reject the idea that Old Testament laws are in any way morally or legally binding on Christians and non-Christians alike, dispensationalists have no place to go in order to discover Bible-mandated social policies. Thomas Ice admitted in a debate with me and Gary DeMar: "Premillennialists have always been involved in the present world. And basically, they have picked up on the ethical positions of their contemporaries."[26] They have had nothing to add because they have no hope in the future, and they reject biblical law.

Dispensationalists have *no earthly hope in the church's future*. This means that dispensational theology lures God's people out of

---

25. *Christianity Today* (Feb. 6, 1987), p. 11-I.

26. April 14, 1988; cited by Gary DeMar, *The Debate Over Christian Reconstruction*, p. 185. Audio tapes of the debate are available for $10 from the Institute for Christian Economics. The debate was Dave Hunt and Tommy Ice vs. Gary North and Gary DeMar.

society. The dispensationalist has no concept of positive social change and positive social transformation because he has no concept of ethical cause and effect in history. He explicitly denies the continuing authority of Deuteronomy 28:1-14. He even denies the continuing authority of the Ten Commandments, as former Dallas Seminary professor S. Lewis Johnson did in 1963:

> At the heart of the problem of legalism is pride, a pride that refuses to admit spiritual bankruptcy. That is why the doctrines of grace stir up so much animosity. Donald Grey Barnhouse, a giant of a man in free grace, wrote: "It was a tragic hour when the Reformation churches wrote the Ten Commandments into their creeds and catechisms and sought to bring Gentile believers into bondage to Jewish law, which was never intended either for the Gentile nations or for the church."[27] He was right, too.[28]

Legitimizing Cultural Retreat

Because he has no faith in the long-term efforts of Christians to transform this world through obedience to God, the consistent dispensationalist retreats from the hard conflicts of society that rage around him, just as the Russian Orthodox Church did during the Russian Revolution of 1917. The existence of this dispensationalist attitude of retreat is openly admitted by dispensational pastor David Schnittger:

> North and other postmillennial Christian Reconstructionists label those who hold the pretribulational rapture position pietists and cultural retreatists. One reason these criticisms are so painful is because I find them to be substantially true. Many in our camp have an all-pervasive negativism regarding the course of society and the impotence of God's people to do anything about it. They will heartily affirm that **Satan is Alive and Well on Planet Earth**, and that this must indeed be **The Terminal Generation**; therefore, any attempt to influence society is ultimately hopeless.

---

27. Citing Barnhouse, *God's Freedom*, p. 134.

28. S. Lewis Johnson, "The Paralysis of Legalism," *Bibliotheca Sacra*, Vol. 120 (April/June, 1963), p. 109.

They adopt the pietistic platitude: *"You don't polish brass on a sinking ship."* Many pessimistic pretribbers cling to the humanists' version of religious freedom; namely Christian social and political impotence, self-imposed, as drowning men cling to a life preserver.[29]

Removing Illegitimate Fears

David Chilton shows in *The Great Tribulation* that Christians' fears regarding some inevitable Great Tribulation for the Church are not grounded in Scripture. Kenneth Gentry shows in this book that the beast of Revelation is not lurking around the corner. Neither is the rapture. Thus, Christians can have legitimate hope in the positive earthly outcome of their prayers and labors. Their sacrifices today will make a difference in the long run. There is *continuity* between their efforts today and the long-term expansion of God's civilization in history ("civilization" is just another word for "kingdom"). Jesus' words are true: there will be no eschatological discontinuity, no cataclysmic disruption, no *rapture* in between today and Christ's second coming at the final judgment:

> Another parable put he forth unto them, saying, The kingdom of heaven is likened unto a man which sowed good seed in his field: But while men slept, his enemy came and sowed tares among the wheat, and went his way. But when the blade was sprung up, and brought forth fruit, then appeared the tares also. So the servants of the householder came and said unto him, Sir, didst not thou sow good seed in thy field? from whence then hath it tares? He said unto them, An enemy hath done this. The servants said unto him, Wilt thou then that we go and gather them up? But he said, Nay; lest while ye gather up the tares, ye root up also the wheat with them. Let both grow together until the harvest: and in the time of harvest I will say to the reapers, Gather ye together first the tares, and bind them in bundles to burn them: but gather the wheat into my barn (Matt. 13:24-31).

The apostles did not understand the meaning of this parable.

---

29. David Schnittger, *Christian Reconstruction from a Pretribulational Perspective* (Oklahoma City: Southwest Radio Church, 1986), p. 7.

Neither do dispensationalists:

> Then Jesus sent the multitude away, and went into the house: and his disciples came unto him, saying, Declare unto us the parable of the tares of the field. He answered and said unto them, He that soweth the good seed is the Son of man; The field is the world; the good seed are the children of the kingdom; but the tares are the children of the wicked one; The enemy that sowed them is the devil; the harvest is the end of the world; and the reapers are the angels. As therefore the tares are gathered and burned in the fire; so shall it be in the end of this world. The Son of man shall send forth his angels, and they shall gather out of his kingdom all things that offend, and them which do iniquity; And shall cast them into a furnace of fire: there shall be wailing and gnashing of teeth. Then shall the righteous shine forth as the sun in the kingdom of their Father. Who hath ears to hear, let him hear (Matt. 13:36-43).

Dispensationalists refuse to hear.

This book presents a message of moral responsibility. Every message of true hope inevitably is also a message of moral responsibility. In God's world, there is no hope without moral responsibility, no offer of victory without the threat of persecution, no offer of heaven without the threat of hell. Deny this, and you deny the gospel. He who has ears to hear, let him hear.

This Book Is About Time

Why would a Christian economics institute publish a book on the beast of revelation and the dating of the Book of Revelation? Because a crucial aspect of all economics, all economic growth, is time perspective. Those individuals and societies that are future-oriented save more money, enjoy lower interest rates, and benefit from more rapid economic growth. A short-run view of the future is the mark of the gambler, the person in poverty, and the underdeveloped society. Those who think in terms of generations and plan for the future see their heirs prosper; those who think in terms of the needs and desires in the present cannot successfully compete over the long haul with those who are willing to forego present consumption for the sake of future growth.

Furthermore, dispensationalists insist, the beast is coming, and so is the antichrist. That horror is just around the corner. The Great Tribulation is imminent. Nothing can stop it. Nothing will resist its onslaught. Nothing we leave behind as Christians will be able to change things for the next generation. It is all hopeless. All we can legitimately hope for is our escape into the heavens at the rapture.

It is no wonder that American Christians have been short-run thinkers in this century. They see failure and defeat in the immediate future, relieved only (if at all) by the rapture of the church into heaven. This is Dave Hunt's message. He sees no earthly hope for the church apart from the imminent return of Christ.

But such a view of the future has inescapable practical implications, although more and more self-professed dispensationalists who have become Christian activists, and who have therefore also become operational and psychological postmillennialists, prefer to believe that these implications are not really inescapable. If the "Church Age" is just about out of time, why should any sensible Christian attend college? Why go to the expense of graduate school? Why become a professional? Why start a Christian university or a new business? Why do anything for the kingdom of God that involves a capital commitment greater than door-to-door evangelism? Why even build a new church?

Here, admittedly, all dispensational pastors become embarrassingly inconsistent. They want big church buildings. Perhaps they can justify this "worldly orientation" by building it with a mountain of long-term debt, just as Dallas Seminary financed its expansion of the 1970's. They are tempted to view the rapture as a personal and institutional means of escape from bill-collection agencies. A person who really believes in the imminent return of Christ asks himself: Why avoid personal or corporate debt if Christians are about to be raptured out of repayment? Why not adopt the outlook of "eat, drink, and be merry, for tomorrow we will be rescued by God's helicopter escape"?

The Helicopter Man

Dave Hunt does not want to become known as "Helicopter Hunt," but that really is who he is. His worldview is the fundamentalists' worldview during the past century, and especially since the Scopes "monkey trial" of 1925,[30] but its popularity is fading fast, just as the back cover copy of his book frankly admits. No wonder. Christians today are sick and tired of riding in the back of humanism's bus. They are fed up with being regarded as third-class citizens, irrelevant to the modern world. They are beginning to perceive that their shortened view of time is what has helped to make them culturally irrelevant.

The older generation of American fundamentalists is still being thrilled and chilled in fits of rapture fever, but not so much the younger generation. Younger fundamentalists are now beginning to recognize a long-ignored biblical truth: *the future of this world belongs to the church of Jesus Christ if His people remain faithful to His Word.* They are beginning to understand Jesus' words of victory in Matthew 28: "And Jesus came and spake unto them, saying, All power is given unto me in heaven and in earth. Go ye therefore, and teach all nations, baptizing them in the name of the Father, and of the Son, and of the Holy Ghost. Teaching them to observe all things whatsoever I have commanded you: and, lo, I am with you alway, even unto the end of the world. Amen" (vv. 18-20). They have at last begun to take seriously the promised victory of the church's Great Commission rather than the past horror of Israel's Great Tribulation. They are steadily abandoning that older eschatology of corporate defeat and heavenly rescue.

In short, Christians are at long last beginning to view Jesus Christ as the Lord of all history and the head of His progressively triumphant church rather than as "Captain Jesus and His angels."

---

30. George Marsden, *Fundamentalism and American Culture: The Shaping of Twentieth-Century Evangelicalism, 1870-1925* (New York: Oxford University Press, 1980).

The Same Argument the Liberals Use

By interpreting Jesus' promise that He would soon return in power and judgment against Israel as if it were a promise of His second coming at the rapture, dispensationalists are caught in a dilemma. They teach that Paul and the apostles taught the early church, in Dave Hunt's words, to "watch and wait for His imminent return,"[31] yet Jesus has delayed returning physically for over 1,950 years. How can we escape the conclusion that the apostles misinformed the early church, a clearly heretical notion, and an argument that liberal theologians have used against Bible-believing Christians repeatedly in this century? But there is no way out of this intellectual dilemma if you do not distinguish between Christ's coming in judgment against Israel in A.D. 70 and His physical return in final judgment at the end of time.

Contrary to Dave Hunt, with respect to the physical return of Jesus in judgment, the early church was told just the opposite: do *not* stand around watching and waiting. "And while they looked stedfastly toward heaven as he went up, behold, two men stood by them in white apparel; Which also said, Ye men of Galilee, why stand ye gazing up into heaven? this same Jesus, which is taken up from you into heaven, shall so come in like manner as ye have seen him go into heaven. Then returned they unto Jerusalem from the mount called Olivet, which is from Jerusalem a sabbath day's journey" (Acts 1:10-12).

Those who prefer figuratively to stand around looking into the sky are then tempted to conclude, as Dave Hunt concludes, that the church today, by abandoning pre-tribulational dispensationalism — as if more than a comparative handful of Christians in the church's history had ever believed in the pre-tribulational rapture doctrine, invented as recently as 1830[32] — has "succumbed once again to the unbiblical hope that, by exerting godly influence upon

---

31. Hunt, *Whatever Happened to Heaven?*, p. 55.

32. Dave McPherson, *The Great Rapture Hoax* (Fletcher, North Carolina: New Puritan Library, 1983).

government, society can be transformed."[33] It is time, he says, for Christians to give up "the false dream of Christianizing secular culture. . . ."[34]

In short, let the world go to hell; we Christians will escape the burning building of because we all have been issued free tickets on God's helicopter escape.

Conclusion

Fear paralyzes people if they see no escape, or if their hoped-for escape is seen by them as a miraculous deliverance by forces utterly beyond their control. Also, a short-run perspective inevitably impoverishes people. The fundamentalist world until the late 1970's had been "immobilized for Jesus" by its all-pervasive dismissal of the "inevitably grim" pre-rapture future and by fundamentalism's rejection of that future. Despairing Christians have believed with all their hearts that anything they could do to improve this world would inevitably be swallowed up by the beast and the antichrist. Then why work, save, and postpone the enjoyments of this world in order to build up a capital base that will be inherited by your enemies? People buried their earthly fears by means of the make-believe dream of God's helicopter escape from the Great Tribulation — a tribulation that ended in A.D. 70. *Fundamentalists buried their talents when they buried the future.* That was the fate of the older dispensationalism: it was buried alive. People's fears could not serve as stimuli to long-term planning and building.

No longer. Fundamentalism's make-believe world of false prophecies regarding ancient events is drawing to a close. This book and its fatter, fully documented companion volume (*Before Jerusalem Fell: Dating the Book of Revelation*), will speed up the process.

It is time for a resurrection: the resurrection of Christian hope. It is time for a parallel resurrection: the resurrection of comprehensive Christian service in every area of life. This means that it

---

33. Hunt, *Whatever Happened to Heaven?*, p. [8].
34. *Idem.*

is time for Christian dominion. It is time to stop asking ourselves "What ever happened to heaven?" and start asking: "What ever happened to the Great Commission and the kingdom of God?"[35] Heaven is for dead men in Christ; earth is for living men in Christ. Our responsibility for this world ends only at the point of our physical death or our complete physical and mental incapacitation. Let those fundamentalists whose primary goal in life is to escape earthly responsibility in the present and surely in the future — and also to "get out of life alive" at the rapture — bury their talents in ceaseless speculations regarding heaven. The rest of us should concentrate on the goal of building the kingdom of God through covenantal faithfulness to God's law.[36] We should begin to take seriously God's promise to the righteous man: "His soul shall dwell at ease; and his seed shall inherit the earth" (Psa. 25:13).

35. Kenneth L. Gentry, Jr., "The Greatness of the Great Commission," *Journal of Christian Reconstruction*, VII (Winter 1981), pp. 19-47.

36. Greg L. Bahnsen, *By This Standard: The Authority of God's Law Today* (Tyler, Texas: Institute for Christian Economics, 1985).

PART I
WHO IS THE BEAST?

INTRODUCTION

Blessed is he who reads and those who hear the words of the prophecy, and heed the things which are written in it . . . (Rev. 1:3a).

Revelation is one of the most fascinating and intriguing books of the Bible. Evidently this has always been the case, for it was one of the most widely circulated of New Testament books in the early centuries of Christianity.[1] Following upon these early Christian centuries, the Middle Ages and the Reformation era experienced an explosion of commentaries on Revelation.[2]

Interest in Revelation shows no sign of slackening today. In fact, as the magic year 2000 looms ever nearer, we are witnessing a reinvigorated interest in prophecy in general, and Revelation in particular. Check any Christian bookstore and you will discover a vast selection of books on eschatology and Revelation.

One of the most interesting questions debated in regard to Revelation is that of the identity of the Beast of Revelation 13 and 17. This terrifying enemy of God and His Church has fascinated both the Christian and non-Christian mind down through the ages.

Who is this nefarious personage?

What is his role in biblical eschatology?

Does his foreboding visage haunt our future?

---

1. Robert Mounce, *The Book of Revelation* (Grand Rapids: Eerdmans, 1977), p. 36; Walter F. Adeney, *New Testament*, vol. 2 of *A Biblical Introduction* (London: Methuen, 1911), p. 461.

2. Henry B. Swete, *Commentary on Revelation* (Grand Rapids: Kregel, [1911] 1977), p. cxcvii.

3

These are questions that are frequently asked by contemporary Christians. These queries must be answered from the one book in Holy Scripture where this evil figure looms large: Revelation. In the Book of Revelation we find God-inspired information regarding the Beast and the essential definitive data to guide us in our inquiry.

Unfortunately, there is much:

Confusion Regarding Revelation

Revelation has been not only one of the most widely circulated, but certainly the most vigorously debated and variously understood of New Testament books. Revelation has proved to be as perplexing as it has been popular. It is lamentable that the vast majority of the prophetic literature, media presentations, films, conferences, seminars, and so forth which has been generated in our era is ill-conceived. Much of it has even been a source of positive embarrassment to the intellectual credibility of the Christian faith.

One of the most interesting analyses exposing the false expectations generated by the modern prophecy movement is Dwight Wilson's 1977 book entitled *Armageddon Now!* He profusely documents a multitude of failed predictions based on careless interpretations of Scripture by well-meaning, Bible-believing Christians in our own century. Most of these failures have been related either directly or indirectly to a radical misunderstanding of the Book of Revelation.

Much of this problem is traceable to a frustrating tendency which David Chilton laments: "Many rush from their first profession of faith to the last book in the Bible . . . finding, ultimately, only a reflection of their own prejudices."[3] Thus, there is a ripe market for tantalizing and dramatic expositions of Revelation. Scripture has a name for this syndrome: "itching ears" (2 Tim. 4:3).

---

3. David Chilton, *Paradise Restored* (Fort Worth, TX: Dominion Press, 1985), p. 153.

Yet there are legitimate:

Reasons for Revelation's Difficulty

Undoubtedly, a major reason for Revelation's difficulty of interpretation is due to its literary form. It is not written as simple historical narrative or didactic instruction. Rather, it is a book of fearsome visions and strange symbols, employing imagery drawn from Old Testament prophecy and ancient culture. Its literary style understandably makes Revelation a difficult work, particularly for modern, Western Christians.

Much of the data concerning the Beast in Revelation is rendered difficult because of the symbolic style John employs. The terrifying visual appearance of the Beast in Revelation 13:1-2 is obviously symbolic, but why does John employ such imagery? The death and resurrection of the Beast in Revelation 13:3 indicate something quite dramatic, but what? The rendering of the Beast's name in numerals in Revelation 13:18 is a unique feature in Scripture, but what does it mean? The Great Harlot in Revelation 17:1-6 is quite mysterious and is somehow connected to the Beast, but who is she and how does she relate to the Beast?

Beyond the widely recognized difficulty of the style of Revelation, there is an equally serious matter that confronts the would-be interpreter. The issue to which we refer is the question of the date of the writing of Revelation.

Basically there are two possibilities regarding the date of Revelation's composition which are open to evangelical Christians: John may have written Revelation prior to the destruction of the Temple, which occurred in A.D. 70. Or possibly he composed it a generation later, around A.D. 95-96, in the last days of the reign of the emperor Domitian. The second view is the majority opinion among contemporary commentators. The first view is the conviction of the present writer and a growing minority of biblical scholars.

Few Christians-in-the-pew realize the importance of this matter for the interpretation of Revelation. This is partially due to the fact that most of the popular literature on Revelation either ignores the issue of dating altogether or too lightly glosses over it.[4] Even the more technical modern commentaries on Revelation tend either to appeal to a majority opinion on the matter or parrot the insufficient evidence for the popular, but erroneous date of Revelation.[5] Yet the matter of Revelation's date of composition is crucial to the correct understanding of the book.

Despite the majority opinion, I believe that two bold claims regarding the date of the writing of Revelation can be made with conviction.

The first is that a misapprehension of the date of its writing can literally turn Revelation on its head, rendering its proper exposition impossible. Whereas the problem of the style of Revelation renders the *exposition of its details difficult*, the adoption of a wrong date for its writing renders its *specific meaning impossible*. If Revelation prophesies events related to the destruction of the Temple in Jerusalem in A.D. 70, then to hold to a date of composition *after* that event would miss John's whole point. I firmly believe this has been done by the majority of Revelation commentators in this century.

My second claim is that Revelation provides more concrete internal information pointing to its date of composition than does any other New Testament book. As we will show, the major reason for dating the book more than a quarter of a century too late is due not to internal indications within Revelation itself, but to church tradition. It is a most unfortunate state of affairs when the self-witness of a biblical book takes the back seat to an inconsistent tradition arising more than a century after its writing.

---

4. See Charles Caldwell Ryrie, *Revelation* (Chicago: Moody Press, 1968), pp. 7-8; William Hendriksen, *More Than Conquerors* (Grand Rapids: Baker, 1967), pp. 19-20; John F. Walvoord, *The Revelation of Jesus Christ* (Chicago: Moody Press, 1966), pp. 13-14; Herman Hoeksema, *Behold, He Cometh!* (Grand Rapids: Kregel, 1969), p. 33.

5. See George Eldon Ladd, *A Commentary on the Revelation of John* (Grand Rapids: Eerdmans, 1972), p. 8; G. R. Beasley-Murray, *The Book of Revelation* (Grand Rapids: Eerdmans, 1978), pp. 37-38; Alan F. Johnson, *Revelation* (Grand Rapids: Zondervan, 1983), p. 12.

Our Purpose

The main purpose of the present work is to ascertain the identity of the Beast of Revelation. I believe that the evidence is there to identify clearly the very name and historical circumstances of the Beast. I also believe that as the reader considers the material to be set forth before him he will find the identification not only persuasive, but surprisingly easy and startling.

An auxiliary purpose will be to provide the reader with a synopsis of some of the arguments for the proper dating of Revelation. As will become evident, the matter of dating is all-important to the identity of the Beast. The concerned student should consult the more extensive and technical research provided in my doctoral dissertation, *The Date of Revelation: An Exegetical and Historical Argument for a Pre-A.D. 70 Composition.* That dissertation, submitted to Whitefield Theological Seminary in Lakeland, Florida, in March, 1988, is also published by the Institute for Christian Economics — under the title *Before Jerusalem Fell: Dating the Book of Revelation* (1989).

1

THE IDENTITY OF THE BEAST

Who is like the Beast, and who is able to wage war with him? . . .
If any one has an ear, let him hear (Rev. 13:4b, 9).

Those readers who like to read the last pages of a book to discover the conclusion to the story will be disappointed in my approach. In this very opening chapter I will identify the Beast. I do this so that you might have his identity in mind as you consider the evidence as it is presented. For those who expect the Beast to appear on the scene of history at any moment, there will also be a surprise. The material in Revelation is quite clear: The Beast has already made his appearance in history past.

All students of Revelation are familiar with the "number of the Beast" (Rev. 13:18a), which is "the number of his name" (Rev. 13:17b). That dreaded number is "666." In that number is contained the specific identity of the Beast, an identity confirmed by a number of lines of additional evidences within Revelation.

Interpretive Principles

Although I will deal specifically with the number of the Beast in a separate chapter, there are several principles for the interpretation of that number which we must keep in mind to govern our thinking. As is evident from the history of the interpretation of 666, we certainly do need something to confine our thinking to the realm of the reasonable! The necessary, textually derived limiting principles are:

9

1. The name-number 666 must be "that of a *man*" (Rev. 13:18b). This excludes any interpretation that would involve demonic beings, philosophical ideas, political movements, or anything other than an individual human person.

2. This man must be someone of an evil, idolatrous, and blasphemous nature. This is required in light of his character traits and evil activities outlined in Revelation 13, particularly verses 4-7.

3. He must also be someone possessing "great authority" (Rev. 13:2, 7). This certainly demands that he be a political figure, particularly in that upon his heads are ten diadems. These first three principles are fairly widely held among evangelical Revelation commentators. The two remaining ones are largely overlooked and are almost certainly the causes of a radical misidentification of the Beast and his mission. These will be simply listed and stated at this juncture. It will be left to later chapters to establish them.

4. The name-number must speak of one of John's *contemporaries*. This is due to the temporal expectation of John. The events of Revelation are to occur "soon"; John insists that "the time is at hand" (Rev. 1:1, 3, 19; 22:6ff). This principle alone will eliminate 99.9% of the suggestions by commentators.

5. The name must be that of someone *relevant* to the first-century Christians in the seven churches to whom John wrote (Rev. 1:4, 11). He expected them to give heed to what he wrote (Rev. 1:3) and to calculate the Beast's number (Rev. 13:18). How could they have done so if the Beast were some shadowy figure far removed from their own situation?

The early establishment of Principles 4 and 5 is essential to the correct understanding of the identity of the Beast. Consequently, we will deal with them at length in Chapter 2.

The Importance of the Limiting Principles

One illustration of the hopeless results gained by ignoring any or all of these obvious limiting factors is found in a dispensational work of the 1970s. In this work we read a vain attempt to explain the number 666: "At all times Satan has had to have one or more Antichrist candidates waiting in the wings, lest the Rapture come suddenly and find him unprepared. That is why so many malevolent world leaders have had names whose letters added up to 666 when combined in certain ways. (Depending on which 666 formula is used, at any given moment there are several hundred thousand men in the world whose names add up to 666. It is from this large pool of candidates that Satan has traditionally chosen his 'man of the moment'.)"[1]

Contrary to as competent a scholar as Leon Morris, we doubt that "the possibilities are almost endless."[2] The limiting factors derived from Revelation's text greatly restrict the realm of possibility.

Dual Imagery

Before we actually point to the one indicated by John's number, a widely recognized problem associated with the Beast imagery must be mentioned. Most commentators agree that the Beast imagery in Revelation shifts between the generic and the specific. That is, sometimes the Beast seems to picture a kingdom, sometimes a particular, individual leader of that kingdom.[3] Nevertheless, it should be understood that the number 666 is itself applied to a particular individual king in that kingdom (Rev. 13:18).

At some places the Beast has seven heads, which are seven kings collectively considered. In Revelation 13:1 John states that

---

1. Raymond Schafer, *After the Rapture* (Santa Ana, CA: Vision House, 1977), p. 55.

2. Leon Morris, *The Revelation of St. John* (Grand Rapids: Eerdmans, 1969), p. 174.

3. This compound idea of generic/specific is not unprecedented in Scripture. For instance, "man" is generic, whereas "Adam" is the specific representative of man. The Church is generic (the Body of Christ), whereas Christ is specific. Here we have the Beast represented as the generic (kingdom) in some places, while receiving specific expression in the ruler of that kingdom in other places.

he "saw a beast coming up out of the sea, having ten horns and seven heads." Revelation 17:10 specifically states that the seven heads represent "seven kings." These seven kings arise in chronological succession; some have already died, one is now reigning, one is yet to come (Rev. 17:10-11). Thus, the *Beast* is generically portrayed as a *kingdom*.

But in the very same contexts the Beast is spoken of as an individual. John urges his readers to "calculate the number of the beast, for the number is that of *a man*" (Rev. 13:18). In Revelation 17:11 the interpretive angel tells John and his readers "the beast which was and is not, is himself also an eighth, and *is one of the seven*." This feature, as frustrating as it may be, is recognized by many commentators of various schools of interpretation.[4]

Introducing the Beast

With these introductory considerations before us I will now state what I believe the Beast to be, in regard to both his generic and his specific identity. I will establish the generic identity in a little more detail at this juncture. Then after only briefly identifying his specific identity, I will develop the proofs of his specific, individual identity in the following chapters.

His Generic Identity

The generic identity of the Beast is the ancient Roman Empire of the first century, under which Christ was crucified and during which John wrote. According to Revelation 17:9, the seven heads of the Beast represent "seven mountains." The seven heads, then, seem clearly to specify a prominent geographical feature. Perhaps no point is more obvious in Revelation than this one: *It is Rome*

---

4. For example: John F. Walvoord, *The Revelation of Jesus Christ* (Chicago: Moody Press, 1966), p. 200; Leon Morris, *The Revelation of St. John*, 1st ed. (Grand Rapids: Eerdmans, 1969), pp. 210-211; R. H. Charles, *A Critical and Exegetical Commentary on the Revelation of St. John* (Edinburgh: T. and T. Clark, 1920), 1:349; Philip Mauro, *Things Which Soon Must Come to Pass*, rev. ed. (Swengel, PA: Reiner Publications, n.d.), p. 402.

that is here symbolized by the seven mountains. After all, *Rome* is the one city in history that has been distinguished by and recognized for its seven mountains. The famous seven hills of Rome are the Palatine, Aventine, Caelian, Esquiline, Viminal, Quirinal, and Capitoline hills.

The Roman writers Suetonius and Plutarch make reference to the first century festival in Rome called *Septimontium, i.e.* the feast of "the seven hilled city." Archaeologists have discovered the Coin of Vespasian (emperor A.D. 69-79) picturing the goddess *Roma* as a woman seated on seven hills. The famed seven hills of Rome are mentioned time and again by ancient pagan writers such as Ovid, Claudian, Statius, Pliny, Virgil, Horace, Propertius, Martial, and Cicero.[5] The seven hills are mentioned by such Christian writers as Tertullian and Jerome, as well as in several of the Sibylline Oracles.[6]

This fact — that Rome was universally recognized as the city on seven hills — is widely recognized by evangelical commentators as having a bearing upon our passage. The referent is virtually beyond doubt: Rome is alluded to in this vision of the seven-headed beast. By everyone's dating, Revelation was written *some-time* during the period of the Roman Empire.

Furthermore, both secular and ecclesiastical history record that the first imperial persecution of Christianity was begun in the seven-hilled city, Rome, by the emperor Nero Caesar in A.D. 64.[7] John himself tells us that he wrote Revelation to seven historical churches in Asia Minor (Rev. 1:4, 11). These churches existed in an age of great trouble (Rev. 1:9; 2:10; 3:10). Moreover, John exhorted these churches to read, hear, and heed the book (Rev. 1:3; 2:7; 2:11, 17, 29; 3:6, 13, 22; 22:7). The subject matter of

---

5. Ovid, *De Tristia* 1:5:69 and *Elegiae* 4; Claudian, *In Praise of Stilicon* 3:135; Statius, *Sylvae* 1; 2:191; Pliny, *Natural History* 3:5, 9; Virgil, *Aeneid* 6:782 and *Georgics* 2:535; Horace, *Carmen Secularae* 7; Propertius 3:10, 57; Martial 4:64; Cicero, *Ad Atticum* 6:5.

6. Tertullian, *Apology* 35; Jerome, *Letter to Marcella*; and *Sibylline Oracles* 2:18; 11:114; 13:45; 14:108.

7. See Chapter 5.

Revelation was critical and relevant to these churches, for John spoke forcefully of the imminent occurrence of the events of Revelation (1:1, 3, 19; 3:10; 22:6ff.).[8]

The matter of the relevancy of the referent in Revelation 17 to the original audience should be a paramount concern for the modern interpreter. In light of the circumstances outlined above, is it at all likely that when John mentioned "the seven mountains" he was not speaking of the Roman Empire? Put yourself in first century sandals: Would *you* think John might be speaking of events occurring untold centuries past the collapse of the empire which was presently engaged in your persecution? Would you suspect that he was not really relating a message about Imperial Rome? Impossible! John exhorted the people to read, hear, and heed the book. He was speaking of the then existing Roman Empire, headquartered in the seven-hilled city of Rome.

His Specific Identity

But who is the Beast *individually* considered? The Beast of Revelation in his personal incarnation is none other than Lucius Domitius Ahenobarbus, better known by his adoptive name, Nero Caesar. He and he alone fits the bill as the specific or personal expression of the Beast. This vile character fulfills all the requirements of the principles derived from the very text of Revelation.

Excluding Julius Caesar, probably no other Roman emperor's name is as well known to the average Christian today as Nero's. Yet his large role in Revelation is virtually unknown among contemporary Christians. Perhaps a brief history of Nero's tumultuous life would serve well in preparing the reader for the proofs of our identification, which will be given in Chapters 2-7.

Nero's Birth and Early Life

The father of Nero[9] was one Enaeus Domitius Ahenobarbus,

---

8. See Chapter 2.

9. We will call Nero by his familiar adoptive name, although it was not granted him until he was twelve years old.

a vicious man from a noted, but cruel, Roman family. The entire family was "notorious for instability, treachery and licentiousness."[10] Nero's father is spoken of as "hateful in every walk of life."[11] Nero's famous, conniving, and ill-fated mother was Agrippina, the sister of Emperor Gaius (also known as "Caligula") and niece of the emperor Claudius.

Nero was born on December 15th, A.D. 37, just nine months after the death of Emperor Tiberius, under whom Christ was crucified. He was born with bright red hair, as was common to his lineage (the name "Ahenobarbus" meant "red-beard").[12] Nero was born feet first; among a superstitious and pagan people this was considered to be an evil omen. This omen did not go unnoticed by Roman historians of the day.[13] Many astrologers "at once made many direful predictions from his horoscope."[14] On the day of his birth even Nero's father predicted that this offspring could only be abominable and disastrous for the public.[15]

Nero's cruel character evidenced itself quite early. At twelve years of age and upon having been adopted by the emperor Claudius Caesar, Nero began to accuse his brother Britannicus of being a "changeling," in order to bring him into disfavor before the emperor. At the same time he even served as a public witness in a trial against his aunt Lepida, in order to ruin her.[16]

Agrippina, Nero's mother, plotted and schemed to secure Nero a high position in imperial Rome. Upon the death of the wife of the emperor Claudius she began to make her moves. She arranged Nero's marriage to the daughter of Claudius, labored to get the Roman law changed to allow her to marry Claudius (her

---

10. Arthur Weigall, *Nero: Emperor of Rome* (London: Thornton Butterworth, 1933), p. 24.
11. Suetonius, *Nero* 5.
12. Weigall, *Nero*, p. 25.
13. Suetonius, *Gaius* 24.
14. *Ibid.*
15. Suetonius, *Nero* 6.
16. Suetonius, *Nero* 7.

uncle), prompted the adoption of Nero by the emperor (A.D. 49), manuevered to get Nero certain high titles to secure his succession to the emperorship, and caused the exile and death of any supporters of Nero's brother, Britannicus. When it became evident that Claudius did not like leaving Britannicus out of his will, as was urged by Agrippina, she poisoned Claudius.[17]

Nero's Adult Years

On the death of Emperor Claudius, Nero, who was then but seventeen years old, had his entry to the Palace to assume the emperorship carefully planned for a specific time. This timing was due to certain bad omens throughout the day.[18] He began to reign on October 13, A.D. 54.

The first five years of his reign were characterized by remarkably good government and prudence. This was due not to his own wisdom or character, but to his being guided by the wise tutors Seneca and Burrus. This era, known as the *quinquennium Neronis*, probably helps us understand Paul's very favorable attitude to the government of the day in Romans 13:1.[19] These tutors attempted to cut off the evil influence of Nero's mother over him. She then began trying to manuever his brother Britannicus into position as the rightful heir to Claudius. Nero responded by poisoning him.

Seneca and Burrus recognized the evil bent in Nero's nature and attempted to let it have expression through private base pleasures, hoping to keep him from causing public harm. Suetonius notes that: "Although at first his acts of wantonness, lust, extravagance, avarice and cruelty were gradual and secret . . . yet even then their nature was such that no one doubted that they were defects of his character and not due to his time of life."[20] But

---

17. S. Angus, "Nero" in James Orr, ed., *The International Standard Bible Encyclopedia*, 1st ed. (Grand Rapids: Eerdmans, [1929] 1956) 3:2134.

18. Suetonius, *Nero* 8; Tacitus, *Annals* 12:68.

19. See Donald B. Guthrie, *New Testament Introduction*, 3rd ed. (Downers Grove, IL: Inter-Varsity Press, 1970), p. 397; and Greg L. Bahnsen, *Theonomy in Christian Ethics*, 1st ed. (Nutley, NJ: Craig Press, 1977), pp. 366-373.

20. Suetonius, *Nero* 26.

Nero descended more deeply into degrading conduct: "He castrated the boy Sporus and actually tried to make a woman of him; and he married him with all the usual ceremonies . . . and treated him as his wife."[21] Suetonius continues: "He even devised a kind of game, in which, covered with the skin of some wild animal, he was let loose from a cage and attacked the private parts of men and women, who were bound to stakes."[22]

Nero even plotted his own mother's murder, despite the fact she was responsible for bringing him to power.[23] Not long after that Burrus died. Later, Nero ordered Seneca to commit suicide, which he did.

Nero divorced his first wife Octavia to marry his mistress, Poppaea. Octavia was banished to an island upon Poppaea's orders and was soon beheaded (A.D. 62). Three years later Poppaea, while pregnant and ill, was kicked to death by Nero.[24]

By enormous, self-glorifying building projects and profligate living, Nero exhausted the imperial treasures inherited from Claudius. Thereupon he began to accuse Roman nobles falsely of various crimes in order to confiscate their estates.[25] Tacitus records that "Nero having butchered so many illustrious men, at last desired to exterminate virtue itself by the death of Thrasea Paetus and Barea Soranus."[26] Suetonius writes that "he showed neither discrimination nor moderation in putting to death whomsoever he pleased on any pretext whatever."[27]

On July 19, A.D. 64, the great Roman fire, which destroyed

---

21. Suetonius, *Nero* 28. An amusing comment is recorded by Suetonius in light of this particularly atrocious activity of Nero: "And the witty jest that someone made is still current, that it would have been well for the world if Nero's father Domitius had had that kind of wife."

22. Suetonius, *Nero* 29.

23. Suetonius, *Nero* 34.

24. Suetonius, *Nero* 35.

25. Suetonius, *Nero* 30-32.

26. Tacitus, *Annals* 16:21ff.

27. Suetonius, *Nero* 37.

most of Rome, broke out.[28] Although he was out of Rome at the time, suspicion was cast upon Nero for causing the fire. Many were convinced that since he deplored the ugliness of Rome he intended to destroy it to make room for more of his own building projects.[29] In order to turn attention from himself, he falsely accused Christians of having started the fire[30] and punished them for being "given to a new and mischievous superstition."[31]

Nero was a lover of music, theater, and the circus, vainly fancying himself to be one of the world's greatest musicians, actors, and charioteers.[32] Suetonius records that "while he was singing no one was allowed to leave the theatre even for the most urgent reasons. And so it is said that some women gave birth to children there, while many who were worn out with listening and applauding . . . feigned death and were carried out as if for burial."[33] He even virtually abandoned direct rule of Rome for a two year visit to Greece (A.D. 67-68) in order to appear in their music festivals.

Nero's Death

Disgusted with his absence from Rome, his excesses in life, and enormous political abuses, a revolt against Nero began in Gaul. But it was quickly put down. Shortly thereafter the revolt broke out anew under Galba in Spain in A.D. 68.[34] Torn with indecision as to what to do in such pressing circumstances, Nero hesitated in acting against Galba. When the revolt had gathered too much strength he talked of suicide, but was too cowardly and again

---

28. Philip Schaff, *History of the Christian Church*, 7 vols., 3rd ed. (Grand Rapids: Eerdmans, 1910) 1:379; B. W. Henderson, *The Life and Principate of Nero* (London: Methuen and Co, 1903), p. 237.

29. Suetonius, *Nero* 38; Tacitus, *Annals* 15:38ff.

30. Tacitus, *Annals* 15:44.

31. Suetonius, *Nero* 16.

32. Suetonius, *Nero* 23-25. See Miriam T. Griffin, *Nero: The End of a Dynasty* (New Haven: Yale University Press, 1984), ch. 9.

33. Suetonius, *Nero* 23.

34. Suetonius, *Nero* 40ff.

hesitated.

As he considered his dire circumstances and the approach of certain death, he is recorded to have lamented: "What an artist the world is losing!"[35] Finally, when he learned that the Senate had voted to put him to death by cruel and shameful means, he secured the assistance of his secretary Epaphroditus to run a sword through his throat.[36] His suicide occurred at the age of 31 on June 9, A.D. 68. With his death the line of Julius Caesar was cut off, and for the first time an emperor of Rome was appointed from outside Rome.

Conclusion

The view to be presented in this work is that the Emperor Nero Caesar is the Beast of Revelation specifically considered and that Rome is the Beast generically considered. As has been shown in our quick survey of his life, Nero was a horrible character in Rome's history. Church historian Philip Schaff speaks of him as "a demon in human shape."[37] As will be shown in the pages to follow, he was the very one whom John had in mind when he wrote of the Beast whose number is 666.

The view I have presented and will be defending is contrary to what the vast majority of Christians believe today. Almost certainly you have been taught a radically different view at some point in your Christian journey. You may even been tempted to scoff at its very suggestion at this point. Nevertheless, I challenge you to bear with me as we wade through the evidence on this matter in Revelation. I am convinced that you will find the evidence quite persuasive.

As we begin our interpretive journey through this issue, may we bear in mind the exhortation of Paul who wrote: "Let God be found true, though every man be found a liar" (Rom. 3:4). May

---

35. Suetonius, *Nero* 49.
36. Suetonius, *Nero* 49.
37. Schaff, *History* 1:379.

we with the faithful Bereans of old "examine the Scriptures daily, to see whether these things" be so (Acts 17:11).

2

THE RELEVANCE OF THE BEAST

The Revelation of Jesus Christ, which God gave Him to show to His bond-servants, the things which must shortly take place; and He sent and communicated it by His angel to His bond-servant John (Rev. 1:1).

One of the most important clues for the proper understanding of Revelation is at the same time one of the most overlooked and neglected. This clue is also a significant key for opening up to us the identity of the Beast. We are speaking of the stated expectation of John in regard to the time of the fulfillment of the prophecies.

The truth of the matter is that *John specifically states that the prophecies of Revelation (a number of which had to do with the Beast) would begin coming to pass within a very short period of time.* He clearly says that the events of Revelation were "shortly to take place" and that "the time is near." And as if to insure that we not miss the point — which many commentators have! — he emphasizes this truth in a variety of ways. Read the following passages and see if you agree.

Emphasis on the Expectation

First, John emphasizes his anticipation of the soon occurrence of his prophecy by *strategic placement* of the time references. He places his boldest time statements in both the introduction and conclusion to Revelation. It is remarkable that so many recent commentators have missed it literally coming and going!

21

The statement of expectancy is found three times in the first chapter — twice in the first three verses: Revelation 1:1, 3, 19. The same idea is found four times in his concluding remarks: Revelation 22:6, 7, 12, 20. *It is as if John carefully bracketed the entire work to avoid any confusion.* It is important to note that these statements occur in the more historical and didactic sections of Revelation, before and after the major dramatic-symbolic visions. You should take time to just quickly read these verses in order to sense John's expectancy. We will look carefully at these below.

Second, his temporal expectation receives *frequent repetition.* His expectation appears seven times in the opening and closing sections of Revelation, and at least three times in the letters to the Seven Churches (Rev. 2:16; 3:10, 11).[1] According to the unambiguous statement of the text, the events were "about to come." John was telling the seven historical churches (Rev. 1:4, 11; 22:16) in his era to expect the events of his prophecy at any moment. He repeats the point for emphasis.

Third, he carefully *varies his manner of expression,* as if to avoid any potential confusion as to his meaning. A brief survey of the three leading terms he employs will be helpful in ascertaining his meaning.

John's Varied Expressions of Anticipation

The first of these terms we come upon in Revelation is the Greek word *tachos,* translated "shortly." John is explaining the purpose of his writing in Revelation 1:1, which reads: "The Revelation of Jesus Christ, which God gave Him to show to His bond-servants, the things which must *shortly* [*tachos*] take place; and He sent and communicated it by His angel to His bond-servant John." The standard Greek lexicon of our era lists the following meanings under the *tachos* entry: "speed," "quickness," "swiftness," "haste," "quickly," "at once," "without delay," "soon," "in

---

1. It should be understood that there are other notes of expectancy elsewhere in Revelation, but those are dependent upon the ones we are considering here in the didactic sections.

a short time," "shortly," "very quickly," and "without delay."[2] If you look up Revelation 1:1 in *any* modern translation you will find that the idea clearly exhibited is that of the very near occurrence of the events of Revelation. This term also occurs in Revelation 2:16; 3:11; and 22:6, 7, 12, 20. Even a cursory reading of these verses unavoidably leads to the conclusion that John expected these things to happen "shortly" or "quickly."

Another term John uses is *eggus* (pronounced *engus*), which means "near" (Rev. 1:3; 22:10). In Revelation 1:3 we read: "Blessed is he who reads and those who hear the words of the prophecy, and heeds the things which are written in it; for the time is *near* [*eggus*]." When used of spatial relationships it means "near," "close to," "close by." When used of temporal relationships it signifies "near," "soon."[3] This term literally means "at hand."[4] Its import in our context is clearly that of temporal nearness. The events bracketed by these statements were expected, by the holy apostle John, to begin taking place at any moment.

The final term we can note is *mello*, which means "about to" (Rev. 1:19; 3:10). When found in both of the verb forms appearing in Revelation 1:19 and 3:10, this term means "be on the point of, be about to."[5] A number of Bible translations confuse the matter when they translate the word properly in Revelation 3:10 but improperly in Revelation 1:19. According to *Young's Literal Translation of the Bible*, Revelation 1:19 reads: "Write the things that thou hast seen, and the things that are, and the things that are *about to come* [*mello*] after these things."[6] The leading interlinear versions

---

2. William F. Arndt and F. Wilbur Gingrich, *A Greek-English Lexicon of the New Testament and Other Early Christian Literature* (Chicago: University of Chicago Press, 1957), p. 814.

3. *Ibid.*, p. 213.

4. The word is derived from the compounding of *en* (in, at) and *guion* (limb, hand). See Joseph H. Thayer, *A Greek-English Lexicon of the New Testament*, 2nd ed. (New York: American Book Co., 1889), p. 164.

5. Arndt-Gingrich, *Lexicon*, p. 502 (1-b).

6. Robert Young, *Young's Literal Translation of the Holy Bible*, 2nd ed. (Grand Rapids: Baker, rep. 1898), p. 167 (New Testament).

of the New Testament concur.[7] This is surely the proper translation of the verse.

The Obvious Is Painful

Unfortunately, right in the very first verse of Revelation certain commentators begin straining to reinterpret the obvious. There are various maneuvers used to get around this and the other terms: Some understand these terms as indicating that whenever the events do start coming to pass, they will occur with great speed, following one upon the other with great rapidity.[8] Others view them as indicating that such events as John prophesied are always imminent.[9] That is, the events are always ready to occur, though they may not actually occur until thousands of years later. Still others see John's references as a measure of God's time, not man's.[10] That is, John is saying that these events will come to pass "shortly" *from God's perspective*. But, then, we must remember that "a day with the Lord is as a thousand years" (2 Pet. 3:8).

Each of these approaches is destroyed by the very fact that John repeats and varies his terms as if to dispel any confusion. Think of it: If these words in these verses do not indicate that John expected the events to occur soon, *what words could John have used to express such?* How could he have said it more plainly?

Another detriment to the strained interpretations listed above is that John is writing to historical churches existing in his own day (Rev. 1:4, 11; 2-3). He and they have already entered the earliest stages of "the tribulation" (Rev. 1:9a). John's message (ultimately from Christ, Rev. 1:1; 2:1; 22:16) calls upon each to

---

7. George Ricker Berry, *The Interlinear Greek-English New Testament* (Grand Rapids: Zondervan, rep. 1961), p. 625; Alfred Marshall, *The Interlinear Greek-English New Testament*, 2nd ed. (Grand Rapids: Zondervan, 1959), p. 959; Jay P. Green, Sr., *The Interlinear Bible*, 2nd ed. (Grand Rapids: Baker, 1983), p. 927.

8. John F. Walvoord, *The Revelation of Jesus Christ* (Chicago: Moody Press, 1966), p. 35.

9. Robert H. Mounce, *The Book of Revelation* (Grand Rapids: Eerdmans, 1977), p. 65.

10. Leon Morris, *The Revelation of St. John* (Grand Rapids: Eerdmans, 1969), p. 45.

give careful, spiritual attention to his words (Rev. 2:7, 11, 17, 29; 3:6, 13, 22). John is deeply concerned with the expectant cry of the martyrs and the divine promise of their soon vindication (Rev. 6:10; cp. Rev. 5:3-5). It would be a cruel mockery of their circumstances for John to tell them that when help comes it will come with swiftness — even though it may not come until two or three thousand years later. Or that the events are always imminent — though the readers may never experience them. Or that God will send help soon — according to the way the Eternal God measures time.

Christ's Comings

Perhaps one of the contextual matters that causes the most confusion is that in several of the passages before us reference is made to Christ's "coming" (Rev. 2:16; 3:11; 22:7, 12, 20). "Behold, I am coming quickly" resounds in these verses. Surely we do not believe the Second Advent came in the first century, do we?

Here is where a good deal of unnecessary confusion arises. Actually there are a number of ways in which Christ "comes." It is true that He will come at the end of history, bringing about the resurrection and the judgment (Acts 1:11; 1 Thess. 4:13ff.; 1 Cor. 15:20-26).[11] But Scripture also teaches that Christ comes to His people in other ways.[12] He comes to us personally in the Holy Spirit (John 16:16, 18, 28),[13] in fellowship by His presence in the

---

11. A view currently gaining popularity teaches that the totality of the Second Advent of Christ occurred in the first-century (bringing about the resurrection, rapture, and judgment) and that history will continue forever. This view is not supported by any creed or any council of the Church in history. All creeds and councils that touch upon the subject of eschatology view history as coming to a final conclusion. It should be noted that much of the literature promoting this view is from the anti-creedal sect of the Campbellites. See Max R. King, *The Spirit of Prophecy* (published by author, 1971), pp. 100-102, 124, 261-262, etc.

12. For an excellent discussion of this, see Roderick Campbell, *Israel and the New Covenant* (Tyler, TX: Geneva Ministries, [1954] 1983), ch. 8.

13. It should be noted that the Greek word occurring in John 16:18, 28 is *erchomai*, which means "come." It is also the word found in Rev. 1:7; 2:5, 16; 3:11; 16:15; 22:7, 12, 17, 20.

Church (Matt. 18:20), to believers at death (John 14:1-3),[14] to God in heaven to receive His kingdom (Dan. 7:13), and in judicial judgment upon men in history (Matt. 21:40, 41; Rev. 2:5).[15] But to which sort of "coming" do the verses mentioned above from Revelation refer?

The references in Revelation to His coming have to do with His coming in judgment, *particularly upon Israel*. This is evident in the theme verse of Revelation found in Revelation 1:7: "Behold, He is coming with the clouds, and every eye will see Him, even those who pierced Him; and all the tribes of the earth will mourn over Him. Even so. Amen." This cloud-coming of Christ in judgment is reminiscent of Old Testament cloud-comings of God in judgment upon ancient historical people and nations (Pss. 18:7-15; 104:3; Isa. 19:1; Joel 2:1, 2; Hab. 1:2ff.; Zeph. 1:14, 15).

Furthermore, it is obvious that this coming is a judgment coming focusing upon first century Israel. Revelation 1:7 says He is coming upon "those who pierced Him." It states that as a consequence all "the tribes of the earth [or Land]" will mourn. The New Testament is emphatic in pointing to first century Israel as responsible for crucifying Christ (John 19:6, 15; Acts 2:22-23, 36; 3:13-15; 5:30; 7:52; 1 Thess. 2:14-15).[16]

Jesus even told the Jewish leaders that they would personally witness this judgment-coming (Matt. 26:64). This coming (Matt. 24:30)[17] was to occur in His generation (Matt. 24:30, 34; cp. Matt. 23:31-36). It was to be witnessed by men who stood and listened

---

14. Here again the Greek word used is *erchomai*.

15. In Matthew 21:40 the Greek word is the aorist tense form of the Greek verb *erchomai*.

16. Early post-apostolic Christianity continued this theme of pointing to the Jews as the ones who pierced Him. See Ignatius (A.D. 50-115), *Magnesians* 11 and *Trallians* 11. Justin Martyr (A.D. 100-165), *First Apology* ch. 35, ch. 38, and *Dialogue with Trypho* 72. More detailed information on Revelation 1:7 may be found in Chapter 9.

17. The Dan. 7:13 context — upon which Matt. 24:30 and 26:64 are based — refers to the Ascension of Christ to take up His kingly rule. The dramatic, historical judgment-experience or witness of the fact of His having ascended is the destruction of the Temple, which event is in view in these and related passages.

to Jesus and was to be in great power (Mark 9:1).

In regard to the Jews (those who "pierced Christ," Rev. 1:7), the Jewish War with Rome from A.D. 67 to 70 brought about the deaths of tens of thousands of the Jews in Judea, and the enslavement of thousands upon thousands more. The Jewish historian Flavius Josephus, who was an eyewitness, records that 1,100,000 Jews perished in the siege of Jerusalem, though this figure is disputed. J. L. von Mosheim, the great ecclesiastical historian, wrote that "throughout the whole history of the human race, we meet with but few, if any, instances of slaughter and devastation at all to be compared with this."[18]

But as awful as the Jewish loss of life was, the utter devastation of Jerusalem, the final destruction of the temple, and the conclusive cessation of the sacrificial system were lamented even more. The covenantal significance of the loss of the temple stands as the most dramatic outcome of the War. It was an unrepeatable loss, for the temple has never been rebuilt. Hence, any Jewish calamity after A.D. 70 would pale in comparison to the redemptive-historical significance of the loss of the temple.

So then, the expectation of a judgment-coming of Christ in the first century is easily explicable in terms of the biblical and historical record.[19] Thus, the point remains: John clearly expected the soon occurrence of the events of Revelation. Obviously, then, the Beast of Revelation must be a contemporary figure who was relevant to the first century audience. Nero was a contemporary political figure who was most relevant to John's hearers.

Conclusion

In light of the clear and emphatic textual evidence, the careful

---

18. John Laurence von Mosheim, *Historical Commentaries on the State of Christianity* (New York: Converse, 1854) 1:125.

19. This expectation of soon occurrence is prevalent throughout the New Testament; something dramatic was looming upon the very horizon of apostolic Christianity: Rom. 13:11, 12; 16:20; 1 Cor. 7:26, 29-31; Col. 3:6; 1 Thess. 2:16; Heb. 10:25, 37; James 5:8, 9; 1 Pet. 4:5, 7; 1 John 2:17, 18.

interpreter of Revelation recognizes that John expected the events prophesied to begin taking place very soon after he wrote. To overlook the repeated statements in Revelation in this regard is to interpret Revelation in defiance of the facts.

This evidence removes any possibility of identifying the Beast with any figure beyond the first century. To assert that the Beast is any contemporary figure existing in our own time is to miss the total point of what John spoke about. Of course, this evidence alone does not demand Nero Caesar as the identity of the Beast. But it does set the stage for his appearance, which will be demonstrated on other grounds.

3

THE NUMBER OF THE BEAST

Here is wisdom. Let him who has understanding calculate the number of the beast, for the number is that of a man; and his number is six hundred and sixty-six (Rev. 13:18).

Following upon an understanding of the necessity for a Beast who is relevant to first century Christians, I come now to material which very particularly points to Nero Caesar. This piece of evidence is drawn from what is probably one of the best known features of Revelation.[1] We speak, of course, of the number 666, which is recorded in Revelation 13:18 quoted above. Who among us has not feared $6.66 coming up on his cash register receipt? Or worse yet, 666 appearing in his Social Security number!

But how is this number helpful to our inquiry? Let us begin with some background research.

The Function of Ancient Alphabets

The usefulness of this number lies in the fact that in ancient days alphabets served a two-fold purpose. Letters functioned, of course, as phonetic symbols. As such, they functioned just as our modern alphabet does. But in ancient times letters also served as numerals, in that the Arabic numbering system was a later devel-

---

1. Mounce introduces his discussion of Revelation 13:18 thus: "No verse in Revelation has received more attention than this one with its cryptic reference to the number of the beast" (Robert Mounce, *The Book of Revelation* [Grand Rapids: Eerdmans, 1977], p. 263).

29

opment of history. Roman numerals are perhaps the most familiar example of this. In Roman numerals the letter "I" possessed the numerical value of 1; "V" was 5; "X" was 10; "C" was 100; and so forth. In the Greek and Hebrew the values of letters followed

**TABLE OF NUMERALS IN USE
DURING THE BIBLICAL PERIOD**

	Hebrew	*Greek*
1	א	α
2	ב	β
3	ג	γ
4	ד	δ
5	ה	ε
6	ו	ς
7	ז	ζ
8	ח	η
9	ט	θ
10	י	ι
20	כ	κ
30	ל	λ
40	מ	μ
50	נ	ν
60	ס	ξ
70	ע	ο
80	פ	π
90	צ	ϙ
100	ק	ρ
200	ר	σ
300	ש	τ
400	ת	υ
500	תק	φ
600		χ
700		ψ
800		ω

Source: J. D. Douglas, ed., *New Bible Dictionary*, 2nd ed. (Leicester, England: Inter-Varsity Press; Wheaton, IL: Tyndale House Publishers, Inc., 1982), pp. 842-843.

the order of the alphabet.[2] The first nine letters represented the values of 1-9; the tenth through nineteenth letters were used for tens (10, 20, 30, etc.); the remaining letters represented values of hundreds (100, 200, 300, etc.).[3]

Due to this ancient phenomenon of the two-fold use of alphabets, riddles employing numbers which concealed names were common. This phenomenon is called a "cryptogram" by modern scholars. Among the Greeks it was called *isopsephia* ("numerical equality"); among the Jews it was called *gimatriya* ("mathematical").[4] Any given name could be reduced to its numerical equivalent by adding up the mathematical value of all of the letters of the name.

Archaeologists have discovered many illustrations of cryptograms as graffiti on ancient city walls that have been excavated. One example has been found in the excavations at Pompeii. There the Greek inscription reads: "*philo es arithmos phi mu epsilon*" ("I love her whose number is 545"). Zahn notes of this example that "The name of the lover is concealed; the beloved will know it when she recognises her name in the sum of the numerical value of the 3 letters *phi mu epsilon*, i.e., 545 ($ph = 500 + m = 40 + e = 5$). But the passing stranger does not know in the very least who the beloved is, nor does the 19th century investigator know which of the many Greek feminine names she bore."[5]

---

2. For Greek, see W. G. Rutherford, *The First Greek Grammar* (London: Macmillan 1935), pp. 143ff. For Hebrew, see E. Kautzsch, ed., A. E. Cowley, trans., *Gesenius' Hebrew Grammar*, 28th ed. (Oxford: Clarendon Press, 1946), p. 30.

3. For readily available evidence of these values in Hebrew and Greek, the reader may consult the appropriate letters at their entries in Francis Brown, S. R. Driver, and Charles A. Briggs, eds., *A Hebrew and English Lexicon of the Old Testament* (Oxford: Clarendon Press, 1972) and G. Abbott-Smith, *A Manual Greek Lexicon of the New Testament* (Edinburgh: T. & T. Clark, 1950).

4. See Alfred Edersheim, *Sketches of Jewish Social Life* (Grand Rapids: Eerdmans, [1876] 1972), pp. 289-290. Examples of Hebrew cryptograms can be found in the ancient Jewish Talmud at *Sanhedrin* 22a, *Yoma* 20a, and *Nazir* 5a.

5. Cited in Oskar Rühle, "*Arithmeo*" in Gerhard Kittel, ed., *Theological Dictionary of the New Testament*, trans. Geoffrey W. Bromiley, vol. 1 (Grand Rapids: Eerdmans, 1964), p. 462.

In the midst of his Latin history, Suetonius records a sample of a Greek lampoon that was circulated after the burning of Rome, which occurred in A.D. 64: "*Neopsephon Neron idian metera apektine.*" The translation of this lampoon is: "A calculation new. Nero his mother slew."[6] J. C. Rolfe notes in the *Loeb Classical Library* edition of Suetonius's works that "the numerical value of the Greek letters in Nero's name (1005) is the same as that of the rest of the sentence; hence we have an equation, Nero = the slayer of his own mother."[7] It is quite interesting to note that there were already anti-Nero cryptograms circulating when John wrote Revelation.

That Jewish Rabbis of old used *gimatriya* is also evident. This may be seen by consultation of the Babylonian Talmud and other ancient Rabbinical writings.[8] In addition, Christian writings often employed gematric riddles. The ancient Christian *Sibylline Oracles* has Jesus' name as equivalent to "888"[9] and makes use of number values to indicate initials of various Roman emperors, including Nero.[10]

When John, then, gave a numerical value as a partial concealment of the name of the Beast (Rev. 13:18), he was engaging in a common practice in his day. If we could decipher the name hidden in the number, we could point to the identity of the Beast.

As we seek to learn the identity of 666, we must recall the several principles of interpretation which we listed in Chapter 1. Those principles were: (1) The name-number 666 must be "that of a *man*" (Rev. 13:18b). (2) The name must be one of John's *contemporaries*. (3) The name must be that of someone *relevant* to the first century Christians to whom John wrote. (4) The name must be that of someone of an evil and blasphemous nature. (5) He

---

6. Suetonius, *Nero* 39.

7. Suetonius, *Lives of the Twelve Caesars*, vol. 2, trans. J. C. Rolfe, ed. E. H. Warmington, *Loeb Classical Library* (Cambridge: Harvard, 1913), p. 158.

8. See *Yoma* 20a, *Nazir* 5a, *Sanhedrin* 22:9 and *Uzkin* 12. See F. W. Farrar, *The Early Days of Christianity* (New York: Cassell and Co., 1884), p. 471.

9. *Sibylline Oracles* 1:327-329.

10. *Sibylline Oracles* 5:1-50.

must also be a political figure possessing great authority (Rev. 13:2, 7).

A good deal of debate has involved the idea I have here designated as my first principle, which is that the number must be that of *a* man. Some scholars interpret the phrase "number of a man" to indicate merely that the number involved is a human number, not a supernatural one.[11] But there is nothing in the context to suggest such. What would be John's point? Why would John tell his readers (whom he had exhorted to read and understand, Rev. 1:3) that he was going to give an intelligible, human number, as opposed to an unintelligible, supernatural one? Others approach the number as purely symbolic of "failure upon failure upon failure"[12] or "a persistent falling short"[13] in that it fails of the number seven, which speaks of completion or qualitative perfection.[14] In response it should be noted that the more natural interpretation of the phrase is "the number of *a* man." Furthermore, the number actually is "six hundred, sixty and six," not "six and six and six."

Identifying 666

Based on what we know of Nero's character and actions, he fits easily within the parameters of the textually derived principles stated above. I will show that, as a matter of fact, Nero *is* indicated by this mysterious number. Two lines of evidence converge on Nero, compelling my choice of him as the candidate.

Nero's Number

Of course, the necessary condition for a candidate is that his

---

11. See discussion in R. H. Charles, *A Critical and Exegetical Commentary on the Revelation of St. John*, 2 vols. (Edinburgh: T. & T. Clark, 1920) 1:364-365; and Mounce, *Revelation*, p. 264.

12. William Hendriksen, *More Than Conquerors* (Grand Rapids: Baker, [1939] 1967), p. 182.

13. Leon Morris, *The Revelation of St. John* (Grand Rapids: Eerdmans, 1969), p. 174.

14. Henry B. Swete, *Commentary on Revelation* (Grand Rapids: Kregel, [1911] 1977), pp. cxxxvi-cxxvii.

name fit the cryptogrammic value. If any given name does not contain the value of 666 then that name must necessarily be excluded from consideration.

Interestingly, several scholars of the last century — Fritzsche, Holtzmann, Benary, Hitzig and Reuss[15] — each stumbled independently upon the name Nero Caesar almost simultaneously. We have seen that the *Greek* spelling of Nero's name has the value 1005. A *Hebrew* spelling of his name was *Nrwn Qsr* (pronounced: Neron Kaiser). It has been documented by archaeological finds that a first century Hebrew spelling of Nero's name provides us with precisely the value of 666.[16] Jastrow's lexicon of the Talmud contains this very spelling.[17] The numerical valuation is as follows:

$$\text{נ} = 50 \quad \text{ר} = 200 \quad \text{ו} = 6 \quad \text{נ} = 50 \quad \text{ק} = 100 \quad \text{ס} = 60 \quad \text{ר} = 200$$

which gives:

$$\text{נְרוֹן. קְסַר} = 666$$

A great number of biblical scholars recognize this name as the solution to the problem. Is it not remarkable that this most relevant emperor has a name that fits precisely the required sum? Is this sheer historical accident?

The Textual Variant 616

If you consult a Bible with marginal references you may notice something of interest regarding Revelation 13:18. Your reference may say something to the effect: "Some manuscripts read 616." The fact is that the number 666 in some ancient manuscripts of Scripture is actually changed to 616. But why? Was it changed accidentally, or on purpose?

---

15. See Charles, *Revelation* 1:367 and Farrar, *Early Days*, p. 471, n. 4.

16. D. R. Hillers, "Revelation 13:18 and A Scroll from Murabba'at," *Bulletin of the American Schools of Oriental Research* 170 (April, 1963): 65.

17. Marcus Jastrow, *A Dictionary of the Targumim, the Talmud Babli and Yerushalmi, and the Midrashic Literature* (London: Judaica Press, 1903). See Charles, *Revelation* 1:367.

The difference surely is no accident of sight made by an early copyist. The numbers 666 and 616 are not even similar in appearance in the original Greek — whether spelled out in words or written out as numerals. The letters representative of the values for 60 and for 10 (which would make the difference between the two readings) are as different as any two letters could be. The letter used as the value for 60 is ξ; the letter for the value 10 is ι. If these values were originally spelled out in words there still would be no similarity. The value for 60 would be indicated thus: *hexekonta*; that for 10 would read: *deka*. There is no way a copyist could confuse the two. As textual scholars agree, it must be intentional.[18] But again we ask, Why? Although we cannot be absolutely certain, a strong and most reasonable case may be made for the following conjecture. As shown above, John, a Jew, used a Hebrew spelling of Nero's name in order to arrive at the figure 666. But when Revelation began circulating among those less acquainted with Hebrew, a well-meaning copyist who knew the meaning of 666 might have intended to make its deciphering easier by altering it to 616. It surely is no mere coincidence that 616 is the numerical value of "Nero Caesar," when spelled in Hebrew by transliterating it from its more common Latin spelling.

Such a conjecture would satisfactorily explain the rationale for the divergence: so that the non-Hebrew mind might more readily discern the identity of the Beast. Even late-date advocate Donald Guthrie, who rejects the Nero theory, grants that this variant gives the designation Nero "a distinct advantage."[19] As renowned Greek scholar Bruce Metzger says: "Perhaps the change was intentional, seeing that the Greek form Neron Caesar written in Hebrew characters (*nrwn qsr*) is equivalent to 666, whereas the Latin form Nero Caesar (*nrw qsr*) is equivalent to 616."[20] Such a possibility

---

18. Bruce M. Metzger, *A Textual Commentary on the Greek New Testament* (London: United Bible Societies, 1971), pp. 751-752.

19. Donald B. Guthrie, *New Testament Introduction*, 3rd ed. (Downer's Grove, IL: Inter-Varsity Press, 1970), p. 959.

20. Metzger, *Textual Commentary*, p. 752.

offers a remarkable confirmation of the designation of Nero.

Is it not conceivable, in light of all that has been noted heretofore, that John, as well, so designated Nero? As you continue reading through the chapters to follow, note how well Nero fits all the requirements of the case.

Objections to Nero

Of course, this view, though widely spread, is not accepted by all scholars. There are certain problems that some see with the Nero designation. Let us mention two of the major ones.

The Silence of Early Church Fathers

It is frequently argued that in one of the earliest treatments of the cryptogram in Revelation 13:18 there is no mention of Nero as a likely candidate. The reference to which we refer is the work *Against Heresies* written by Irenaeus, Bishop of Lyons, around A.D. 180.

Not only does Irenaeus not mention Nero, but he mentions other possibilities: *Euthanos, Laetinos,* and *Teitan*.[21] If Nero was the actual meaning of the riddle, why did not Irenaeus know this, since he wrote about the matter 100 years later? Why do no other church fathers suggest it?

This would certainly appear to be a reasonable objection to our theory.[22] In fact, it is *the* strongest argument against it. However, in the final analysis it cannot overthrow the positive evidence for the theory, for two reasons.

First, this argument is really a two-edged sword. The very fact that Irenaeus, writing just 100 years after Revelation, cannot be sure of the proper designation demonstrates that the true interpretation, whatever it was, had very quickly been lost. If this is true of Irenaeus in A.D. 180, it is certainly true of the later fathers.

Second, had Irenaeus offered with conviction and assurance a

---

21. Irenaeus, *Against Heresies* 5:30:3.

22. This objection, however, would apply to *any* modern exposition of the name, for no modern commentator adopts Irenaeus's suggestions!

specific alternative, the case against the Nero theory would have been more seriously challenged. Interestingly, Irenaeus suggests the hopelessness of determining the proper understanding: "It is therefore more certain, and less hazardous, to await the fulfillment of the prophecy, than to be making surmises, and casting about for any names that may present themselves, inasmuch as many names can be found possessing the number mentioned; and the same question will, after all, remain unsolved."[23] *Irenaeus admits his own ignorance on the matter.* How can that prove the Nero theory wrong? None of the later church fathers does more than guess at the solution. Did the riddle have *no* answer?

The Problem of the Hebrew Spelling

Some have argued that since John writes to Gentile churches in Asia Minor, the mechanical maneuver necessary to derive the name from its Hebrew spelling would be too difficult for the audience. Though reasonable at first glance, this objection also fails to undermine the Nero theory.

First, although John wrote in Greek, Revelation has long been recognized as one of the more "Jewish" books of the New Testament. All technical commentaries on Revelation recognize this. For instance, in his commentary R. H. Charles includes a major section entitled "A Short Grammar of the Apocalypse." Section 10 of this "Grammar" is entitled "The Hebraic Style of the Apocalypse."[24] There Charles well notes of John's unusual syntax: "The reason clearly is that, *while he writes in Greek, he thinks in Hebrew.*"[25] As J. P. M. Sweet puts it: "The probability is that the writer, thinking in Hebrew or Aramaic, consciously or unconsciously carried over Semitic idioms into his Greek, and that his 'howlers' are deliberate attempts to reproduce the grammar of classical Hebrew at certain points."[26] Some scholars have even suggested

23. *Against Heresies* 5:30:3.
24. Charles, *Revelation* 1:cxvii, cxlii.
25. *Ibid.*, p. cxliii.
26. J. P. M. Sweet, *Revelation* (Philadelphia: Westminster Press, 1979), p. 16.

John originally wrote it in Aramaic, a cognate language to Hebrew.[27]

Second, in fact there are other very Hebraic names in Revelation. For instance, the words "Abaddon" (Rev. 9:11) and "Armageddon" (Rev. 16:16) are Hebrew words which are given Greek equivalents. The Hebrew word "Satan" is used by John, but is interpreted into Greek as "the devil" (Rev. 12:9). Other Hebrew words appear, as well: "Amen" is said to mean "truthfully" (Rev. 3:14). The Hebrew "hallelujah" is not even translated into a Greek equivalent (Rev. 19:1, 3, 4, 6). How natural, it would seem, to adopt a Hebraic spelling for the basis of the cryptogram.

Third, Asia Minor was well populated by Jews. As a matter of fact "long before the Christian era the Jews had formed a considerable factor in the population of the Asian cities."[28] Indeed, the Jews "were a notable part of the population of Alexandria. They were strongly rooted in Syria and Asia Minor. . . . Few cities of the empire were without their presence."[29] The audience could well have been composed of at least a significant minority of Jews.

And why should John not use an Hebraic riddle? Was not John himself a Jew? Was not he, the writer of Revelation, sent "to the circumcised" (Gal. 2:9)? Despite the brevity of each of the Seven Letters, in them are prominent allusions to Jewish situations (Rev. 2:9, 14; 3:9). In the book itself are very definite allusions to Jewish matters, such as the twelve tribes of Israel (Rev. 7 and 14).

Conclusion

The role of Nero Caesar in Revelation is written large. As all roads lead to Rome, so do they all terminate at Nero Caesar's Palace. The factors pointing to Nero in Revelation are numerous

---

27. Charles C. Torrey, *The Apocalypse of John* (New Haven: Yale University Press, 1958), pp. 27-58.

28. Swete, *Revelation*, p. lxvi.

29. Williston Walker, *A History of the Christian Church*, 3rd ed. (New York: Scribner's, 1970), p. 16.

and varied. I have shown that his name perfectly fits the certain reading of the text in Revelation 13:18, which is 666. His name even fits the corrupted reading, 616. In later chapters additional evidences will be brought forth to provide an even greater enhancement of the interpretation of Nero as 666.

It is difficult to discount the many ways in which Nero fits the expectations of Revelation. *He is the only contemporary historical figure that can possibly fulfill all of the requirements.* Contrary to some commentators who fear that the key to Revelation's "666" is lost, I suggest that the key is actually in the keyhole, the last place to look!

4

THE CHARACTER OF THE BEAST

And the beast which I saw was like a leopard, and his feet were like those of a bear, and his mouth like the mouth of a lion. And the dragon gave him his power and his throne and great authority (Rev. 13:1-2).

In Revelation 13 the one behind the 666 riddle is specifically designated a "beast." The word for "beast" in Greek is *therion*, a term frequently used of "wild animals," of "dangerous animals."[1] *Therion* is often used of the wild, carnivorous animals employed in the cruel Roman arenas.[2] Because of its natural association, the term is often quite aptly used figuratively of persons with "a 'bestial' nature, *beast, monster*."[3]

Not only is the name "Beast" employed by John in this passage, but he even symbolically represents this fearsome being with horrible, beastly imagery. This Beast is a compound of such feared and destructive carnivores as the leopard, bear, and lion. Almost all commentators agree that this vision of the Beast is reflective of

---

1. William F. Arndt and F. Wilbur Gingrich, *A Greek-English Lexicon of the New Testament and Other Early Christian Literature* (Chicago: University of Chicago Press, 1957), p. 361. In Lev. 26:6 the beasts of the land are symbolic of evil; in Lev. 26:22 God promises their return to plague Israel and to bereave her of her children if she is unfaithful to the covenant. Messianic blessedness vanquishes the evil beasts (Isa. 11:6-9; Ezek. 34:25).

2. Josephus, *The Wars of the Jews* 7:38; *Martyrdom of Polycarp* 2:4; 3ff.; 11:1ff; Ignatius, *Romans* 4:1ff.; 5:3; *Smyrnaens* 4:2; *Diognetus* 7:7; Hermas, *Visions* 3:2:1.

3. Arndt-Gingrich, *Lexicon*, p. 361.

Daniel's vision of the Four Beasts (Dan. 7). John's Beast even has ten horns like Daniel's fourth beast (Dan. 7:7; Rev. 13:1). However, John compounds the lion, bear, and leopard — three of Daniel's beasts — into one Beast. Daniel emphasizes the fearsome terror of his beast: "After this I kept looking in the night visions, and behold, a fourth beast, dreadful and terrifying and extremely strong; and it had large iron teeth. It devoured and crushed, and trampled down the remainder with its feet" (Dan. 7:7).

The Pagan Evidence of Nero's Nature

Now it is almost universally agreed that Nero was one who was possessed of a "bestial nature." Nero was even feared and hated by his own countrymen. A perusal of the ancient literature demonstrates that Nero "was of a cruel and unrestrained brutality."[4]

His bestial cruelty is evidenced in the writings of the Roman historian Suetonius (A.D. 70-160), who speaks of Nero's "cruelty of disposition" evidencing itself at an early age.[5] He documents Nero's evil and states: "neither discrimination nor moderation [were employed] in putting to death whosoever he pleased on any pretext whatever."[6] Suetonius notes that Nero "compelled four hundred senators and six hundred Roman knights, some of whom were well to do and of unblemished reputation, to fight in the arena."[7] He also mentions that Nero was a sodomist, who is said to have castrated a boy named Sporus and married him.[8] He enjoyed homosexual rape and torture.[9] He ruthlessly killed his mother, brother, wife, aunt, and many others close to him and of

---

4. Sir Paul Harvey, *The Oxford Companion to Classical Literature* (Oxford: Clarendon Press, 1937), p. 287.

5. Suetonius, *Nero* 7:1.

6. *Ibid.* 27:1.

7. *Ibid.* 12:1.

8. *Ibid.* 28, 29.

9. *Ibid.*

high station in Rome.[10]

Roman historian Tacitus (A.D. 55-117) spoke of Nero's "cruel nature" that "put to death so many innocent men."[11] Roman naturalist Pliny the Elder (A.D. 23-79) described Nero as "the destroyer of the human race" and "the poison of the world."[12] Roman satirist Juvenal (A.D. 60-140) speaks of "Nero's cruel and bloody tyranny."[13] Elsewhere he calls Nero a "cruel tyrant."[14] Nero so affected the imagination that the pagan writer Apollonius of Tyana (*ca.* 4 B.C-A.D. 96) specifically mentions that Nero was called a "beast": "In my travels, which have been wider than ever man yet accomplished, I have seen many, many wild beasts of Arabia and India; but this beast, that is commonly called a Tyrant, I know not how many heads it has, nor if it be crooked of claw, and armed with horrible fangs. . . . And of wild beasts you cannot say that they were ever known to eat their own mother, but Nero has gorged himself on this diet."[15]

Among the ancient pagan written traditions exhibiting a hatred and mockery of Nero are those by such Roman and Greek writers as: Suetonius, the writer of *The Octavia*, Pliny the Younger, Martial, Statius, Marcus Aurelius, Aulus Persius Flaccus, Vulcacius, Epictetus, Marcus Annaeus Lucan, and Herodian.[16] Nero scholar Miriam T. Griffin analyzes the presentation of Nero in the ancient tragedy *The Octavia*: "Nero is, in fact, the proverbial tyrant, robbed of any personal characteristics, a mere incarnation of the

---

10. *Ibid.* 33-35. See also Dio, *Roman History* 61:1:2; *Ascension of Isaiah* 4:1; *Sibylline Oracles* 5:30; 12:82.

11. *Histories* 4:7; 4:8.

12. Pliny, *Natural History* 7:45; 22:92.

13. Juvenal, *Satire* 7:225.

14. *Satire* 10:306ff

15. Philostratus, *Life of Apollonius* 4:38.

16. Suetonius, *Domitian* 14; *The Octavia*; Pliny the Younger, *Panegyricus* 53; Juvenal, 4:38; Martial, *Epigrams* 7:21; 21:33; Statius, *Silvae* 2:7; Marcus Aurelius, 3:16; Aulus Persius Flaccus in Suetonius's *On Poets – Aulus Persius Flaccus*; Vulcacius, *Life of Cassius* 8:4; *Capitolinus* 28:10; Epictetus, 4:5,17; Marcus Annaeus Lucan in Suetonius's *On Poets – Lucan*; Herodian, 3:4, *Historial Augusta*; Martial, *Book of Spectacles* 2.

will to evil, unaffected by advice or influence."[17]

In the Jewish *Sibylline Oracles* Nero is spoken of as a "terrible snake, breathing out grievous war. . . . He will also cut the mountain between two seas and defile it with gore. But even when he disappears he will be destructive. Then he will return declaring himself equal to God."[18] Later it speaks of him as a notoriously "savage-minded mighty man, much-bloodied, raving nonsense."[19] Another of the *Sibylline Oracles* mentions him as "terrible and frightful . . . a terrible snake."[20]

Many of the early Christians remembered Nero with loathing. I will cite just a few. Clement of Rome (A.D. 30-100) speaks of Nero's persecution as one which claimed "a vast multitude of the elect . . . through many indignities and tortures."[21] In Book 8 of the Christian *Sibylline Oracles* (A.D. 175) Nero is fearfully designated a "great beast."[22] Tertullian (A.D. 160-220) satirically states: "We glory in having our condemnation hallowed by the hostility of such a wretch."[23] Eusebius (A.D. 260-340) echoes this hatred of Nero when he speaks of Nero's "depravity," "the coarseness of the man's extraordinary madness, under the influence of which . . . [he] accomplished the destruction of so many myriads without any reason" and his being "the first of the emperors who showed himself an enemy of the divine religion."[24]

Lactantius (A.D. 240-320) observes of Nero: "He it was who first persecuted the servants of God . . . and therefore the tyrant, bereaved of authority, and precipitated from the height of empire, suddenly disappeared."[25] Lactantius also speaks of Nero as "an

---

17. Miriam T. Griffin, *Nero: The End of a Dynasty* (New Haven: Yale, 1984), p. 100.
18. *Sibylline Oracles* 5:29, 33-35.
19. *Ibid.* 5:96.
20. *Ibid.* 12:79, 81.
21. *1 Clement* 6:1.
22. *Sibylline Oracles* 8:157.
23. Tertullian, *Apology* 5:3; cp. *To the Nations* 1:7.
24. Eusebius, *Ecclesiastical History* 2:25:2,3.
25. *On the Death of the Persecutors* 2:2.

execrable and pernicious tyrant" and a "noxious wild beast."[26] Sulpicius Severus (A.D. 360-420) writes that Nero was "the basest of all men, and even of wild beasts," that "he showed himself in every way most abominable and cruel," and that "he first attempted to abolish the name of Christian."[27] He even associates Nero with the prophecy of Revelation: "It was accordingly believed that, even if he did put an end to himself with a sword, his wound was cured, and his life preserved, according to that which was written regarding him, – 'And his mortal wound was healed,' [Rev. 13:3] – to be sent forth again near the end of the world, in order that he may practice the mystery of iniquity."[28]

Nero and Modern Historians

From such evidence as presented above many modern historians feel the terror and dread among the early Christians. Noted church historian John Laurence von Mosheim writes of Nero:

> Foremost in the rank of those emperors, on whom the church looks back with horror as her persecutors, stands Nero, a prince whose conduct towards the Christians admits of no palliation, but was to the last degree unprincipled and inhuman. The dreadful persecution which took place by order of this tyrant, commenced at Rome about the middle of November, in the year of our Lord 64.
>
> . . . .
>
> This dreadful persecution ceased but with the death of Nero. The empire, it is well known, was not delivered from the tyranny of this monster until the year 68, when he put an end to his own life.[29]

B. W. Henderson notes that Nero was especially feared by Christians:

> An early Church tradition identified St Paul's "man of sin" and

---

26. *Ibid.*

27. Sulpicius Severus, *Sacred History* 2:28.

28. *Sacred History* 2:29. Although he asserts that John wrote Revelation under Domitian, 2:31.

29. John L. von Mosheim, *History of Christianity in the First Three Centuries* (New York: Converse, 1854) 1:138, 139.

"son of perdition" and "mystery of iniquity" with the Emperor Nero; and of St Augustine's contemporaries some believed that he was still alive in the vigour of his age, others that he would rise again and come as Antichrist. Lactantius, St Chrysostom, St Jerome, and other Christian writers accept and repeat the theory that Nero is the Antichrist to come. The horrors of the first martyrdoms combined with the Nero-legend to produce the Christian tradition, and I doubt if the belief is any more dead to-day than in the eleventh century, though it cannot now as then obtain a Pope's sanction. Nero, after Judas, becomes the most accursed of the human race. "The first persecutor of the Church must needs be the last, reserved by God for a final and a more awful vengeance."

Thus Nero became a Type, the type of inconceivable wickedness and unnatural horror.[30]

Miriam Griffin observes that "[t]he picture of him as the incarnation of evil triumphed as Christianity triumphed." She speaks at length of Nero's infamy:

Commenting on the unanimity of opinion about the Emperor Nero that prevails among the ancient authorities, the historian Charles Merivale wrote, "With some allowance only for extravagance of colouring, we must accept in the main the verisimilitude of the picture they have left us of this arch-tyrant, the last and the most detestable of the Caesarean family. . . . Nero was the first Princeps to be declared a public enemy by the Senate."[31]

. . . .

In European literature Nero has served as the stock example of unnatural cruelty, a matricide in Shakespeare's *Hamlet*, a fratricide in Racine's *Britannicus*. The hero of the Marquis de Sade, he has fascinated decadent writers as the *incredibilium cupitor* longing to overcome human limits through extremes of luxury, cruelty and depravity. . . . Certainly no serious historian has been tempted to whitewash the tyrant.[32]

---

30. B. W. Henderson, *The Life and Principate of the Emperor Nero* (London: Methuen, 1903), pp. 420-421.

31. Griffin, *Nero*, p. 15.

32. *Ibid.*, p. 16.

Conclusion

The Beast of Revelation is a being possessed of an incredibly wicked character. Nero well fits the requirements, being one of the most evil of the Roman emperors. Interestingly, Nero was as destructive and fearsome as such carnivores as leopards, lions, and bears, which were used in the cruel Roman arenas and which John compounded in his imagery of the Beast. Surely Nero is the Beast of Revelation, specifically considered.

I will close this chapter with one last reference from Suetonius's history. The following quotation reinforces the aptness of the Beast imagery as applied to Nero. Speaking of Nero, Suetonius relates the following story: "He so prostituted his own chastity that after defiling almost every part of his body, he at last devised a kind of game, in which, covered with the skin of some wild animal, he was let loose from a cage and attacked the private parts of men and women, who were bound to stakes, and when he had sated his mad lust, was dispatched by his freedman Doryphorus."[33] The beasts of the arena were imitated by the Beast of Revelation, Nero Caesar.

---

33. Suetonius, *Nero* 29.

5

THE WAR OF THE BEAST

And there was given to him a mouth speaking arrogant words and blasphemies; and authority to act for forty-two months was given to him. . . . And it was given to him to make war with the saints and to overcome them; and authority over every tribe and people and tongue and nation was given to him (Rev. 13:5, 7).

In this chapter we note that the Beast is said to "make war with the saints and to overcome them" (Rev. 13:7). In fact, he is said to conduct such blasphemous warfare for a specific period of time: 42 months (Rev. 13:5). If the Beast is Nero it will be necessary to show that: (1) he did, in fact, make war with (or persecute) Christians, (2) he persecuted them *as Christians* ("saints"), and (3) he did so for a period of 42 months.

It seems clear enough to most commentators that Revelation evidences the fact that cruel imperial persecution against the faith has already begun as John writes. In addition to the statement here in Revelation 13, which is indicative of persecution, there are several others pointing in this direction. Particularly significant in this regard is a verse taken from John's opening statements: Revelation 1:9.

In Revelation 1:9 John clearly indicates he was writing Revelation while he was banished for his faith: "I, John your brother and fellow-partaker in the tribulation and kingdom and perseverance which are in Jesus, was on the island called Patmos, because of the word of God and the testimony of Jesus." This speaks of the

47

present reality of persecution. This persecution has already begun as he writes, for he informs his original audience that he is their "brother and fellow-partaker in the tribulation" (Rev. 1:9a). And since only Rome had the power to banish someone and since Patmos was an island used by Rome as a penal settlement,[1] this must indicate Roman involvement. Most probably this persecution is in its earliest stages, for (1) it is only beginning to be felt in Asia Minor (Rev. 2:10; 3:10) and (2) John points out that it will continue only for a brief period of 42 months (Rev. 13:4).

Let us consider the suitability of the Neronic persecution as the proper historical eventuation of the Beast's "war against the saints." This will serve as strong evidence for the identity of the Beast as Nero.

The Horror of the Neronic Persecution

As I have noted, John and his Christian readers were entering what John himself designates "the tribulation" (Rev. 1:9). The Neronic persecution is tremendously significant to the history and development of early Christianity. It could not but leave a lasting impression upon later Christianity for a number of reasons.

The Significance of Nero's Persecution

First, this persecution, which was initiated by Nero in A.D. 64, was the first ever *Roman* assault on Christianity. Earlier Paul had safely appealed to Caesar (Nero) and in A.D. 62 had been acquitted and released.[2] Christianity was not being persecuted by Rome at that time. Furthermore, this A.D. 64 persecution was specifically directed against Christians as Christians. As Eusebius (A.D. 260-340) notes of Nero, he was famous for being the first imperial persecutor of Christianity: "Nero was the *first* of the emperors who

---

1. Pliny (A.D. 23-79), *Natural History* 12:4-13, 23; Tacitus, *Annals* 3:68; 4:30; 15:71.

2. J. N. D. Kelly, *A Commentary on the Pastoral Epistles* (London: Harper, 1963), pp. 6ff.; William Hendriksen, *I-II Timothy and Titus* (Grand Rapids: Baker, 1957), pp. 39ff.

showed himself an enemy of the divine religion."[3] Sulpicius Severus (A.D. 360-420) concurs: "He *first* attempted to abolish the name of Christian."[4]

As an imperial persecution (as opposed to the Jewish persecutions witnessed in Acts) it had the effect of removing early Christianity's protected status as a *religio licita* ("legal religion"). Until this time Christianity was assumed to be a sect of Judaism and thus protected under the umbrella of Judaism as a "legal religion." In his classic study on persecution, Workman confidently asserts that

> we can date with some certainty this distinction in the official mind between Jew and Christian as first becoming clear in the summer of 64. The acquittal of St. Paul in 61 or 62 — an event we may fairly assume as probable — is proof that in that year Christianity, a distinct name for which was only slowly coming into use, could still claim that it was a *religio licita* . . . still recognized as a branch of Judaism. . . . At any rate, both Nero and Rome now [in A.D. 64] clearly distinguished between the *religio licita* of Judaism and the new sect. . . . The destruction of Jerusalem would remove the last elements of confusion.[5]

This protected status during Christianity's infancy was vitally important in that it gave apostolic Christianity time to spread and gain a solid footing in the Empire. From the time of the Neronic persecution, however, Christianity would be distinguished from Judaism and would be exposed to the unprovoked cruelty of Rome.

That this persecution was against Christians as such may be proved not only from Christian but pagan sources. In his *Annals* Roman historian Tacitus (A.D. 56-117) points to those who were

---

3. Eusebius, *Ecclesiastical History* 2:25:3.

4. Sulpicius Severus, *Sacred History* 2:28. See also Tertullian (A.D. 160-220), *On the Mantle* 4; *Apology* 5; Paulus Orosius (A.D. 385-415), *The Seven Books of History Against the Pagans* 7:7.

5. Herbert B. Workman, *Persecution in the Early Church* (Oxford: Oxford University Press, [1906] 1980), p. 22.

persecuted as "those who . . . were vulgarly called Christians."[6] Roman historian Suetonius (A.D. 70-160) concurs, for in a list of the few "positive" contributions of Nero as emperor, he includes the fact that Nero persecuted Christians: "During his reign many abuses were severely punished and put down, and no fewer new laws were made: . . . Punishment was inflicted on the Christians, a class of men given to a new and mischievous superstition."[7]

No imperial persecution other than the very first would be more important to establishing the durability of the faith. No imperial persecution more urgently required a word of exhortation and consolation to the beleaguered faith, a word such as that offered in Revelation.

> To all appearance, at Rome, the Christian Church was drowning in its own blood in Nero's reign. We must consider the feeling of the ordinary Christian — the man in the street, so to speak — and look at it from his point of view. In later persecutions men had got to know that the Church could survive the furious edicts of Rome. But that was just the doubt which presented itself to the mind of the average Christian man in Nero's time.[8]

The Beast's "war with the saints" — i.e., the Neronic persecution — was: (1) the first such "war," (2) contemporary with John's life, (3) relevant to the first century Christians, and (4) could not be overlooked.

The Severity of Nero's Persecution

Second, in addition to being the first imperial persecution, which set the stage for later persecutions, the Neronic assault on Christianity was also one of the severest. Noted church historian Philip Schaff comments that the Neronian persecution was "the

---

6. Tacitus, *Annals* 15:44.

7. Suetonius, *Nero* 16.

8. James J. L. Ratton, *The Apocalypse of St. John* (London: R. and T. Washbourne, 1912), p. 87.

most cruel that ever occurred."[9]

The earliest evidence for Nero's persecuting wrath upon the Christians is found in an epistle from the first century Christian leader Clement of Rome (A.D. 30-100). His letter was written to the Corinthians and is designated *1 Clement*. Not only is his letter very early evidence for the persecution, but it is from one who lived in Rome and who knew many of those who were slain by Nero. In *1 Clement* 6 Clement tells us that under Nero Christians suffered "through *many indignities and tortures*" and endured "cruel and unholy insults."

Tacitus gives a most detailed and terrifying account of the beginning of the persecution. His account deserves recitation:

> But by no human contrivance, whether lavish distributions of money or of offerings to appease the gods, could Nero rid himself of the ugly rumor that the fire was due to his orders. So to dispel the report, he substituted as the guilty persons and inflicted unheard-of punishments on those who, detested for their abominable crimes, were vulgarly called Christians. . . .
>
> So those who first confessed were hurried to the trial, and then, on their showing, an immense number were involved in the same fate, not so much on the charge of incendiaries as from hatred of the human race. And their death was aggravated with mockeries, insomuch that, wrapped in the hides of wild beasts, they were torn to pieces by dogs, or fastened to crosses to be set on fire, that when the darkness fell they might be burned to illuminate the night. Nero had offered his own gardens for the spectacle, and exhibited a circus show, mingling with the crowd, himself dressed as a charioteer or riding in a chariot. Whence it came about that, though the victims were guilty and deserved the most exemplary punishment, a sense of pity was aroused by the feeling that they were sacrificed not on the altar of public interest, but to satisfy the cruelty of one man.[10]

9. Philip Schaff, *History of the Christian Church*, 3rd. ed., 7 vols. (Grand Rapids: Eerdmans, 1910) 1:386.

10. Tacitus, *Annals* 15:44.

In his *Sacred History*, Christian writer Sulpicius Severus (A.D. 360-420) reserves two chapters to a consideration of Nero's reign, and only three sentences to Domitian's. Severus extols the sainted life of Martin of Tours by noting that even though he did not suffer martyrdom, he would gladly have done so. He then chooses two of the worst persecutors of the Church to exalt Martin's willingness: "But if he had been permitted, in the times of Nero and of Decius, to take part in the struggle which then went on, I take to witness the God of heaven and earth that he would freely have submitted."[11]

Thus, we learn from both pagan and Christian sources that Christians were punished in huge numbers. Tacitus speaks of an "immense number";[12] Clement a "vast multitude of the elect."[13] Of Tacitus's observation that the spectacle ultimately elicited pity from the Roman populace, William M. Ramsay notes that: "It can have been no inconsiderable number and no short period which brought satiety to a populace accustomed to find their greatest amusement in public butcheries, frequently recurring on a colossal scale."[14]

The Impact of Nero's Persecution

Third, it was under the Neronic persecution that Christianity lost two of its greatest leaders, Peter and Paul,[15] and had another, John, banished.[16] This would certainly be a blow to nascent Christianity. As such, it would intensify the dreadful impact of the assault against the Church.

---

11. Sulpicius Severus, *Letters* 3 (To Deacon Aurelius).

12. *Annals* 15:44.

13. *1 Clement* 6.

14. William M. Ramsay, *The Church in the Roman Empire Before A.D. 170* (New York: G. P. Putnam's Sons, 1893), p. 241.

15. Clement of Rome (A.D. 30-100), *1 Clement* 5; Tertullian (A.D. 160-220), *On the Exclusion of Heretics* 36; Lactantius (A.D. 240-320), *On the Death of the Persecutors* 2; Eusebius (A.D. 260-340), *Ecclesiastical History* 3:1:3.

16. See Revelation 1:9; the Syriac *History of John the Son of Zebedee*; the Syriac versions of Revelation. See also Chapter 13 below.

The Length of the Neronic Persecution

Remarkably, the Neronic persecution of Christianity lasted almost precisely the length of time mentioned in Revelation 13:5. The persecution began after the destructive burning of Rome, which began on July 19, A.D. 64.[17] Soon after Rome's near destruction rumors began circulating that Nero himself intentionally caused the fires.[18]

Although Nero's unsuccessful efforts to dispel the rumors by his frantic largess must have taken a little time, he could not afford to wait for an extensive period of time to quell the politically damaging accusations. So in the latter part of November, A.D. 64, furious persecution broke out upon the innocent church.[19] This persecution continued against the church for several years, ultimately claiming the lives of Peter and Paul, as noted previously, in either A.D. 67 or 68.[20]

This persecution finally ended with the death of Nero, which occurred on the ninth of June, A.D. 68.[21] Noted church historian Mosheim wrote of Nero's persecution: "Foremost in the rank of those emperors, on whom the church looks back with horror as her persecutors, stands Nero, a prince whose conduct towards the Christians admits of no palliation, but was to the last degree unprincipled and inhuman. The dreadful persecution which took place by order of this tyrant, commenced at Rome about the middle of November, in the year of our Lord 64. . . . This

---

17. Tacitus, *Annals* 15:41. See discussion in Schaff, *History* 1:379.

18. Tacitus, *Annals* 15:39; Suetonius, *Nero* 38.

19. John Laurence von Mosheim, *Historical Commentaries*, vol. 1, trans. Robert Studley Vidal (New York: S. Converse, 1854), p. 138; Moses Stuart, *Commentary on the Apocalypse*, 2 vols. (Andover: Allen, Morrill, and Wardwell, 1845) 2:279.

20. Merrill F. Unger, *Archaeology and the New Testament* (Grand Rapids: Zondervan, 1963), p. 323. See also A. T. Robertson, "Paul, the Apostle" in James Orr, ed., *The International Standard Bible Encyclopedia* (Grand Rapids: Eerdmans, 1956) 3:2287; Richard Longenecker, *The Ministry and Message of Paul* (Grand Rapids: Zondervan, 1971), pp. 85-86.

21. Stuart, *Apocalypse*, 2:469. See also Justo L. Gonzalez, *The Early Church to the Dawn of the Reformation* (San Francisco: Harper and Row, 1984), p. 36.

dreadful persecution ceased but with the death of Nero. The empire, it is well known, was not delivered from the tyranny of this monster until the year 68, when he put an end to his own life."[22] At that time the empire was embroiled in civil war and could not afford to be distracted by the Christians.

But for a few days, this represents a period of 42 months! How significant! Not only does Nero's name fit the number of the Beast, but his persecution lasted the very time required by the Beast's "war with the saints."

A Common Objection

Most commentators agree that Revelation definitely breathes the atmosphere of violent persecution. But the question arises: Which persecution? The Neronic or the Domitianic? Although a number of commentators argue that the persecution background of Revelation is that of Domitian, this view is not supported by the evidence.

Unfortunately for those who claim a Domitianic persecution background for Revelation, there is a good deal of debate as to whether Domitian even persecuted Christians! George E. Ladd is a capable New Testament scholar who believes Revelation was written during Domitian's reign. Nevertheless, he warns against the use of evidence drawn from the persecution motif for proving that John wrote the book under Domitian: "The problem with this theory is that there is no evidence that during the last decade of the first century there occurred any open and systematic persecution of the church."[23] Reginald H. Fuller also argues for a Domitianic date of Revelation, but he advises that "there is otherwise no evidence for the persecution of Christians in Asia Minor" under Domitian.[24] Leon Morris also laments: "While later Christians

22. von Mosheim, *Historical Commentaries* 1:138, 139.

23. George Eldon Ladd, *A Commentary on the Revelation of John* (Grand Rapids: Eerdmans, 1972), p. 8.

24. Reginald H. Fuller, *A Critical Introduction to the New Testament* (Letchworth: Duckworth, 1971), p. 187.

sometimes speak of a persecution under Domitian the evidence is not easy to find."[25]

Many scholars understand Domitian's violent conduct in A.D. 95 as a paranoid outburst. It seems not to have been directed against Christians, but rather against "selected individuals whom he suspected of undermining his authority."[26] A major problem with the evidence for a "persecution" under Domitian is that it proceeds solely from Christian sources – sources somewhat later than the events. A Domitianic "persecution" is not mentioned by *any* secular historian of the era. Furthermore, it is remarkable that though Roman historian Suetonius praises Nero for the persecution of Christians, he makes no mention at all of Domitian's alleged persecution.[27] It would seem that since he viewed the punishment of Christians as praiseworthy under Nero, any general persecution of them under Domitian would have deserved comment.

Thus, the evidence for the persecution of Christianity under Domitian is questionable. Such is not the case, however, with the persecution under Nero. As I have shown, the evidence for the Neronic persecution is overwhelming and is documentable from heathen, as well as Christian, sources.

Conclusion

It is evident that the initial, paradigmatic role, extreme cruelty, and length of Nero's persecution of Christianity fit well the role required in Revelation for the Beast. Nero did wage "war with the saints" to "overcome them" (Rev. 13:7). And he is the only Roman emperor of the first century to have done such. Not only

---

25. Leon Morris, *The Revelation of St. John* (Grand Rapids: Eerdmans, 1969), pp. 36-37.

26. Glenn W. Barker, William L. Lane, and J. Ramsey Michaels, *The New Testament Speaks* (New York: Harper and Row, 1969), p. 368.

27. *Nero* 16.

so but he did it for the length of time specified in the Revelational record: 42 months. Surely Nero is before us in Revelation 13 as the specific manifestation of the Beast.

6

THE WORSHIP OF THE BEAST

And they worshiped the dragon, because he gave his authority to the beast; and they worshiped the beast, saying, "Who is like the beast, and who is able to wage war with him?" (Rev. 13:4).

If Nero is indeed the personal incarnation of the Beast of Revelation, as I have been demonstrating, then it must be that he was worshiped. This is necessary in that a number of references in Revelation speak of the worship of the Beast. These are found in scattered places: Revelation 13:4, 8, 12, 15; 14:9, 11; 16:2; 19:20; 20:4. The most noteworthy passage is found in Revelation 13, where worship of the "beast" is spoken of repeatedly and is compelled. Revelation 13:4, cited as the chapter heading above, will suffice as a sample.

The worship of the Roman emperor through what is known as "the emperor cult" is a familiar feature of Roman imperial history. Let us briefly survey the origins and early history of emperor worship before we set forth the evidence for the worship of Nero.

The Early History of the Emperor Cult

Julius Caesar

Emperor worship had its roots in the rule of Julius Caesar, the first emperor of Rome. As a matter of fact, Julius was granted by the Roman Senate the title "Jupiter Julius." This act put him on a level with Jupiter, the leading god among the Romans.[1]

The evidence for emperor worship does not end here, however. Archaeologists have discovered an interesting inscription at Ephesus, one of the very cities to which Revelation is addressed. Julius was described in this inscription as "god manifest and common saviour of the life of man."[2] His statue was placed in the temple of Quirinius, and was inscribed: "To the invincible God."[3] Roman historian Suetonius notes in this regard that "he allowed honours to be bestowed on him which were too great for mortal man: . . . temples, altars, and statues beside those of the gods; a special priest, an additional college of the Superci, and the calling of one of the months by his name."[4] The senate decreed that a special temple be built for the *clementia Caesaris.* "There Caesar and his divine *clementia* were to be set up and worshipped."[5]

After Julius's death the Roman Senate voted him into the company of the gods. From that time forth he began to be called "*Divus Iulius,*" that is, "divine Julius."[6] In addition, a formal cult of *Divus Iulius* was established and "an altar to him was erected in the forum."[7]

Suetonius records for us that "some write that three hundred men of both orders were selected from the prisoners of war and sacrificed on the Ides of March like so many victims at the altar raised to the Deified Julius."[8] Here we find at least this one

---

1. H. H. Scullard, *From the Gracchi to Nero*, 2nd ed. (New York: Barnes and Noble, 1963), p. 152.

2. *Ibid.*, p. 152.

3. James J. L. Ratton, *The Apocalypse of St. John* (London: R. and T. Washbourne, 1912), p. 48. See Dio Cassius, 47:18:33.

4. Suetonius, *Julius* 76.

5. Ethelbert Stauffer, *Christ and the Caesars* (Philadelphia: Westminster Press, 1955), p. 50.

6. See the Roman writers Cicero (*Philippi* 2:110), Suetonius (*Julius* 38), and Dio Cassius (*Roman History* 44:6:4).

7. Scullard, *Gracchi*, p. 152.

8. Suetonius, *Augustus* 15.

occurrence of the slaying of men as altar victims for the deified Caesar.

After Julius's death, several men set up a twenty foot high marble column inscribed with "To the Father of his Country." Suetonius notes that "at the foot of this they continued for a long time to sacrifice, make vows, and settle some of their disputes by an oath in the name of Caesar."[9] He was said to have been accepted as a god not only by a formal decree of the senate, "but also in the conviction of the common people."[10]

Augustus Caesar

Although Rome's second emperor, Augustus, forbade divine honors to himself in Rome,[11] the Roman historians Tacitus and Suetonius note that he sanctioned his worship and the erection of altars elsewhere.[12] Even as early as 29 B.C. Augustus allowed such, giving the annually elected high priest of the cult much dignity in the provinces.[13]

Scullard commented regarding Octavian (*i.e.* Augustus):

In one respect Octavian had long been unique: since 42 B.C. and the consecrations of Divus Julius he had been the son of a god, "Divi filius." After Actium his birthday was celebrated as a public holiday; libations were poured in his honour at public and private banquets; from 29 B.C. his name was added to those of the gods in hymns; two years later he received the title of Augustus; his Genius, perhaps in 12 B.C., was inserted in official oaths between the names of Jupiter and the Di Penates; in A.D. 13 an altar was

9. Suetonius, *Julius* 85.

10. *Ibid.* 88.

11. He disdained the title "*Dominius*" ("Lord") because he preferred to be known as the governor of free men rather than the master of slaves.

12. Suetonius, *Augustus* 52-53; Tacitus, *Annals* 1:10.

13. Edward Selwyn, *The Christian Prophets and the Prophetic Apocalypse* (London: Macmillan, 1900), pp. 122-123. For a helpful study of the socio-political implications of the "genius" of Caesar, see R. J. Rushdoony, *The One and the Many* (Fairfax, VA: Thoburn, [1971] 1978), ch. 5.

dedicated by Tiberius in Rome to the Numen Augusti.[14]

Beckwith notes that on his death the Senate voted Augustus among the gods and that a temple was erected in the Palatine area of Rome. Furthermore "his worship spread rapidly in both the Asian and western provinces, so that the Jewish philosopher Philo (*ca.* 20 B.C.-A.D. 50) could say, that 'everywhere honors were decreed to him equal to those of the Olympian gods.'"[15]

Archaeologists have in their possession a most interesting decree of the Synod of the Province of Asia, which is dated about 9 B.C. This decree is preserved in a letter of the proconsul to the cities of Asia:

> [W]hether the natal day of the most divine Caesar is to be observed most for the joy of it or for the profit of it – a day which one might justly regard as equivalent to the beginning of all things, equivalent, I say, if not in reality, at any rate in the benefits it has brought, seeing that there was nothing ruinous or that had fallen into a miserable appearance that he has not restored. He has given another aspect to the universe, which was only too ready to perish, had not Caesar – a blessing to the whole of mankind – been born. For which reason each individual may justly look upon this day as the beginning of his own life and physical being, because there can be no more of the feeling that life is a burden, now that he has been born. . . .

> Resolved by the Greeks of the province of Asia, on the proposal of the High-priest Apollonius . . . : Whereas the Providence which orders the whole human life has shown a special concern and zeal and conferred upon life its most perfect ornament by bestowing Augustus, whom it fitted for his beneficent work among mankind by filling him with virtue, sending him as a Savior, for us and for those who come after us, one who should cause wars to cease, who should set all things in fair order, and whereas Caesar, when he

---

14. Scullard, *Gracchi*, p. 242.

15. Isbon T. Beckwith, *The Apocalypse of John: Studies in Introduction* (Grand Rapids: Baker, [1919] 1967), p. 199.

appeared, made the hopes of those who forecast a better future [look poor compared with the reality], in that he not only surpassed all previous benefactors, but left no chance for future ones to go beyond him, and the glad tidings which by his means went forth into the world took its rise in the birthday of the God. . . .[16]

Tiberius Caesar

The third emperor of Rome was Tiberius. It is in response to just this issue — emperor worship — that Christ's remarks during the reign of Tiberius regarding the tribute money must be understood (Matt. 22:15-22; Mark 12:13-17; Luke 20:20-26). Here Christ taught that lovers of the true God should "render unto God" those things which are God's (*i.e.* worship), and only "render unto Caesar" those things which are rightfully his (*i.e.* taxes). This clearly is a tacit protest against emperor worship under Tiberius (ruled A.D. 14-37).

At Tiberius's death "eleven cities of Asia struggled for the honour of erecting a temple to his memory."[17] The Senate finally awarded the temple to Smyrna,[18] one of the seven cities to which one of the Seven Letters in Revelation was written.

Gaius ("Caligula") Caesar

The fourth Roman emperor was Gaius Caesar, also known by his nickname "Caligula." Gaius was clearly a madman possessed with the conviction of his own deity. He placed the head of his own statue on that of Jupiter, had himself saluted as Jupiter, and had temples erected to himself.[19]

The Jewish historian Josephus records the deluded pretensions

16. Howard Clark Kee, *The Origins of Christianity: Sources and Documents* (Englewood, NJ: Prentice-Hall, 1973), p. 76. See also Stauffer, *Christ and the Caesars*, chs. 5-7.

17. Herbert B. Workman, *Persecution in the Early Church* (Oxford: Oxford University Press, [1906] 1980), pp. 39ff.

18. Edward C. Selwyn, *The Christian Prophets and the Prophetic Apocalypse* (London: Macmillan, 1900), p. 123.

19. Suetonius, *Caligula* 21.

of Gaius (here spelled: "Caius"): "All who were subject to the Roman empire built altars and temples to Caius, and in other regards universally received him as they received the gods."[20] His infamous plan to have his image erected in the temple at Jerusalem and the providential prevention of it is well-known, thanks to Josephus.[21] That attempt, prevented by his death, would certainly have issued forth in war with the Jews.

Claudius Caesar

The fifth emperor, the immediate forerunner of Nero, was Claudius Caesar. Suetonius and Tacitus both record the up and down position of Claudius as a god. He was voted a god upon his death only to have his enrollment among the gods annulled by Nero but later restored by Vespasian![22] Even during his life a temple was erected to him at Colchester.[23]

Summary

Church historian Kurt Aland comments: "In the first century of the Christian Era all the emperors claim this supreme achievement [*i.e.*, divinity] for themselves." He even remarks that "the emperors after Augustus especially promoted the cult of the emperor."[24] As a matter of fact, A. S. Peake notes that "the practice in its worst form, that is the worship of the living emperor, had been known in Asia as early as the reign of Augustus."[25]

Clearly then, the emperor cult had a prominent role in the political and social life of the Roman empire. Let us turn now to a consideration of the matter from the perspective of Nero's reign

20. *Antiquities* 18:8:1. See also Eusebius, *Ecclesiastical History* 2:5-6.

21. Josephus, *Antiquities* 18:8:2.

22. Suetonius, *Claudius* 45; *Nero* 9; Tacitus, *Annals* 12:69.

23. Workman, *Persecution*, p. 40.

24. Kurt Aland, *A History of Christianity* (Philadelphia: Fortress Press, 1985) 1:18, 19.

25. A. S. Peake, *The Revelation of St. John* (London: Joseph Johnson, 1919), p. 84.

in particular.

The History of the Emperor Cult in Nero's Reign

Nero was surely the most notorious Roman emperor of the first century, excelling both the insane Caligula and the paranoid Domitian in notoriety. He was also jealously vain in his proud appreciation of his own artistic talents.[26] How could such a vain character neglect the opportunities afforded by the emperor cult? As a matter of historical record, he did not.

The Roman dramatist and statesman Seneca (4 B.C.-A.D. 65) was one of young Nero's tutors and a powerful influence in Nero's early rule. Seneca convinced Nero that he was destined to become the very revelation of the divine Augustus and of the god Apollo.[27] Speaking as Apollo, Seneca praised Nero: "He is like me in much, in form and appearance, in his poetry and singing and playing. And as the red of morning drives away dark night, as neither haze nor mist endure before the sun's rays, as everything becomes bright when my chariot appears, so it is when Nero ascends the throne. . . . He restores to the world the golden age."[28]

Suetonius remarks of Nero that "since he was acclaimed as the equal of Apollo in music and of the Sun in driving a chariot, he had planned to emulate the exploits of Hercules as well."[29] An inscription from Athens speaks of him as "all powerful Nero Caesar Sebastos, a new Apollo."[30]

Nero's portrait appears on coins as Apollo playing the lyre. He appears with his head radiating the light of the sun on copper coins struck in Rome and at Lugdunum. One type has Genius (a

---

26. Miriam T. Griffin, *Nero: The End of a Dynasty* (New Haven: Yale University Press, 1984), chs. 9 and 10.

27. Seneca, *On Clemency* 1:1:6; *Apocolocyntosis* (or *Pumpkinification*) 4:15-35.

28. Stauffer, *Christ and the Caesars*, p. 52.

29. Suetonius, *Nero* 53.

30. Mary E. Smallwood, *Documents Illustrating the Principates Gaius Claudius and Nero* (Cambridge: University Press, 1967), p. 52 (entry #145).

Roman tutelary deity) sacrificing over an altar on the reverse side; another has Apollo on the reverse. As Bo Reicke notes of Nero's Apollo fascination: "All this was more than pomp and show: Nero strove with deadly seriousness to play the role of Augustus and Apollo politically, the former primarily from 54 to 61, the latter from 62 to 68."[31]

As early in his reign as 55 the senate erected a huge statue of Nero in the Temple of Mars in Rome.[32] The statue was the same size as that of Mars in Mars's own Temple.

That Nero actually was worshiped is evident from inscriptions found in Ephesus in which he is called "Almighty God" and "Savior."[33] Reference to Nero as "God and Savior" is found in an inscription at Salamis, Cyprus.[34] Indeed, "as his megalomania increased, the tendency to worship him as ruler of the world became stronger, and in Rome his features appeared on the colossus of the Sun near the Golden House, while his head was represented on the coinage with a radiate crown. Members of the imperial house also began to receive unheard of honours: . . . Nero deified his child by Poppaea and Poppaea herself after their deaths. All this was far removed from the modest attitude of Augustus."[35]

Regarding the imperial development of the emperor cult, Caligula (Gaius) and Nero "abandoned all reserve"[36] in promoting emperor worship. In fact, "Caligula and Nero, the only two of the Julio-Claudians who were direct descendants of Augustus, de-

---

31. Bo Reicke, *The New Testament Era: The World of the Bible from 500 B.C. to A.D. 100* (Philadelphia: Fortress Press, 1968), p. 70.

32. See Tacitus, *Annals* 13:8:1.

33. Ratton, *Apocalypse*, p. 48.

34. Smallwood, *Documents Illustrating the Principates*, p. 142 (entry #142).

35. Scullard, *Gracchi*, p. 371.

36. Eduard Lohse, *The New Testament Environment*, trans. John E. Steely (Nashville: Abingdon, 1976), p. 220.

manded divine honors while they were still alive."[37]

Perhaps this demand for worship by Nero can best be seen in the following incident. In A.D. 66 Tiridates, King of Armenia, approached Nero in devout and reverential worship, according to Roman historian Dio Cassius (A.D. 150-235):

> Indeed, the proceedings of the conference were not limited to mere conversations, but a lofty platform had been erected on which were set images of Nero, and in the presence of the Armenians, Parthians, and Romans Tiridates approached and paid them reverence; then, after sacrificing to them and calling them by laudatory names, he took off the diadem from his head and set it upon them.
>
> . . . .
>
> Tiridates publicly fell before Nero seated upon the rostra in the Forum: "Master, I am the descendant of Arsaces, brother of the kings Vologaesus and Pacorus, and thy slave. And I have come to thee, my god, to worship thee as I do Mithras. The destiny thou spinnest for me shall be mine; for thou art my Fortune and my Fate."[38]

By this action this king actually worshiped "the image of the Beast" (Rev. 13:15).

Dio Cassius notes also the fate of one senator who did not appreciate Nero's "divine" musical abilities: "Thrasaea was executed because he failed to appear regularly in the senate, . . . and because he never would listen to the emperor's singing and lyre-playing, nor sacrifice to Nero's Divine Voice as did the rest."[39] This senator failed to worship the Beast and was executed. This reflects Revelation 13:15 which says "as many as do not worship the image of the beast" are "to be killed."

In A.D. 67 Nero went to Greece, where he remained for more

---

37. Joseph Ward Swain, *The Harper History of Civilization* (New York: Harper, 1958) 1:229.

38. Dio Cassius, *Roman History* 62:5:2.

39. *Ibid.* 62:26:3.

than a year performing as a musician and an actor in the Grecian festivals. The response of the Greeks is given by Arthur Weigall, as he comments upon the history of Rome written by Dio Cassius: "Soon Nero was actually deified by the Greeks as 'Zeus, Our Liberator.' On the altar of Zeus in the chief temple of the city they inscribed the words 'to Zeus, our Liberator' namely Nero, for ever and ever; in the temple of Apollo they set up his statue; and they called him 'The new Sun, illuminating the Hellenes,' and 'the one and only lover of the Greeks of all time.'"[40]

When Nero returned to Rome from Greece in A.D. 68, he returned to the triumphant praise of the city as he entered the Palace and Apollo's Temple on the Palatine. Dio Cassius records the scene thus: "The city was all decked with garlands, was ablaze with lights and reeking with incense, and the whole population, the senators themselves most of all, kept shouting in chorus: 'Hail, Olympian Victor! Hail, Pythian Victor! Augustus! Augustus! Hail to Nero, our Hercules! Hail to Nero, our Apollo! The only Victor of the Grand Tour, the only one from the beginning of time! Augustus! Augustus! O, Divine Voice! Blessed are they that hear thee.'"[41]

During the Roman Civil Wars, begun with the death of Nero in June A.D. 68, the emperor Vitellius even offered sacrifices to the spirit of the deceased Nero. To better secure his own emperorship, Emperor Vespasian, who overthrew Vitellius, had to make the effort to check this Nero cult.[42]

Conclusion

The appearance of emperor worship in Revelation is evidence that we are on the right track in specifying the Roman empire as

---

40. Arthur Weigall, *Nero: Emperor of Rome* (London: Thornton Butterworth, 1933), p. 276.

41. Dio Cassius, *Roman History* 62:20:5.

42. *Ibid.* 65:4.

the Beast, particularly as it is incarnate in Nero Caesar. There is abundant testimony to emperor worship at various stages of development well before Nero. And Nero himself actually demanded such worship in a way unsurpassed by any previous emperor, except, perhaps, for Caligula.

7

THE REVIVAL OF THE BEAST

And I saw one of his heads as if it had been slain, and his fatal wound was healed. And the whole earth was amazed and followed after the beast. . . . And the beast which was and is not, is himself also an eighth, and is one of the seven (Rev. 13:3; 17:11a).

A most interesting and perplexing aspect of the Beast is that which indicates his death and revivification. The specific verses of Revelation which contain allusions to this phenomenon are Revelation 13:3, 14 and 17:8, 11. Two of these are cited at the heading of the present chapter.

The Death of the Beast

The manner of Nero's death corresponds with the prophecy of Revelation 13:10: "If anyone is destined for captivity, to captivity he goes; if any one kills with the sword, with the sword he must be killed." In the context of speaking of the Beast, John gives encouragement to those whom the Beast was presently afflicting: "Here is the perseverance and the faith of the saints," *i.e.* that the Beast who slays by the sword would also be slain by the sword. Revelation 13:14 also mentions his death by sword.

That Nero did in fact kill by the sword is well-attested fact. Paul, for example, is said to have died under Nero by decapitation by means of the sword.[1] Tertullian credits "Nero's cruel sword"

---

1. Eusebius, *Ecclesiastical History* 2:25:5; Tertullian, *The Exclusion of Heretics* 36; the Syriac *The Teaching of the Apostles*.

as providing the martyr's blood as seed for the church.[2] He urges his Roman readers: "Consult your histories; you will there find that Nero was the first who assailed with the imperial sword the Christian sect."[3]

Just as well-attested is the fact of Nero's own death by sword. According to Suetonius, he "drove a dagger into his throat, aided by Epaphroditus, his private secretary."[4] He not only killed others by the sword, but himself, as Revelation prophesies.

This evidence alone cannot compel the conclusion that Nero is in mind; many emperors died by the sword, even Domitian. But it quite harmoniously lends its voice to the chorus of other evidences, both major and minor.

The Revival of the Beast

We now come to a consideration of the Beast's revival after his death. At first glance this detail regarding the Beast in Revelation may seem fatal to my designation of the Beast as Rome (corporately) and Nero Caesar (specifically). But looks are deceiving. As a matter of fact, this aspect of the Beast's function in Revelation is further and quite satisfying confirmation to my position. It is a confirmation that is, when properly understood, not only historically verifiable, but also inappropriate to any other time in Rome's history than that of the A.D. 60s, the imperial era dominated by Nero Caesar. Let us see how this is so.

The Beast's Two-fold Referent

As we consider the proper interpretation, it will be necessary to remember that John allows some shifting in his imagery of the Beast: The one Beast has seven heads (Rev. 13:1; 17:3), which at some places are seven kings collectively considered (Rev. 17:9-10a), or seven kings who arise in chronological succession (cf.

---

2. Tertullian, *Exclusion* 21.
3. Tertullian, *Apology* 5.
4. *Nero* 49.

Rev. 17:10b-11). Thus, the *Beast* is generically portrayed as a *kingdom*. But in the very same contexts the Beast is spoken of as an individual (he is a man with a specific name, Rev. 13:18) and as but one head among the seven (Rev. 17:11). This unusual feature, as noted before, is recognized by a number of commentators.[5]

As I begin consideration of the matter it must be recognized that it is *one* of the heads which received a death blow: "And I saw one of his heads as if it had been slain, and his fatal wound was healed" (Rev. 13:3). I demonstrated earlier that Nero Caesar is the "head" which is in view here.[6] John prophesies that Nero will die by the sword (Rev. 13:10, 14). Nero is the one mysteriously numbered "666" (Rev. 13:18).

Recognizing these factors takes us a long way toward resolving the interpretive issue before us. The mortal sword wound to *one* of the heads is a wound that should have been fatal to *the Beast, generically considered*. This explains why it is that after the wound was healed and *the Beast* continued alive, "the whole earth was amazed and followed after the beast" (Rev. 13:3b). The seven-headed Beast seems indestructible, for the cry goes up: "Who is like the beast, and who is able to wage war with him?" (Rev. 13:4b).

Now how does all of this imagery have anything to do with Rome and Nero Caesar?

The Historical Fulfillment

At this point we need to reflect upon a most significant series of historical events of the A.D. 60s. A perfectly reasonable and historical explanation of the revived Beast lies before the interpreter. Here is where so many faddish interpretations of Revelation go wrong. They forget the *original audience relevance* factor and, consequently, overlook the history of the era.

---

5. See pages 11-12 *supra*.
6. See Chapter 3. More discussion of this may be found in Chapter 10 below.

When Nero committed suicide on June 9, A.D. 68, two major inter-related historical situations presented themselves to the world. Both carried with them catastrophic consequences.

First, with the death of Nero, the Julio-Claudian line of emperors perished from the earth. In other words, the Roman Empire's founding family vanished from rule. The blood line that had given birth to, extended, stabilized, brought prosperity to, and had received worship from the Roman Empire was suddenly cut off forever. In superstitious, pagan fashion Suetonius notes that "many portents" foreshadowed the tragedy that was to be, *i.e.* that "the race of the Caesars ended with Nero."[7] This was a grave and serious matter to the Roman Empire.

Second, catastrophe upon catastrophe followed the death of Nero and the extinction of the Julian line. Immediately, the Roman Empire was hurled into civil wars of great ferocity and dramatic proportions. In fact, the civil wars almost destroyed the empire, seriously threatening to reduce "eternal Rome" to rubble. The peril Rome faced and the upheaval that shook the empire were well known in that era. As Josephus notes of these Roman civil wars: "I have omitted to give an exact account of them, because they are well known by all, and they are described by a great number of Greek and Roman authors."[8]

These civil wars are of tremendous importance in first-century world history — and ecclesiastical history, as well. Since the book of Revelation was written during Nero's reign and in regard to the Neronic evils, as the wealth of evidence demands,[9] we should expect that prophetic allusions to Rome's civil wars would appear. And they do!

---

7. Suetonius, *Galba* 1.

8. Josephus, *The Wars of the Jews* 4:9:2.

9. See Part 2 of the present work for a popular summation of the pre-A.D. 70 composition of Revelation. For a more rigorous treatment see my doctoral dissertation, published under the title: *Before Jerusalem Fell: Dating the Book of Revelation* (Tyler, TX: Institute for Christian Economics, 1989).

In introducing the months following the death of Nero, Tacitus (A.D. 56-117) wrote:

> The history on which I am entering is that of a period rich in disasters, terrible with battles, torn by civil struggles, horrible even in peace. Four emperors failed by the sword;[10] there were three civil wars, more foreign wars and often both at the same time. There was success in the East,[11] misfortune in the West. Illyricum was disturbed, the Gallic provinces wavering, Britain subdued and immediately let go. The Sarmatae and Suebi rose against us; the Dacians won fame by defeats inflicted and suffered; even the Parthians were almost roused to arms through the trickery of a pretended Nero. Moreover, Italy was distressed by disasters unknown before or returning after the lapse of ages. Cities of the rich fertile shores of Campania were swallowed up or overwhelmed; Rome was devastated by conflagrations, in which her most ancient shrines were consumed and the very Capitol fired by citizens' hands. Sacred rites were defiled; there were adulteries in high places. The sea was filled with exiles, its cliffs made foul with the bodies of the dead. In Rome there was more awful cruelty. . . . Besides the manifold misfortunes that befell mankind, there were prodigies in the sky and on the earth, warnings given by thunderbolts, and prophecies of the future, both joyful and gloomy, uncertain and clear. For never was it more fully proved by awful disasters of the Roman people or by indubitable signs that gods care not for our safety, but for our punishment.[12]

Tacitus's detailed account of the ruin wreaked upon Rome almost equals in psychological horror, cultural devastation, and human carnage that which befell Jerusalem during the Jewish War, as recorded by Josephus and Tacitus.[13] The Roman civil wars were the firstfruits of Nero's death.

---

10. Nero died June 8, A.D. 68; Galba was murdered January 15, A.D. 69; Otho committed suicide April 17, A.D. 69; and Vitellius was slain on December 20, A.D. 69.

11. The Jewish War, which ended with the destruction of the Temple in A.D. 70.

12. Tacitus, *Histories* 1:2-3.

13. Josephus, *Wars of the Jews,* and Tacitus, *Histories* 5:10ff. See also Eusebius, *Ecclesiastical History,* 3:5-8.

These civil wars would, to all appearance, strike the citizens, subjects, neighbors, and enemies of the vast empire — Christian and pagan alike — as being the *very death throes of Rome*, the Beast generically considered. Indeed, in Tacitus's estimation it very nearly was so: "This was the condition of the Roman state when Serius Galba, chosen consul for the second time, and his colleague Titus Vinius entered upon the year that was to be for Galba his last and *for the state almost the end.*"[14]

Before the world's startled eyes, the seven headed Beast (Rome)[15] was toppling to its death as its sixth head (Nero)[16] was mortally wounded with the sword. As Suetonius viewed the long months immediately following Nero's death, the empire "for a long time had been unsettled, and as it were, drifting, through the usurpation and violent death of three emperors."[17]

Josephus records the matter as perceived by the Roman generals Vespasian and Titus, while they were engaged in the Jewish War in A.D. 69: "And now they were both in suspense about the public affairs, the Roman empire being then in a fluctuating condition, and did not go on with their expedition against the Jews, but thought that to make any attack upon foreigners was now unseasonable, on account of the solicitude they were in for their own country."[18] The reports of the destruction and rapine were so horrible that it is reported of General Vespasian: "And as this sorrow of his was violent, he was not able to support the torments he was under, nor to apply himself further in other wars when his native country was laid waste."[19]

According to the pseudo (after-the-fact) prophecy of *4 Ezra* 12:16-19, written around A.D. 100, the Empire was "in danger of

---

14. Tacitus, *Histories* 1:11. Emphasis added.

15. See Chapter 10.

16. For proof that the sixth head/king is Nero, see Chapter 10.

17. Suetonius, *Vespasian* 1.

18. Josephus, *Wars* 4:9:2.

19. *Ibid.* 4:10:2.

falling": "In the midst of the time of that kingdom great struggles shall arise, and it shall be in danger of falling; nevertheless it shall not fall then, but shall regain its former power."[20]

Josephus agrees that during this time Rome was brought near to utter "ruin."[21] He notes that "about this time it was that heavy calamities came about Rome on all sides."[22] Josephus writes elsewhere that "the Roman government [was] in a great internal disorder, by the continual changes of its rulers, and [the Germans] understood that every part of the habitable earth under them was in an unsettled and tottering condition."[23] Men everywhere understood that "the state of the Romans was so ill."[24]

But what eventually occurred at the end of these death throes? The rest of Suetonius's quotation begun above informs us that "the empire, which for a long time had been unsettled and, as it were, drifting through the usurpation and violent death of three emperors, was at last taken in hand and given stability by the Flavian family."[25] Josephus sets forth this view of things when he writes, "So upon this confirmation of Vespasian's entire government, which was now settled, and upon *the unexpected deliverance of the public affairs of the Romans from ruin*, Vespasian turned his thoughts to what remained unsubdued in Judea."[26] Thus, after a time of grievous civil wars, *the Empire was revived by the ascending of Vespasian to the purple.*

James Moffatt states the matter well when he writes regarding Revelation 13:3: "The allusion is . . . to the terrible convulsions which in 69 A.D. shook the empire to its foundations (Tac. *Hist.*

---

20. For an excellent analysis of *4 Ezra*, see Bruce M. Metzger, "The Fourth Book of Ezra," in James H. Charlesworth, ed., *The Old Testament Pseudepigrapha*, 2 vols. (Garden City: Doubleday, 1983) 2:517 ff.

21. Josephus, *Wars* 4:11:5

22. *Ibid.* 4:10:1.

23. *Ibid.* 7:4:2.

24. *Ibid.* 7:4:2.

25. *Vespasian* 1.

26. *Wars* 4:11:5. Emphasis added.

i.11). Nero's death with the bloody interregnum after it, was a wound to the State, from which it only recovered under Vespasian. It fulfilled the tradition of the wounded head. . . . The vitality of the pagan empire, shown in this power of righting itself after the revolution, only added to its prestige."[27]

The relevant verses in Revelation regarding the death and revivification of the Beast can properly be understood as prophesying the earth-shaking historical events of the late A.D. 60s era. Rome died, as it were, and returned again to life. In light of John's original audience (Rev. 1:4, 11), his call for their careful consideration (Rev. 1:3; 13:9), and his contemporary expectation (Rev. 1:1, 3), we must wonder why commentators project themselves into the distant future seeking some other fulfillment of these events. All the evidence heretofore dovetails nicely with this revivification factor.

An Objection Considered

The reference to the "eighth" king in Revelation 17:11 has caused some commentators to stumble here. There we read: "And the beast which was and is not, is himself also an eighth, and is one of the seven. . . ." In response to a view such as I am presenting, some commentators note that the eighth emperor of Rome was actually Otho, the second of the rulers during Rome's awful civil wars. Thus, they point out, this head does not refer to Vespasian. Given the interpretive approach presented above, it would appear that the eighth head (according to my calculation) is one of the *destroying* elements of Rome, not one who actually stabilized the Empire, causing its revival. Consequently, the supposed imagery fails.

This problem should not deter acceptance of the view I have presented. A consultation of the Greek text helps alleviate the apparent tension in the view. Exegetically, the chronological line

---

27. James Moffatt, *The Revelation of St. John the Divine*, vol. 5 in W. Robertson Nicoll, ed., *The Expositor's Greek Testament* (Grand Rapids: Eerdmans, rep. 1980), p. 430.

of heads/kings is spoken of with careful exactness by use of the definite article, "the." That is, if we translate John with exact literalness, he writes of the "kings" (emperors) in Revelation 17:10 as follows: "*the* five fell, *the* one is, *the* other not yet come, and whenever he comes a little [while] him it behooves to remain."[28]

But the definite article is conspicuously absent in a literal translation of the reference to the eighth head/king in Revelation 17:11: "And the beast which was and is not, even he *an* eighth is."[29] The definite article that clearly and repetitively defined the chronological series of head/kings ("*the* five," "*the* one," "*the* one to come") vanishes before the eighth is mentioned. Thus, this eighth king is "*an* eighth," *i.e.* it refers not to any one particular individual, but to the revival of the Empire itself under one who is outside of the originally specified seven kings. The Roman Empire is arising from ruin.

There is a very important sense in which the revival of the Empire under Vespasian, was a revival under "an eighth," who is, nevertheless, "of the seven." It is the same Roman Empire which is brought to life from the death of the civil wars that is in view here; it is not some new empire. John's concern is particularly with the contemporaneous events: the Roman civil wars that occurred within the compass of the reign of the seven kings. The eighth is beyond his most pressing and immediate concern (although it is not unimportant), and thus is not specified and detailed.

In addition, the number eight is the number of resurrection.[30] The *eighth* day is the beginning of a new week. Thus, Jesus was resurrected on the first or eighth day (John 20:1). This reestablishment of the Roman Empire under Vespasian offers a new beginning (the Julio-Claudian line was gone) and a revival of the

---

28. Literal translation taken from Alfred Marshall, *The Interlinear Greek-English New Testament*, 2nd ed. (Grand Rapids: Zondervan, 1959), p. 1007.

29. *Ibid.*

30. Gary North, *The Dominion Covenant: Genesis*, 2nd ed. (Tyler, TX: Institute for Christian Economics, 1987), ch. 5; E. W. Bullinger, *Number in Scripture* (London: Eyre and Spottiswoode, n.d.).

Roman Empire, which had been through death throes. That recovery will come shortly after the demise of *the* original seven when *an* eighth arises.

Conclusion

Despite the pervasive view among modern evangelicals, Revelation was a crucially relevant book to the apostolic era church. We have seen how many roads lead to the Rome/Nero view of the Beast. Perhaps the most difficult piece of prophetic material for the Rome/Nero view of the Beast is that which speaks of the Beast's death and revival. Yet again, however, an understanding of the circumstances of the first century is immensely helpful to our interpretation.

With the death of Nero and the ensuing civil wars which plagued Rome, the world witnessed what surely was to be the final demise of mighty Rome. But to the surprise of friend and foe alike, Rome arose anew under Vespasian to assert its vitality and to demonstrate its power. Under the next two emperors – Vespasian and Titus – Christianity would be left in peace for more than a decade. John clearly spoke of the events of his era as a true prophet of God and as one concerned for his "fellow-partakers in the tribulation" (Rev. 1:9). He did not overlook the earth-shaking events of his own era; he spoke directly to them.

PART II
WHEN WAS REVELATION WRITTEN?

8

THE IMPORTANCE OF
THE DATE OF REVELATION

I, John, your brother and fellow-partaker in the tribulation and kingdom and perseverance which are in Jesus, was on the island called Patmos, because of the word of God and the testimony of Jesus (Rev. 1:9).

The Issue

The present section of this book is given over to the vitally important question of the date of the composition of Revelation, which was written while John was banished to Patmos. The reader should recall that in the Introduction I noted that this matter is a major difficulty confronting the student of Revelation. The position taken on this issue has a great bearing on the interpretive possibilities available to the interpreter. Indeed, the view of the Beast presented heretofore could well be affected by the question we now approach.

The Debate

Unfortunately, there is much lively debate over the question of the date of Revelation. In fact, scholarly opinion has shifted back and forth between two major viewpoints. The two leading views held by New Testament scholars are: (1) The early date view, which holds that John wrote Revelation prior to the August, A.D. 70, destruction of the temple. (2) The late-date view, which

81

argues that John composed his work around A.D. 95-96, in the last days of the principate of Domitian Caesar, who was assassinated September 18, A.D. 96.

My Position

The position I will set forth in the following pages is that of an early date prior to A.D. 70,[1] somewhere in the time-frame of late-A.D. 64 (after the initial outbreak of the Neronic persecution) to A.D. 67 (prior to the Jewish War with Rome). For too long, popular commentaries have brushed aside the evidence for the early date for Revelation. Despite the majority opinion of current scholarship, the evidence for an early date for Revelation is clear and compelling.

Almost invariably the major reason for the dismissal of the early date for Revelation is due to one statement by an early church father named Irenaeus. Other supportive evidences for a late-date are brought into the discussion later. *Initially*, however, almost all commentators begin with and depend upon Irenaeus's statement in his late second century worked entitled *Against Heresies*.[2] Pick a Revelation commentary off your shelves and see for yourself.

There is one particularly frustrating aspect of the debate for early date advocates. When one mentions that he affirms a date for Revelation prior to the destruction of the temple, a predictable response all too often heard is: "Aren't you aware that all scholars agree it was written at the end of the first century?" Or, if talking with a seminarian, the reply might be: "Don't you realize Irenaeus clearly settled this question?" In such encounters the early date proponent is deemed intellectually naive and historically misinformed. He is thought to be throwing objective evidence and assured conclusions out the window on the basis of sheer presump-

---

1. I would like to thank Dr. George W. Knight III for his suggestions on the following order of arrangement, which differ from my dissertation's order.

2. One notable exception is Leon Morris in his *The Revelation of St. John* (Grand Rapids: Eerdmans, 1969).

tion or theological bias.

Early Date Advocates

Holding to an early date for Revelation does not, however, prove one is in defiance of "historical facts." This should be evident in the list of names of those who have held to an early date. An appeal to venerated scholarship cannot settle the issue, to be sure. But the very fact that a good number of astute biblical scholars hold to a minority position should at least forestall too hasty a dismissal of that position.

We herewith list a number of noted scholars who have discounted the late-date for Revelation in favor of an earlier date. Some of the following are noted liberal scholars, some orthodox. The historical facts of the matter are not necessarily determined by a particular school of thought. In fact, that some of the scholars are liberals is quite remarkable in that the liberal view usually tends to push the dates of biblical books to a later, not an earlier, period.

We list these names in alphabetical, rather than chronological, order: Jay E. Adams, Luis de Alcasar, Karl August Auberlen, Greg L. Bahnsen, Arthur S. Barnes, James Vernon Bartlet, F. C. Baur, Albert A. Bell, Jr., Willibald Beyshclag, Charles Bigg, Friedrich Bleek, Heinrich Bohmer, Wilhelm Bousset, F. F. Bruce, Rudolf Bultmann, W. Boyd Carpenter, David Chilton, Adam Clarke, William Newton Clarke, Henry Cowles, W. Gary Crampton, Berry Stewart Crebs, Samuel Davidson, Edmund De Pressense, P. S. Desprez, W. M. L. De Wette, Friedrich Dusterdieck, K. A. Eckhardt, Alfred Edersheim, George Edmundson, Johann Gottfried Eichhorn, G. H. A. Ewald, F. W. Farrar, Grenville O. Field, George P. Fisher, J. A. Fitzmeyer, J. Massyngberde Ford, Hermann Gebhardt, James Glasgow, R. M. Grant, James Comper Gray, Samuel G. Green, Heinrich Ernst Ferdinand Guerike, Henry Melville Gwatkin, Henry Hammond, H. G. Hartwig, Karl August von Hase, B. W. Henderson, Johann Gottfried von Herder, Adolf Hilgenfeld, David Hill, F. J. A. Hort, H. J. Holtzmann, John

Leonhard Hug, William Hurte, A. Immer, Theodor Keim, Theodor Koppe, Max Krenkel, Johann Heinrich Kurtz, Victor Lechler, Francis Nigel Lee, J. B. Lightfoot, Gottfried C. F. Lucke, Christoph Ernst Luthardt, James M. Macdonald, Frederick Denison Maurice, Charles Pettit M'Ilvaine, John David Michaelis, Theodor Mommsen, A. D. Momigliano, Charles Herbert Morgan, C. F. D. Moule, John Augustus Wilhelm Neander, Bishop Thomas Newton, A. Niermeyer, Alfred Plummer, Edward Hayes Plumtree, T. Randell, James J. L. Ratton, Ernest Renan, Eduard Wilhelm Eugen Reuss, Jean Reville, J. W. Roberts, Edward Robinson, John A. T. Robinson, J. Stuart Russell, W. Sanday, Philip Schaff, Johann Friedrich Schleusner, J. H. Scholten, Albert Schwegler, J. J. Scott, Edward Condon Selwyn, Henry C. Sheldon, William Henry Simcox, D. Moody Smith, Arthur Penrhyn Stanley, Edward Rudolf Stier, Moses Stuart, Milton S. Terry, Friedrich August Gottreu Tholuck, Charles Cutler Torrey, Cornelius Vanderwaal, Gustav Volkmar, Foy E. Wallace, Jr., Arthur Weigall, Bernhard Weiss, Brookes Fost Westcott, J. J. Wetstein, Karl Wieseler, Charles Wordsworth, Herbert B. Workman, Robert Young, and C. F. J. Zullig.[3] Can it be that these scholars are intellectually careless and historically naive?

My Approach

Since I have already begun swimming against the tide of contemporary opinion on this point, why not continue the swim? Whereas most approaches to the question of Revelation's date begin with the evidence from *church tradition* (often called "external evidence"), I will begin with evidence drawn from Revelation's *self-witness* (usually called "internal evidence"). Holding to an unshakable conviction regarding Scripture's divine inspiration, I also affirm its inherent authority, infallibility, and inerrancy. Hence, I am convinced the self-witness is the superior and determinative evidence. I will turn to the evidence from tradition in due time,

---

3. For source documentation, see my *Before Jerusalem Fell: Dating the Book of Revelation* (Tyler, TX: Institute for Christian Economics, 1989).

however.

The reader should note that this part of the book is a condensation and popularization of a fuller, more technical doctoral dissertation.[4] In the larger work will be found much fuller exegetical and historical argumentation.

The Significance of the Issue

If the earlier date for Revelation be adopted, an interesting result presents itself to the interpreter: Most of the judgment visions in Revelation (chs. 4-19) could easily be applied to the historical turmoil which came to a head shortly after John wrote. The fulfillment of the majority of its prophecies would then apply to the very beginning of Christianity, rather than to its conclusion. Contained in Revelation might be prophetic allusions to the first Roman persecution of Christianity (A.D. 64-68), the Jewish War with Rome (A.D. 67-70), the death of Christianity's first persecutor (Nero Caesar, d. A.D. 68), the Roman Civil Wars (A.D. 68-69), and the destruction of Jerusalem and the temple (A.D. 70).[5]

If such were the case, then the fulfillment of many of Revelation's prophecies would be subject to documentation from history. Furthermore, the book would then be intensely relevant to the suffering churches to which John addressed it (Rev. 1:4, 11; chs. 2-3; 22:16). Revelation's initial purpose would have been to steel infant Christianity against the tribulation into which it was entering (Rev. 1:9; cp. 2:10, 22; 3:10; 6:9-11). In addition, John would also be explaining to the early Christians and to us the spiritual and historical significance of the destruction of Jerusalem and the temple and the demise of Judaism. Such a preparation of first-century Christianity would be of immense practical and spiritual

4. See footnote 2 above.

5. Adherents to this view include: David Chilton, *The Days of Vengeance: An Exposition of the Book of Revelation* (Fort Worth, TX: Dominion Press, 1987); Cornelius Vanderwaal, *Search the Scriptures*, trans. Theodore Plantinga, 10 vols. (St. Catherines, Ontario: Paideia Press, 1978), vol. 10; and Philip Schaff, *History of the Christian Church*, 3rd ed. (Grand Rapids: Eerdmans, 1910), vol. 1.

importance. Apostolic Christianity tended to focus around Jerusalem and the temple (Luke 24:47; Acts 1:8, 12; 3:1, 2, 11; 5:12-16, 42; 8:1; 11:1, 2; 15:1, 2) and the early converts to Christianity were predominantly from Judaism (Acts 2:14, 41, 47; 4:1-4).

If the late-date of around A.D. 95-96 were accepted, a wholly different situation would prevail. The events of the mid- and late 60s of the first century would be *absolutely excluded* as possible fulfillments. The prophecies within Revelation would be opened to an abundance of speculative scenarios, which could be extrapolated into the indefinite future. Revelation might outline the course of Church history according to any number of outlines or to certain general principles.[6] Or it might focus exclusively on the end of history, which would begin approaching thousands of years after John's time, either before, after, or during the tribulation or the millennium.[7]

The purpose of Revelation would then be to show early Christians that things will get worse, that history will be a time of constant and increased suffering for the Church. This understanding, of course, would be tempered by references within Revelation to the spiritual reality of heaven above to which the martyrs go upon departing this life. And, in the case of premillennial systems, the latter chapters would hold forth the ultimate hope of Christ's intervention in the course of history to impose His triumphant kingdom over the agelong harriers of the Church.

Conclusion

The impact of the question of the dating of Revelation is of great significance. Though the majority of current scholars calls

---

6. Adherents to this outline-of-history view include: Albert S. Barnes, *Barnes' Notes on the New Testament* (Grand Rapids: Kregel, rep. 1962); and W. Boyd Carpenter, "The Revelation of St. John," in John C. Ellicott, *Ellicott's Commentary on the Whole Bible* (Grand Rapids: Zondervan, rep. n.d.).

7. For example, John F. Walvoord, *The Revelation of Jesus Christ* (Chicago: Moody Press, 1966); Herman Hoeksema, *Behold, He Cometh!* (Grand Rapids: Kregel, 1969); and Robert H. Gundry, *The Church and the Tribulation* (Grand Rapids: Zondervan, 1973).

for a Domitianic date for Revelation (A.D. 95-96), there is a growing movement away from such a position to the more conservative Neronic dating which predominated in the late 1800s. I trust that this section of the present study will be used in some small way to interest Christians in the important debate. I hope that the evidence rehearsed below will draw many to the early date view of the writing of Revelation.

9

THE THEMATIC EVIDENCE

Behold, He is coming with the clouds, and every eye will see Him, even those who pierced Him; and all the tribes of the earth will mourn over Him. Even so. Amen (Rev. 1:7).

As should be obvious, an author's stated theme is of great importance for understanding his message. Fortunately, there is a broad consensus among commentators regarding the basic *theme* of Revelation. The determination of the theme of Revelation holds much potential value for our inquiry as to its date. Yet, although the *fact* of Revelation's theme is widely agreed upon, the *nature* of the fulfillment of the fact is not so broadly held. The proper interpretation of it will have to be shown from the evidence.

Determination of the Theme

The theme of Revelation is found in its introduction at Revelation 1:7, cited above. A great number of scholars point to this verse as the theme of Revelation. Among them we could list Moses Stuart,[1] Friedrich Dusterdieck,[2] Bernhard Weiss,[3] Justin A. Smith,[4]

---

1. Moses Stuart, *Commentary on the Apocalypse*, 2 vols. (Andover: Allen, Morrill, and Wardwell, 1845) 1:273.

2. Friedrich Dusterdieck, *Critical and Exegetical Handbook to the Revelation of John*, trans. Henry E. Jacobs (3rd ed: New York: Funk and Wagnalls, 1886), p. 28.

3. Bernhard Weiss, *A Manual of Introduction to the New Testament*, 2 vols., trans. A. J. K. Davidson (New York: Funk and Wagnalls, 1889) 2:71.

4. Justin A. Smith, *Commentary on the Revelation* in Alvah Hovey, ed., *An American Commentary on the New Testament* (Valley Forge: Judson, [1884] rep. n.d.), p. 18.

Milton S. Terry,[5] J. Stuart Russell,[6] T. D. Bernard,[7] Donald W. Richardson,[8] George E. Ladd,[9] Charles C. Ryrie,[10] G. R. Beasley-Murray,[11] and David Chilton.[12]

That this note regarding the coming of Christ is Revelation's theme is evident in the emphasis placed on it, for it is a constant refrain in the personal letters to the Seven Churches (Rev. 2:5, 16, 25; 3:3, 11, 20) and elsewhere (Rev. 16:15; 22:7, 12, 20). The theme, introduced dramatically with a "Behold!," not only introduces Revelation (Rev. 1:7), but closes it as well (Rev. 22:20).

Clearly there is the expectation of this event, an event that is of tremendous import. But exactly what is it that is expected? And how is it anticipated? Further, how does it assist in our determination of the date of Revelation?

Explication of the Theme

The event prophesied in Revelation 1:7 is a "cloud-coming" of Christ: "Behold! He is coming with the clouds." Here it is necessary to understand the Old Testament imagery that forms the backdrop to the idea. In the Old Testament clouds are frequently emblems of divine wrath and judgment. This is because God is surrounded with thick, foreboding clouds due to His unap-

5. Milton S. Terry, *Biblical Apocalyptics* (New York: Eaton and Mains, 1898), p. 280.

6. J. Stuart Russell, *The Parousia: A Study of the New Testament Doctrine of Our Lord's Second Coming*, 2nd ed. (Grand Rapids: Baker, [1887] 1983), p. 368.

7. Thomas Dehany Bernard, *Progress of Doctrine in the New Testament* (Grand Rapids: Eerdmans, [1864] 1949), p. 213.

8. Donald W. Richardson, *The Revelation of Jesus Christ* (Richmond, VA: John Knox, 1964), p. 28.

9. George Eldon Ladd, *A Commentary on the Revelation to John* (Grand Rapids: Eerdmans, 1972), p. 28.

10. Charles C. Ryrie, *Revelation* (Chicago: Moody Press, 1968), p. 15.

11. G. R. Beasley-Murray, *The Book of Revelation* (Grand Rapids: Eerdmans, 1978), p. 58.

12. David Chilton, *The Days of Vengeance: An Exposition of the Book of Revelation* (Fort Worth, TX: Dominion Press, 1987), p. 64.

proachable holiness and righteousness (Gen. 15:17; Ex. 13:21-22; 14:19-20; 19:9, 16-19; Deut. 4:11; Job 22:14; Pss. 18:8ff; 97:2; 104:3; Isa. 19:1; Ezek. 32:7-8). Thus, God is poetically portrayed as *coming in clouds* in historical judgments upon men (Pss. 18:7-15; 104:3; Isa. 19:1; Joel 2:1, 2; Nah. 1:2ff.; Zeph. 1:14, 15). Likewise, the New Testament speaks of Christ's coming in clouds of judgment (Matt. 24:30; 26:64) and at His Second Coming at the end of world history (Acts 1:11).

According to our theme, Christ's cloud-coming is a judgment which causes men to "mourn." But upon whom does this cloud-coming fall? And when? And how?

Fortunately, cues exist within the theme text to assist us in our inquiry. Also cues may be found in the other New Testament allusions to this same passage (which is a conflation of Dan. 7:13 and Zech. 12:10). Along with these cues we may surmise the objects of His wrath: The passage clearly states that Christ will come to and cause mourning among "those who pierced Him," even upon "all the tribes of the earth." I am convinced that these references speak directly to the first century Jews. Let me lay before the judicious reader the following evidence in this regard.

"Those Who Crucified Christ"

First, though it is true that the Romans were responsible for physically nailing Christ to the cross[13] (John 18:30-31), nevertheless, when covenantally considered the onus of the divine curse falls squarely upon those who instigated and demanded it: the Jews. The biblical record is quite clear and emphatic: the *Jews* are the ones who sought His death (John 11:53; Matt. 26:4; 27:1), paid for His capture (Matt. 26:14-15, 47; 27:3-9), brought false witnesses against Him (Matt. 27:59-62), initially convicted Him (Matt. 27:65-66), turned Him over to Roman civil authority (Matt.

---

13. The very fact that He died of crucifixion (a Roman punishment) and not stoning (a Jewish punishment) is by itself indicative of the physical involvement of the Roman judicial apparatus.

27:2, 11, 12; Acts 3:13), and even called down His blood upon their own heads (Matt. 27:24-25). John even tells us in his Gospel that the Roman procurator, Pontius Pilate, sought to free Jesus, finding no fault in Him (John 18:38; 19:12; cp. Acts 3:13). But the Jews demanded that the robber Barabbas be released instead (John 18:39, 40) and that Christ be immediately crucified (John 19:6, 15). They even threatened Pilate's tenuous Roman procuratorship by affirming "we have no king but Caesar" (John 19:14-15), suggesting that Pilate was allowing Christ to supplant Caesar. And Jesus Himself, during the course of these events, specifically pointed out to Pilate that "he who delivered Me up to you has the greater sin" (John 19:11). This should settle the matter of culpability, but there is more — much more.

In Peter's pentecostal sermon at Jerusalem in Acts 2:22-23, 36 the blame is laid wholly on Israel: "Men of Israel, listen to these words: Jesus the Nazarene . . . *you nailed to a cross* by the hands of godless men and put Him to death. . . . Therefore let all the house of Israel know for certain that God has made Him both Lord and Christ — this Jesus whom *you crucified*." He does the same in his next sermon in Acts 3:13-15a: "The God of Abraham, Isaac, and Jacob, the God of our fathers, has glorified His servant Jesus, the one whom *you* delivered up, and disowned in the presence of Pilate, when he had decided to release Him. But *you* disowned the Holy and Righteous One, and asked for a murderer to be granted to you, but put to death the Prince of life." He repeats this to the Jews in Acts 5:30 where he proclaims: "The God of our fathers raised up Jesus, whom *you* had put to death by hanging Him on a cross."

Stephen, in Acts 7:52, declares the same truth: that the Jews were the "betrayers and murderers" of Christ. Paul concurs in 1 Thessalonians 2:14-15 when he speaks of "the *Jews, who both killed the Lord Jesus* and the prophets, and drove us out."

This consistent and constant witness against the Jews in the canon of the New Testament continues into post-apostolic Church history. I will quote a few samples from the early fathers to illustrate the matter.

Ignatius (A.D. 50-115) quite frequently drives home the point of Jewish culpability regarding Christ's death when he refers to the Jews as "Christ-killing Jews,"[14] "those murderers of the Lord,"[15] and "the Jews fighting against Christ."[16] Justin Martyr (A.D. 100-165) plays the same theme of Jewish liability when he writes: "Jesus Christ stretched forth His hands, being crucified by the Jews,"[17] "all these things happened to Christ at the hands of the Jews,"[18] and "the Jews deliberated about the Christ Himself, to crucify and put Him to death."[19] Irenaeus (A.D. 130-202) concurs when he says of the Jews: "[God] sent in Jesus, whom they crucified and God raised up,"[20] and "to the Jews, indeed, they proclaimed that the Jesus who was crucified by them was the Son of God."[21] Other church fathers who return to this theme include: Melito of Sardis (d. A.D. 190), Tertullian[22] (A.D. 160-220), Hippolytus[23] (A.D. 170-236), Cyprian[24] (A.D. 200-258), Lactantius[25] (A.D. 240-320), to name but a few.[26]

"The Tribes of the Earth"

Second, this view is reinforced in the Revelation 1:7 passage

---

14. *Epistle to the Magnesians* 11.

15. *Epistle to the Trallians* 11.

16. *Epistle to the Smyrnaeans* 2.

17. *First Apology* 35.

18. *Ibid.* 38.

19. *Dialogue with Trypho* 72.

20. *Against Heresies* 3:12:2.

21. *Ibid.* 3:12:13.

22. *Apology* 21 and 26; *On Idolatry* 7; *An Answer to the Jews* 9 and 13; *Against Marcion* 3:6; 3:25; 5:15.

23. *Treatise on Christ and Antichrist* 30 and 57; *Expository Treatise Against the Jews* 1, 2, and 7; and *Against Noetus* 18.

24. *Treatises* 9:7; 10:5; Introduction to *Treatise* 12; 12:2:14; 12:2:20.

25. *Divine Institutes* 4:18; *Epitome of the Divine Institutes* 46; *On the Manner in Which the Persecutors Died* 2.

26. Additional references can be found in my *Before Jerusalem Fell: Dating the Book of Revelation* (Tyler, TX: Institute for Christian Economics, 1989).

when it speaks of the mourning of "the tribes of the earth." The Greek word for "tribe" is *phule*, which in Scripture most frequently refers to the Jewish tribes. In fact, the Septuagint "with few exceptions . . . has *phule*, so that this becomes a fixed term for the tribal system of Israel."[27] The word for "tribe" is a common designation of the twelve-fold division of Israel (see Rev. 5:5; 7:4-8; Acts 26:6, 7). The "tribes" found their home in Palestine; these are "the tribes of the Land." The Jews were so attached to their land that of Jerusalem it may be said: "To the Jew this was the true home of his soul, the centre of his inmost life, the longing of his heart."[28]

The reference to the "tribe of Judah" in Revelation 5:5 definitely carries that connotation. The term obviously has that import in Revelation 7:4ff. (where it is used of each of the specifically named Twelve Tribes) and in Revelation 21:12 (where John refers to "the twelve tribes of the children of Israel"). Of course, where the term is found in connection with "every kindred, tribe, tongue, and nation" in Revelation, such would not be the exclusive reference (cf. Rev. 5:9; 7:9; 11:9; 13:7; 14:6).

"The Earth, or Land"

Third, in addition, the Greek word for "earth" in Revelation 1:7 is *ge*.[29] This common word, which appears over 80 times in Revelation, has five related meanings. Two of its basic meanings are: (1) "earth" and (2) "land." It is used in both senses in the New Testament, as well as in Revelation.

---

27. Christian Maurer, *"phule"* in *Theological Dictionary of the New Testament*, ed. Gerhard Kittle and Gerhard Friedrich, trans. Geoffrey W. Bromiley (Grand Rapids: Eerdmans, 1974) 9:246. See also Burton Scott Easton, "Tribe," in *The International Standard Bible Encyclopaedia*, ed. James Orr (Grand Rapids: Eerdmans, 1956) 4:3010. It should be noted, in addition, that the Arndt-Gingrich *Lexicon* (p. 876) and the Thayer *Lexicon* (p. 660) both list "tribe," as in Israel, as their first lexical entries.

28. Edersheim, *Sketches of Jewish Social Life*, p. 63.

29. See Arndt and Gingrich, *Lexicon*, p. 156; Thayer, *Lexicon*, pp. 114-115; Abbott-Smith, *Lexicon*, p. 91.

In a number of places in the New Testament this word is used to speak of the Promised Land. In these places it is found in such phrases as "the land of Judah" (Matt. 2:6), "the land of Judea" (John 3:22), and "the land of Israel" (Matt. 2:20). It can be used with the definite article alone and without any modifiers. In these cases it means simply "the land" (Greek: *he ge*), signifying the famous Promised Land. This usage is found in Matthew 27:45; Mark 15:33; Luke 4:25; 21:23 (see v. 21); Romans 9:28 (see v. 27); and James 5:17. Thus, upon purely lexical considerations, the term can be understood as designating the Promised Land.

The significance of this translation of *he ge* may be discerned from spiritual-cultural situations, such as noted of the ancient Rabbis by Edersheim: "For, to the Rabbis the precise limits of Palestine were chiefly interesting so far as they affected the religious obligations or privileges of a district. . . . Indeed, viewing the question from this point, Palestine was to the Rabbis simply 'the land,' all other countries being summed up under the designation of 'outside the land.'"[30]

As a matter of fact, literal translations of the Scripture lean in this direction, with such translations as: "Lo, he doth come with the clouds, and see him shall every eye, even those who did pierce him, and wail because of him shall all the tribes of the land. Yes! Amen!"[31] and "Behold he comes with the clouds, and will see him every eye and [those] who him pierced, and will wail over him all the tribes of the land. Yes, amen."[32]

Christ's usage of the phrases found in Revelation 1:7 ties the occurrence to Palestine, when he warns His believers in *Jerusalem* and *Judea* to flee (Luke 21:20, 21, 27).

In addition, that such is the referent of *he ge* in Revelation 1:7

30. Edersheim, *Sketches of Jewish Social Life*, p. 14. Edersheim's entire second chapter is helpful reading along these lines.

31. Robert Young, *Young's Literal Translation of the Holy Bible*, 2nd ed. (Grand Rapids: Baker, [1898] n.d.), p. 167.

32. Alfred Marshall, *The Interlinear Greek-English New Testament*, 2nd ed. (Grand Rapids: Zondervan, 1959), p. 956.

seems to be indicated by the fact that the verse is a blending of Daniel 7:13 and Zechariah 12:10.[33] The Zechariah 12:10 passage indisputably refers to the land of Israel: "And I will pour out on the house of David and on the inhabitants of Jerusalem, the Spirit of grace and of supplication, so that they will look on Me whom they have pierced; and they will mourn for Him, as one mourns for an only son, and they will weep bitterly over Him, like the bitter weeping over a first-born. In that day there will be great mourning in Jerusalem, like the mourning of Hadadrimmon in the plain of Megiddo. And the land will mourn, every family by itself."

Gospel Confirmation

That these phrases in Revelation 1:7 speak of *the Promised Land of the first century* is evident in Jesus' teaching. There we find a recurring emphasis upon the culpability of the generation of Jews *then living* — those who actually crucified the Messiah, the Lord of Glory. In Matthew 23 He calls down a seven-fold woe upon the scribes and Pharisees, those who "sit in the chair of Moses" (Matt. 23:2). In this woeful passage He distinctly and clearly warns (Matt. 23:32-38): "*Upon you* [will] fall the guilt of all the righteous blood shed on earth [or: "on the land"]. . . . *Truly I say to you, all these things shall come upon this generation.* O Jerusalem, Jerusalem, who kills the prophets and stones those who are sent to her! How often I wanted to gather your children together, the way a hen gathers her chicks under her wings, and you were unwilling. Behold, your house is being left to you desolate!"

Christ then goes on to describe the desolation of Israel's "house" (temple) in Matthew 24. In Matthew 24:1-2 He clearly and distinctly makes reference to the destruction of the temple. And in the following context He expands on this as involving the

---

33. An early note should be recalled at this point. Daniel 7:13 has original reference to the ascension of Christ to glory. Here John is not interpreting Daniel 7:13, but merging it with Zechariah 12:10 in application to the theme of his prophecy: the judgment-coming upon Israel that resulted from the ascension-coming to the Father to take up His rule.

"abomination of desolation" in the temple (v. 15) and the "great tribulation" (v. 21), which signify "the Son of Man coming on the clouds of the sky with power and great glory" (v. 30). These events are said to be coming upon "this generation" (v. 34), *i.e. the very generation which rejected and "pierced" Him.* The crucifixion took place in Israel in its very capital, Jerusalem (Matt. 20:17-19; Luke 9:31; 13:33-34; 18:31; 24:18-10). Indisputably, it was *that generation* which was to be destroyed in His judgment-coming.

Drawing Conclusions

With these several contextual indicators before us, it seems certain that the theme of Revelation deals with Christ's judgment-coming *upon the generation of those Jews who crucified Him.* Clearly, the judgment-coming of Christ upon "those who pierced Him" was to be upon the Jews, according to the repeated and uniform witness both of the New Testament and of early church history. As Chilton observes: "Verse 7 [*i.e.,* of Revelation 1] announces the theme of the book, which is not the Second Coming of Christ, but rather the Coming of Christ in judgment upon Israel, in order to establish the Church as the new Kingdom."[34] Desprez notes of this theme verse in conjunction with the temporal expectations of the book: "No scriptural statement is capable of more decided proof than that the coming of Christ is the destruction of Jerusalem, and the close of the Jewish dispensation."[35]

We know as a matter of indisputable historical fact that the temple was destroyed by Titus's August, A.D. 70, siege of the temple.[36] Hence, as Jesus bears His cross to Calvary He exhorts the "daughters of Jerusalem" to weep for themselves because of the coming judgment (Luke 23:28-31, cp. Rev. 6:16).

Such being the case, only a pre-A.D. 70 date could be expected, for what events subsequent to the A.D. 70 destruction of

---

34. Chilton, *Days of Vengeance,* p. 64.

35. P. S. Desprez, *The Apocalypse Fulfilled,* 2nd ed. (London: Longman, Brown, Green, Longmans, 1855), p. 9.

36. Josephus, *The Wars of the Jews* 7:1:1.

the temple parallel the magnitude and covenantal significance of this event? Surely the destruction of the Jewish temple (accomplished now for over 1900 years) and the gruesome Jewish War with Rome *must* be in view here. In terms of Jewish calamity and woe, what events near the reign of Domitian could equal those which transpired just after Nero's reign? Surely Revelation 1:7 indicates that "the *Jewish people* are most evidently intended, and therefore the whole verse may be understood as predicting the destruction of the Jews; and is a presumptive proof that the Apocalypse was written *before* the final overthrow of the Jewish state."[37]

As we press on with our case for a pre-A.D. 70 date for Revelation, we move to consideration of Israel's condition as evidenced in Revelation. We will discover that her condition bespeaks a time pre-A.D. 70.

Coming Judgment in the Land

With these observations before us, it would seem certain that the theme of Revelation deals with Christ's judgment-coming *upon the generation of those Jews who crucified Him.* And it was a judgment-coming upon them, particularly as they dwelt in "the Land," the Promised Land God had given them. We might well expect that the theme would recur throughout Revelation – and it does. I will cite just one illustration of the fact that Revelation looks to the Jewish War with Rome of A.D. 67-70.[38]

The Sealing of the Saints

In Revelation 7:1-8 we find an interesting temporary divine protection of "the Land" where four angels are seen holding back the winds of destruction. We will translate the Greek words nor-

---

37. Adam Clarke, *Clarke's Commentary on the Whole Bible* (Nashville: Abingdon, rep. n.d.) 6:971.

38. For additional information in this regard, see my larger work, *Before Jerusalem Fell: Dating the Book of Revelation.*

mally translated "the earth" by our preferred translation "the Land":

> After this I saw four angels standing at the four corners of the Land, holding back the four winds of the Land, so that no wind should blow on the Land or on the sea or on any tree. And I saw another angel ascending from the rising sun, having the seal of the living God; and he cried out with a loud voice to the four angels to whom it was granted to harm the Land and the sea, saying, "Do not harm the Land or the sea or the trees, until we have sealed the bond-servants of our God on their foreheads."

Then follows the sealing of the 144,000 from the Twelve Tribes of Israel.

Clearly the reference to those who are sealed is to *Christians*. This must be the case because (1) God intervenes to protect them, and (2) they are called "bond-servants of our God." These cannot be unbelieving Jews. Furthermore, these would have to be Christian *Jews* for (1) they are from Israel's Twelve Tribes (Rev. 7:4), (2) they are in "the Land" (Rev. 7:1, 2), and (3) they are contrasted with the "great multitude" from "every nation" who praise God (Rev. 7:9).

The designation of the "Twelve Tribes" is another common means by which to refer to the "the tribes of the Land" (cp. Rev. 1:7). Here, however, it is not the entirety of the Twelve Tribes that is protected, the whole race of Israel, as such. Rather, it is only 144,000 of them: a perfect number[39] representing the "cream of the crop," *i.e.* those Jews who have converted to Christ. They are sealed "out of" or "from among" (Greek: *ek*) "every tribe of the sons of Israel" (Rev. 7:4).

Why are these 144,000 designated as being from Jewish tribes? Because the pending "wind of destruction" was threatened against

---

39. The number 144,000 is derived from the number symbolic of quantitative fullness (10), which is trebled (10 x 10 x 10), and then multiplied by the number of tribes squared (12 x 12).

Judea, the land where the city of Jerusalem is found, in which the Lord was crucified (Rev. 11:1, 2, 8).

The Destruction in the Land

The fact that an angel intervenes in order to prevent their being destroyed along with the Land surely indicates the era prior to the devastation of Israel in A.D. 70 (remember the expectation of soon occurrence that we noted in Chapter 2 above). Were "the Land" already destroyed (as it was in August, A.D. 70), such a promised protection would have been embarrassingly anachronistic.

In the Olivet Discourse Jesus spoke of the destruction of the very temple to which the disciples could physically point (Matt. 24:1-2). He warned His disciples that they should flee *Judea* (Matt. 24:16) when it was time for these things to come to pass (which occurred in A.D. 70). He added further that they should accept His promise that these horrendous events would be cut short (Matt. 24:22), and that he who endured to the end would be saved through it all (Matt. 24:13). He also clearly taught that all of these things would happen to "this generation" (Matt. 24:32). Indeed, this coming event was to be "the great tribulation" (Matt. 24:21) – the very tribulation in which John finds himself enmeshed even as he writes (Rev. 1:9; cp. 7:14).

The protection of Jewish Christians in Jerusalem is thus indicated in Revelation 7:1-7 via the symbolism of sealing. This refers to the providential protection of those Christians of Jewish lineage who were "in the Land."

An extremely interesting and famous piece of history informs us that the Jewish Christians in Jerusalem escaped the city before it was too late, possibly either at the outset of the War or during one of its providential lulls. Church historian Eusebius (A.D. 260-340) records the situation thus:

> But the people of the church in Jerusalem had been commanded by a revelation, vouchsafed to approved men there before the war,

to leave the city and to dwell in a certain town of Perea called Pella. And when those that believed in Christ had come thither from Jerusalem, then, as if the royal city of the Jews and the whole land of Judea were entirely destitute of holy men, the judgment of God at length overtook those who had committed such outrages against Christ and his apostles, and totally destroyed that generation of impious men.[40]

Thus, Revelation 7, which provides supplemental evidence to John's overarching theme, is strongly indicative of a pre-fall Judea. This must be so because after the Jewish War "Palestine was proclaimed a Roman province, and a great part of the land became the personal property of the emperor. But the country was in ruins, its once flourishing towns and villages almost without inhabitants, dogs and jackals prowling through the devastated streets and houses."[41]

Conclusion

The theme of Revelation involves Christ's judgment upon first-century Israel for its rejection of His Messianic kingship. This is evident from the various terms used in the thematic statement of Revelation 1:7: Christ is to come upon (1) those who pierced Him, *i.e.* the Jews, (2) those who are of "the tribes," *i.e.* the Jews, and (3) those who dwell in "the Land," *i.e.* the Promised Land. All of this comes about as a fulfillment of His own prophecies in Matthew 21:33-45; 23:1ff; 24:1-34; Luke 21:5-28; 23:27-31; and elsewhere. And all of this was to come upon "this generation" (Matt. 23:36; 24:34). Or, using John's terminology, these events were "near" (Rev. 1:3) and were to occur "shortly" (Rev. 1:1; 22:6ff).

The events to which Christ and John point were those associ-

---

40. *Ecclesiastical History* 3:5:3.

41. Rufus Learsi, *Israel: A History of the Jewish People* (New York: World, 1949), p. 178.

ated with the Jewish War with Rome in A.D. 67-70. Particularly in view is the destruction of the temple, which was destroyed in August, A.D. 70. Consequently, Revelation must have been written prior to that destruction.

10

THE POLITICAL EVIDENCE

Here is the mind which has wisdom. The seven heads are seven mountains on which the woman sits, and they are seven kings; five have fallen, one is, the other has not yet come; and when he comes, he must remain a little while (Rev. 17:9-10).

In this chapter I will be considering what I believe to be *the* leading objective evidence for Revelation's date of composition. That evidence is contained in the statement regarding the "seven kings" in Revelation 17, which is cited above. Here we are given what I believe to be a concrete political statement of an historically datable quality that clearly establishes a time-frame for the dating of Revelation. As I will show, that time-frame not only precludes a Domitianic date for Revelation, but firmly establishes a Neronic one.

The prominent features of the chapter bearing upon our inquiry are: (1) There is the imagery of the Beast with seven heads (Rev. 17:3, 7, 9; cp. 13:2). (2) These seven heads are said to represent both seven mountains and seven kings (17:9, 10). (3) Of the seven kings, "five have fallen," "one is" reigning, and one is to come to rule for "a little while" (17:10).

Let us consider this evidence carefully in demonstration of Revelation's date.

The Line of Kings

Earlier, in Chapter 1, I showed that the seven mountains represented by the seven heads spoke of the peculiar geography of Rome. Rome was familiar to all of the ancient world as the "the city on Seven Hills." This geographical clue in the vision, coupled with the expectation of soon occurrence and the relevance of the letter to its original audience, necessarily limit us to the broad historical era of the ancient Roman Empire.[1]

But there is a more particular aspect to the vision, an aspect which confines the outer reaches of the time-frame to the early date era. I speak of the *political* reference to the line of the kings. John writes of the seven heads that they are not only "seven mountains" but: "They are seven kings; five have fallen, one is, the other has not yet come; and when he comes, he must remain a little while." Here is described for us a sequence of seven kings of Rome. This statement, as we will see, closely fixes the time of composition of Revelation. All we need to do is to determine the identity of these seven kings, and which ones are alive as John writes. I lay before the careful student the following evidences, supportive of the early date position.

First, it may be dogmatically asserted that the sixth king is alive and ruling even as John writes. John clearly states that the first five "have fallen." In this verse is used a verb in the past tense:[2] The five that "have fallen" are *past* rulers. For whatever reasons, these five have already fallen from power as "kings." He continues by noting that the sixth king "is." Here John uses the present tense.[3] The sixth king is presently in control of the kingdom. The seventh "has not yet come;[4] and when he comes, he must remain a little while" (Rev. 17:10). The coming to power of the seventh is not yet a present reality.

This obviously speaks of the past deaths of the first five kings

---

1. See Chapter 2.

2. The form of the Greek verb *pipto* ("fall") is the second aorist active indicative.

3. The Greek is the present indicative form of the verb *eimi* ("to be").

4. Here John uses the "prophetic second aorist active of *erchomai*" according to A. T. Robertson, *Word Pictures in the New Testament*, 6 vols. (Nashville: Broadman, 1933) 6:432.

and the present reign of the sixth one. It is also anticipatory of a coming seventh king, who will immediately follow the sixth. Whoever these kings are, the sixth one is indisputably alive and in control *as John writes*, while in exile for his faith (cp. Rev. 1:9).

Second, history documents for us that *Nero was the sixth emperor of Rome*. Nero reigned in Rome from October 13, A.D. 54, to June 9, A.D. 68 — well before the A.D. 90s required by the late-date theory. He was the sixth ruler to bear the name "Caesar." The list of the Caesars is as follows:

1. Julius Caesar (49-44 B.C.)

2. Augustus Caesar (31 B.C.-A.D. 14)

3. Tiberius Caesar (A.D. 14-37)

4. Gaius Caesar, also called "Caligula" (A.D. 37-41)

5. Claudius Caesar (A.D. 41-54)

6. *Nero Caesar* (A.D. 54-68)

Nero fits the bill perfectly in terms of the enumeration of the emperors of Rome. But there is more.

Third, John says of the seventh king that he "has not yet come; and when he comes, he must remain a little while" (Rev. 17:10). In my enumeration this seventh king must be reckoned with. It is a remarkable and indisputable fact of Roman imperial history that upon Nero's death by suicide in the summer of A.D. 68, the empire was cast into a leadership turmoil and struggle. The next ruler to appear after Nero was Galba. *And Galba reigned only seven months!* His rule lasted from June, A.D. 68, to January 15, A.D. 69.

By almost any standard, Galba's brief rule of seven months was a "little while." The Greek term in Revelation 17:10 for "little" is *oligon*. We get our term "oligarchy" (which means "a rule by a few") from this word. When Galba's rule is compared to any of the preceding six emperors (see the listing above), it is obvious that his is indisputably the shortest imperial reign theretofore.

This evidence from Revelation 17 fits the reign of Nero, then, in more than one respect. The correspondence to the history of the era is perfect. But not all commentators accept this view. Let us survey the major objections against our position.

Objections to the Nero View

There are several major objections that have been argued against the view presented above. Initially these seem to be quite formidable objections. But a careful analysis of them will dispel any real force they may appear to have.

The Call for Wisdom

Some commentators point to the fact that Revelation is full of imagery that might not be so obvious. Regarding the present matter in particular, they argue that the text even cautions against too easy an interpretation. Immediately before our verse is the following statement: "here is the mind which has wisdom" (Rev. 17:9a). In this regard, John F. Walvoord writes: "The explanation of the beast introduced by the unusual phrase 'here is the mind which hath wisdom' anticipates the difficulty and complexity of the revelation to follow. The reader is warned that spiritual wisdom is required to understand that which is unfolded."[5]

Despite his observation, it appears that Walvoord is once again turning a matter in Revelation on its head (as we noted earlier regarding John's temporal expectation). The context of John's statement clearly suggests that this phrase is introducing an *elucidation* of the matter. It is not a warning about an additional difficulty to be added by verses 9 and 10. The angel who shows John the harlot seated on the seven-headed Beast, notes John's wonder and confusion about the vision (Rev. 17:1, 7a). Then the angel tells John that he will interpret the matter for him: "Why do you wonder? I shall tell you the mystery of the woman and of

---

5. John F. Walvoord, *The Revelation of Jesus Christ* (Chicago: Moody Press, 1966), p. 250. See also Henry B. Swete, *Commentary on Revelation* (Grand Rapids: Kregel, [1911] 1977), pp. 219-220 and Alan F. Johnson, *Revelation* (Grand Rapids: Zondervan, 1983), p. 158.

the beast that carries her, which has the seven heads and the ten horns" (Rev. 17:7). What follows is the angel's exposition of the vision. *He is not providing John with more difficult material, but is explaining the confusing aspect of the vision.* This experience, then, is reminiscent of an earlier situation in which an "elder" (an angel of some sort) explains to John the vision of the "great multitude" in Revelation 7:9, 13, 14. In both Revelation 7 and 17 the angelic explanation is provided as a *help* to the interpretation of a vision.

The difficulty of the vision requiring "wisdom" is that the interpretation of the imagery involves a *two-fold* referent. "The seven heads are [1] seven mountains on which the woman sits, *and* they are [2] seven kings" (vv. 9-10a). This feature would doubtless escape the interpreter without the angelic explication. It would appear, therefore, that the expression "here is the mind which has wisdom" is introducing the *interpretation* of a vision. Consequently, it is the case that he who follows the angelic interpretation "has wisdom." To argue that the following statements become more difficult would go contrary to the stated purpose of the angelic explanation. Therefore, we may expect to be able to easily understand the statements in Revelation 17:9, 10. And these statements point to the reign of Nero.

Identifying the First King

Many scholars argue that the line of the emperors of Rome officially began with Augustus, whom I have numbered the second king. Technically this may be true, in that Julius Caesar was not legally an emperor. But the historical evidence still points to the legitimacy of starting the count with Julius Caesar. As a matter of fact, Julius Caesar did claim the title *Imperator*, according to Roman historian Suetonius.[6] Furthermore, the subsequent rulers of Rome, who were technically emperors, called themselves by the name "Caesar," indicating a continuity with Julius Caesar.

But even more persuasive is the fact that records from the era

---

6. Suetonius, *Julius* 76.

in which John wrote show that Julius was commonly recognized as the first emperor of the Empire. The Roman historian Suetonius (A.D. 70-160) entitles his famous history of the emperors from the beginning up until his time, *Lives of the Twelve Caesars*. His work begins with Julius Caesar. Roman historian Dio Cassius (A.D. 150-235) also begins the count of the emperors with Julius.[7]

Other works from the same general era follow suit. Among the more prominent ones we could include *4 Ezra*, *The Epistle of Barnabas*, and various *Sibylline Oracles*.[8] Theophilus of Antioch (A.D. 115-168),[9] a Christian writer praised by Eusebius for his pastoral fidelity,[10] is quite clear in his designation: "The annual magistrates ruled the Romans, as we say, for 453 years. Afterwards those who are called emperors began in this order: first, Caius Julius, who reigned 3 years 4 months 6 days; then Augustus, 56 years 4 months 1 day; Tiberius . . . ," etc.[11]

Even more important, however, is the reckoning of the emperors by the Jewish historian Flavius Josephus. He counts Julius as the first emperor.[12] Josephus is most significant in that (1) he was a Jew, as was John, (2) he lived and wrote during John's lifetime (Josephus's dates are A.D. 37-101), (3) he even participated in the Jewish War, which seems to be the subject matter of much of Revelation, and (4) he wrote his history while at Rome.

In summary, while modern historians may often begin their count of the Roman emperors with Augustus, ancient ones began with Julius. Since the Book of Revelation is an ancient, not a modern book, it is obvious which method of counting we must use in its interpretation. The objection regarding the enumeration of

---

7. Dio Cassius, *Roman History* 5.

8. *4 Ezra* 11:13ff; 12:13ff; *Barnabas* 4:4; *Sibylline Oracles* 5:12; 8:135-138; 11:261ff.

9. His dates are conjectural. I have followed the suggestion of Marcus Dods, which is found in Alexander Roberts and James Donaldson, eds., *The Ante-Nicene Fathers*, 10 vols. (Grand Rapids: Eerdmans, [n.d] rep. 1975) 2:87-88.

10. Eusebius, *Ecclesiastical History* 4:24.

11. Theophilus, *To Autolycus* 3:28.

12. Josephus, *Antiquities of the Jews* 19:1:11; cp. 18:2:2; 18:6:10.

the kings does not, therefore, overthrow our analysis.

Interestingly, however, even *if* we begin counting with Augustus, we would still end up in the era pre-A.D. 70. For in such a counting, we would be left with the sixth king being Galba, who reigned seven months in A.D. 68-69. The seventh king would then be Otho, who reigned an even shorter period of time (January 15 to April 17, A.D. 69). Still, the evidence requires the count to begin with Julius Caesar. And that evidence lands us in the era pre-A.D. 70, before Nero's death (June, A.D. 68).

The Civil War Emperors

Another objection comes from those who suggest that the three brief reigning emperors of the Roman Civil War — Galba, Otho, Vitellius — should not be counted. This would remove three kings in the enumeration. If we then started with Augustus we would have Vespasian (emperor from A.D. 69-79) as the sixth king. This objection fails to overthrow the early date case, as well. I have already shown the improbability of starting the count from Augustus. And we should note that this counting still does not bring us to the late-date period of Domitian's rule (A.D. 95). Even Vespasian's reign begins pre-A.D. 70.

But there is more: This objection is based on two grounds: (1) Roman historian Suetonius speaks of the brief reigns of Galba, Otho, and Vitellius as but a "rebellion."[13] (2) The short reigns of these three would have been inconsequential to the far-flung provinces of the Roman Empire.[14] The ease with which we may dispose of these objections is surprising, in light of the widespread employment of them.

In regard to Suetonius's statement, it must not escape our notice that he does, nevertheless, list these three emperors in his

---

13. Suetonius, *Vespasian* 1.

14. G. R. Beasley-Murray, *The Book of Revelation* (Grand Rapids: Eerdmans, 1978), pp. 256-257; Robertson, *Word Pictures*, 5:432; James Moffatt, *The Revelation of St. John the Divine*, vol. 5 in W. Robertson Nicoll, ed., *The Expositor's Greek Testament* (Grand Rapids: Eerdmans, rep. 1980), p. 318.

Lives of the Twelve Caesars! In addition these three are recognized as emperors by Roman historian Tacitus, the pro-Roman, Jewish historian Josephus, the Christian pastor Theophilus of Antioch, the writer of *4 Ezra*, and one of the *Sibylline Oracles*.[15]

In response to the notion that these three emperors would be inconsequential to the Roman provinces in Asia Minor, nothing could be more mistaken. These three emperors almost destroyed the city of Rome and nearly caused the collapse of the empire.[16] Inconsequential?

Emperors as "Kings"

Some might object to the interpretation I am defending on the grounds that John calls these men "kings," whereas the Roman imperial rulers were properly designated "emperors." Though formally correct, this complaint overlooks the ancient tendency to call the emperors "kings."

In non-biblical Christian writings and in pagan literature the emperors were often designated kings. The Roman poet Martial (A.D. 40-104) and Nero's court philosopher, Seneca (4 B.C.-A.D. 65), both call Nero "king."[17] The *Sibylline Oracles* of the first two centuries call various emperors "kings."[18] The early Christian writings entitled *The History of John the Son of Zebedee, The Giving Up of Pontius Pilate,* and *The Acts of the Holy Apostle and Evangelist John the Theologian,* and the fifth century Christian writer Sulpicius Severus[19] all call certain emperors "kings."

More importantly, in Scripture itself we find emperors called kings! In John 19:15 the priests reject Christ before Caesar by

---

15. Tacitus, *Histories* 1:1ff; 2:10; Theophilus, *To Autolycus* 2:28; Josephus, *Wars of the Jews* 4:9:2; *Sibylline Oracles* 5:35; and *4 Ezra* 12:20ff.

16. See Chapter 7.

17. Seneca, *On Clemency* 2:12 (cited from Miriam T. Griffin, *Nero: The End of a Dynasty* [New Haven: Yale University Press, 1984], p. 95); and Martial, *Book of Spectacles* 2.

18. See *Sibylline Oracles* 4:119; 5:138ff; 8:131ff; 11:286; 12:25ff; 13:15.

19. Sulpicius Severus, *Sacred History* 2:28.

saying, "We have no king but Caesar." The accusers of Jason in Acts 17:7 warn of Jason's receiving Christians into their homes: "Jason has welcomed them, and they all act contrary to the decrees of Caesar, saying that there is another king, Jesus."

Clearly, this objection is without merit.

Conclusion

In light of all the evidence presented above, we may safely conclude that Revelation 17:9-10 provides objectively verifiable information supportive of the early date composition of Revelation. The sixth king, who is presently reigning (Rev. 17:9), is Nero Caesar, whom we have shown in Part I of this work to be the specific identity of the Beast.[20] Thus, the latest possible date which we may ascribe to Revelation is before June, A.D. 68, the date of Nero's death.

---

20. For a discussion of the 8th king. See pages 75-77, *Supra.*

11

THE ARCHITECTURAL EVIDENCE

And there was given me a measuring rod like a staff; and someone said, "Rise and measure the temple of God, and the altar, and those who worship in it. And leave out the court which is outside the temple, and do not measure it, for it has been given to the nations; and they will tread under foot the holy city for forty-two months" (Rev. 11:1-2).

Another very helpful evidence for the dating of Revelation is found in Revelation 11 (cited above), where we discover a reference to a temple complex. If we can determine the identity of this temple, and if it is a temple that exists in history, then we may be able to point to it as hard (no pun intended) evidence for a particular date for Revelation.

The most important question to consider for our present purpose is that of the *identity* of this temple complex. Basically there are three views as to the identity of this temple: Some have argued that this temple complex stands as a purely symbolic representation of the Church.[1] Others understand John's vision to refer to a future, yet-to-be-built temple.[2] Still others see the temple reference here as indicative of the earthly temple of Herod, which existed

---

1. William Hendriksen, *More Than Conquerors* (Grand Rapids: Baker, 1967), pp. 153ff; Herman Hoeksema, *Behold, He Cometh!* (Grand Rapids: Kregel, 1969), pp. 362-370; J. M. P. Sweet, *Revelation* (Philadelphia: Westminster Press, 1979), pp. 183-184.

2. John F. Walvoord, *The Revelation of Jesus Christ* (Chicago: Moody Press, 1966), pp. 175-178; Charles C. Ryrie, *Revelation* (Chicago: Moody Press, 1968), pp. 71-72.

during Jesus' day.[3] I will defend the last view in the following remarks.

The most natural identity of the temple, which suggests itself to the unbiased reader, is that this is a reference to the literal temple in Jerusalem in Jesus' day. This temple, known as Herod's temple, was familiar to the readers of the New Testament. Let us consider the merits of this view. During the course of the demonstration, the inferiority of the other positions will become evident.

Herod's Temple

Its Historical Location

First, the temple complex is said to be located in a particular city. This city is clearly *historical Jerusalem* of the first century, which, for a time, housed the last temple of Israel, known to us as the Herodian temple. That the "holy city" is *Jerusalem* is evident in that Jerusalem is called the "holy city" in both the Old and New Testaments (Isa. 48:2; 52:1; Neh. 11:1-18; Matt. 4:5; 27:53). What other city besides Jerusalem ever had a just claim to be called "the holy city" in Scripture? It was historically known as the "city of God" (Pss. 46:4; 48:1, 8; 87:3), "my holy mountain" (Isa. 11:9; 56:7; 57:13: 65:11, 25), the "city of the Great King" (Pss. 48:2; Matt. 5:35), and other such sacred and intimate designations in Scripture. Interestingly, coins minted during the Jewish War of A.D. 67-70 (the era of the early date's concern) bore the legend "Jerusalem the Holy."[4]

That the city mentioned is *literal* Jerusalem – and not a symbol for the Church – is indicated in that it could be trodden down in war, as per the text's demands. "And leave out the court which is outside the temple, for it has been given to the nations; and they

---

3. Jay E. Adams, *The Time Is Fulfilled* (Phillipsburg, NJ: Presbyterian and Reformed, 1966), p. 68; Milton S. Terry, *Biblical Hermeneutics* (Grand Rapids: Zondervan, n.d. [1906]), pp. 473ff.

4. George Adam Smith, *Jerusalem: The Topography, Economics, and History from the Earliest Times to A. D. 70* (London: Hodder and Stoughton, 1907) 1:270.

will tread under foot the holy city for forty-two months" (Rev. 11:2). It was not a symbol, but an historical reality subject to destruction.

Moreover, there is a contextual clue that specifically demands we understand this "holy city" to be literal, historical (not spiritual) Jerusalem. Revelation states that the city — which was to be trodden underfoot and wherein the temple was located — was the place "where also their Lord was crucified" (Rev. 11:8): "And their dead bodies will lie in the street of the great city which mystically is called Sodom and Egypt, where also their Lord was crucified."

Notice that the literal city also is referred to mystically as "Sodom and Egypt" (v. 8). In the Old Testament we find precedent for rebellious Jerusalem's being designated by the pagan name "Sodom" (Isa. 1:9-10; Ezek. 16:46-49). The names applied to Jerusalem in Revelation are representative of the evil enemies of the Old Testament people of God. They are applied to historical Jerusalem because the greatest crime of all history was perpetrated there: It was at historical Jerusalem that the Lord Jesus Christ was crucified (Matt. 16:21; Mark 8:31; 10:32-34; Luke 9:22; 13:32; 17:11; 19:28). Through spiritual metamorphosis the once "holy city" had been transformed into a mutant, unholy "Sodom and Egypt."

That the same city can be called "holy" in one verse and "Sodom and Egypt" in a following verse does not indicate that reference is being made to two distinct cities. This is simply John's way of saying, "the faithful city has become an harlot" (Isa. 1:22a).

Thus, the *symbolic* references are "Egypt" and "Sodom." The modifying clause — "where also their Lord was crucified" — is given to ensure the proper, historical identifying of the city. This *literal*, geographical referent is not another symbol, but specifies the historical city Jerusalem. Clearly, the city cannot be a symbol of the Church or the heavenly Jerusalem because of both the historical nature of the reference, as well as the inappropriateness of an evil, mutated "Jerusalem" representing such.

That the city is Jerusalem of the *first century* is demanded by the soon occurrence expectation of John (Rev. 1:1, 3, 19; 3:10; 22:6ff). No Jerusalem in the distant future could be in view, in light of John's own stated temporal restrictions. In addition, the reference to Jerusalem's being the place where the Lord was crucified would seem more appropriate for the first century Jerusalem than for the twentieth- or twenty-first-century Jerusalem.

Since historical, first century Jerusalem is in view, we should expect that the prominent, historical feature of that city should be in view, as well: the Herodian temple complex.

The Thematic Demand

Second, the theme of the book suggests the appearance of a literal temple in Jerusalem. We must remember that Revelation was written to warn that "those who pierced Him" (the Jews of the first century, see Chapters 2 and 9) would experience His cloud-judgment coming upon them (Rev. 1:7). Again, we must recall that the judgment would be soon (Rev. 1:1, 3, 19; 3:10; 22:6ff.), not thousands of years later. Hence, the potential significance of the literal, historical temple – the place of Jewish worship – in this passage, which speaks of the place where the Lord was "pierced."

Scripture Interprets Scripture

Third, Scripture elsewhere speaks of the destruction of the historic temple existing in Jesus' day, and with language closely corresponding to that found in Revelation 11. John uses the future tense when he speaks of the nations treading down the city ("they will tread," Rev. 11:2b). This is not a reminiscence of a past event, but rather a future expectation.

Revelation 11:1-2 clearly reflects the prophecy of Christ as recorded in Luke 21:24. The prophecy in Luke 21 (like its parallels in Matt. 24 and Mark 13) is widely held to refer to the destruction of Jerusalem and the temple in A.D. 70. Indeed, this *must* be the case, for at least two reasons: (1) The very occasion of the prophetic discourse arises from the disciples' pointing out the beauty of the material temple to Christ. (2) That very temple to which they pointed was destroyed in A.D. 70 in a manner which precisely fulfilled the terms of the prophecy.

Note that in Luke 21:5-7a the disciples pointed out the actual features of that historical structure: "And while some were talking about the temple, that it was adorned with beautiful stones and votive gifts, He said, 'As for these things which you are looking at, the days will come in which there will not be left one stone upon another which will not be torn down.' And they questioned Him, saying, 'Teacher, when therefore will these things be?'" The prophecy that follows the disciples' remarks was definitely spoken by the Lord as the historical temple stood! In Luke's record of the Olivet Discourse, Christ specifically speaks of the dismantling of the temple and destruction of Jerusalem in terms which form the basis of those in Revelation 11.

A little further into the context, we read in Luke 21:24: "and they will fall by the edge of the sword, and will be led captive into all the nations; and *Jerusalem will be trampled underfoot by the Gentiles* until the times of the Gentiles be fulfilled." Compare this to Revelation 11:2b, which reads: "it has been given to the *nations*; and they will *tread under foot* the *holy city* for forty-two months." In these two passages the correspondences are so strong, they surely bespeak historical identity, rather than mere accidental similarity:

Luke 21:24 / Revelation 11:2

Jerusalem = the holy city

Gentiles (*ethne*) = nations (*ethnesin*)

trampled underfoot (*patoumene*) = tread under foot (*patesousin*)

It is evident that these verses in both John's Revelation and Luke's Gospel look to the same events.[5] And these events were literal occurrences that happened to historical institutions and

---

5. This may explain why John's Gospel is the only Gospel which does not record Christ's Olivet Discourse, which pointed to the destruction of the Temple. See Matthew 24; Mark 13; Luke 21.

structures. These events had not already occurred, but lay in the future for both Jesus (whose words Luke records) and John (in Revelation). The context of Luke demands a literal Jerusalem (Luke 21:20) and temple (Luke 21:5, 6) besieged by literal armies (Luke 21:20) in literal Judea (Luke 21:21). As a matter of indisputable historical record this occurred in the events leading up to A.D. 70, *not after.*

The Natural Interpretation

The most natural interpretation of Revelation 11, then, suggests that the reference is to the literal temple, for only in literal Jerusalem did God have His temple. In light of these factors certain questions arise.

Even recognizing that the part of the temple to be preserved has a spiritual referent (see discussion below), how could John be commanded to measure symbolically that which did not exist with the idea of preserving (in some sense) a part and destroying the rest? If Revelation were written in the A.D. 90s, why would there be no reference to the temple's already having been destroyed, particularly in such a work as this, that treats of divine judgment upon Judaism? Early, post-apostolic Christianity made much of the fact of the destruction of the temple as evidence of God's rejection of the Jew. Let us survey a few early Christian references to the destruction of the temple.

The Epistle of Barnabas is dated between A.D. 75 and 100. In *Barnabas* 16:1ff. we read: "Moreover I will tell you likewise concerning the temple, how these wretched men being led astray set their hope on the building, and not on their God that made them, as being a house of God. . . . So it cometh to pass; for because they went to war it was pulled down by their enemies." It is indisputably clear that *Barnabas* makes much of the fact of Jerusalem's fall as an apologetic for Christianity.

Ignatius wrote around A.D. 107. And although clear and explicitly detailed reference is not made to Jerusalem's fall in Ignatius's letters, there is what seems to be an allusion to the matter. In his *Epistle to the Magnesians* 10 we read: "It is absurd to speak of Jesus Christ with the tongue, and to cherish in the mind a Judaism which has now come to an end." With the demise of the temple, Judaism is incapable of worshiping in the manner prescribed in the Law of God; it "has now come to an end." This is used by Ignatius to enhance the role of Christianity against that of now defunct *Bible-based* Judaism.

Justin Martyr wrote his *The First Apology of Justin* about A.D. 147. In this work we read at Chapter 32: "For of all races of men there are some who look for Him who was crucified in Judea, and after whose crucifixion the land [i.e. Israel] was straightway surrendered to you as spoil of war." In chapter 53 he writes: "For with what reason should we believe of a crucified man that He is the first-born of the unbegotten God, and Himself will pass judgment on the whole human race, unless we had found testimonies concerning Him published before He came and was born as man, and unless we saw that things had happened accordingly – the devastation of the land of the Jews."

In the fragments of the works of Melito of Sardis (written about A.D. 160-180), we read of his words against the Jews: "Thou smotest thy Lord: thou also hast been smitten upon the earth. And thou indeed liest dead; but He is risen from the place of the dead, and ascended to the height of heaven."

Hegesippus, in the fragments of his *Commentaries on the Acts*, writes (A.D. 170-175): "And so he suffered martyrdom; and they buried him on the spot, and the pillar erected to his memory still remains, close by the temple. This man was a true witness to both Jews and Greeks that Jesus is the Christ. And shortly after that Vespasian besieged Judaea, taking them captive." He ties in the persecution of Christ's apostle James to the destruction of Jerusalem.

Clearly, early Christianity made much of the fall of Jerusalem and the Jews. Furthermore, where is there any reference to a rebuilding of the temple in Revelation so that it could be again destroyed (as per the dispensationalist argument)? If there is no reference to a rebuilding of the temple and the book was written about A.D. 95, how could the readers make sense of its prophecies? John definitely speaks of the temple as still standing.

It is a matter of indisputable historical record – confirmed in both archaeology and ancient literature – that the temple in Jerusalem was destroyed in August, A.D. 70, by the Roman general Titus. And yet in Revelation 11:1-2 we read of the temple standing while John wrote. John looks to its *future* destruction. Hence, John must have written prior to A.D. 70.

We need to realize how obvious it is that this temple is Herod's temple. The conclusion is so strong that this passage has played prominently in the various liberal critical theories of Scripture. These (erroneous) liberal approaches view Revelation as a hodge-podge collection of older and newer traditions from both Jewish and Christian sources. These traditions, it is alleged, were strung together, rather disjointedly, by one or more editors. For instance, James Moffatt viewed this particular section of Revelation as a pre-A.D. 70 Jewish fragment, and claimed that this is "widely recognised by critics and editors."[6] Thus, the particular "tradition" preserved in Revelation 11:1-2, he alleges, had to have been written by some Jewish zealot during the Jewish War against Rome before the temple was destroyed.

Obviously the presence of this temple in Revelation 11 is a remarkable fact, even if the liberals handle it wrongly. It is an indicator of the early date for Revelation, not for a patch-work view of Revelation's composition.

Objections

There are several objections that have been raised against the position outlined above. Let us briefly mention and respond to these.

6. James Moffatt, *The Revelation of St. John the Divine*, vol. 5 in W. Robertson Nicoll, ed., *The Expositor's Greek Testament* (Grand Rapids: Eerdmans, rep. 1980), pp. 287ff., 414, etc.

The Preservation of a Portion of the Temple

A major objection to our view is that Revelation seems to indicate that the temple in view will be partially preserved, while history shows clearly that the temple was leveled to the ground. How are we to understand the commands for John to measure the temple but not to measure its court? That is, how are we to understand this partial preservation of the temple (that which is "measured") in Revelation if the first-century temple is meant?

The proper understanding of the passage *requires* that we recognize a mixture of the figurative and literal, the symbolic and historical. This is true in virtually every interpretive approach to the passage, even the attempted alleged literalistic hermeneutic of dispensationalism. This may be why dispensationalist John F. Walvoord is prone to agree that "careful students of the book of Revelation will probably agree with Alford that chapter 11 'is undoubtedly one of the most difficult in the whole Apocalypse.'"[7]

In preparation for commenting on Revelation 11, Walvoord writes that "the guiding lines which govern the exposition to follow regard this chapter as a legitimate prophetic utterance in which the terms are taken normally."[8] By "normally" he means "literalistically." Interestingly, Walvoord is conspicuously silent on the matter of John's literally scaling the walls of the temple, with a physical reed in hand, and his gathering the worshipers together to measure them. And he fails to interpret verse 5 as demanding that literal fire issue forth from the mouths of the two witnesses.[9] Even fellow premillennialist (though non-dispensationalist) Robert Mounce notes: "The measuring of the temple is a symbolic way of declaring its preservation."[10]

It is apparent that there is a mixture of the symbolic inter-

---

7. Walvoord, p. 175.
8. *Ibid.*
9. *Ibid.*, p. 180.
10. Robert Mounce, *The Book of Revelation* (Grand Rapids: Eerdmans, 1977), p. 219.

spersed with the literal in Revelation 11. This should not surprise us in a book such as Revelation. As I will show, this mixture of literal and figurative draws a contrast between that which is material and non-essential to the worship of God and that which is internal and essential to the worship of God. Such a mixture of figurative and literal is neither unprecedented nor uncommon in Scripture (for example: 2 Kings 21:12, 13; Amos 7:8, 9; Isa. 34:11; Lam. 2:8).

John is commanded to not "measure" the outer court of the temple. In fact, the outer court is commanded instead to be "cast out." The Greek of Rev. 11:2a is *ekbale*, a stronger term than "leave out," as in the New American Standard Bible. The outer court is not destined for preservation, "for it has been given to the nations." Neither is Jerusalem, for the nations "will tread under foot the holy city for forty-two months" (Rev. 11:2b). The prior prophecy of Christ regarding the destiny of the temple (Luke 21:6, 24) absolutely prohibits any expectation of even its partial preservation. Thus, John here reveals the prophetic certainty of the destruction of the external, material temple ("the court which is outside").

On the other hand, John's measuring is for the preservation of its innermost aspects: the inner temple (Greek: *naos*), altar, and worshipers within (Rev. 11:1). Here the portions of the temple measured seem to symbolize the inner-spiritual idea of the temple. In the New Covenant era — the Christian era — the spiritual inner-temple supercedes the material temple of the Old Covenant era.

John prophesies that judgment is about to be brought upon literal Jerusalem and the temple (the court is to be cast out and the city trodden down). Nevertheless, his prophecy promises the preservation of God's Church, the new inner-temple (Greek: *naos*, Eph. 2:19ff.; 1 Cor. 3:16; 6:19; 2 Cor. 6:16; 1 Pet. 2:5ff). In the Old Testament those who worshiped at the altar were priests (Ex. 28:43; 29:44). In Revelation John calls Christians "priests" (Rev. 1:6; 5:10) who offer prayers at the altar of incense (Rev. 5:8; 6:9-10; 8:3-4).

It is important to remember that the Christian Church (the

spiritual inner-temple) had its birth in and was originally head-quartered at historical Jerusalem (Luke 24:47; Acts 1:8, 12; 3:1, 2, 11; 5:12-16, 42; 8:1; 11:1-2; 15:1-2). Furthermore, the early converts to Christianity were predominantly from Judaism (Acts 2:14, 41, 47; 4:1-4). Hence, the need for protection of the Church during the work of destruction.

Revelation 11:2 parallels the idea in Revelation 7:1-8. There Christian Jews are sealed for protection, before the destruction of the Land. As such, both of these prophecies — Revelation 7:1-8 and 11:1-2 — teach the truth for Christians that was contained in Christ's prior prophecy: "Yet not a hair of your head will perish" in Jerusalem's destruction (Luke 21:18). Heeding Christ's command to "flee to the mountains" (Luke 21:21), Christians were protected from the destruction that fell upon Jerusalem. Early church history records that Christians fled to Pella and were spared.[11]

Also we should notice that after the 42-month treading down of Jerusalem, the altar is seen no longer in earthly Jerusalem, but in heaven (Rev. 11:18). This is significant because it is there Christ's kingdom originates (John 18:36; Heb. 1:3). It is there that Christians have their ultimate citizenship (Eph. 2:6; Col. 3:1-2; Heb. 12:22).

Although it is recognized on all sides that there is an obvious involvement of the symbolic in the passage, there surely must be some historical reality that forms the basis of the symbol. After all, the symbolic names "Egypt" and "Sodom" refer to the histori-cal city Jerusalem (Rev. 11:8). If John wrote about literal Jerusa-lem ("where also their Lord was crucified") twenty-five years after the destruction of the literal temple (as per the evangelically formulated late-date argument), it would seem most improbable that he would speak of the temple as if it were still standing. The

11. See the church history of Eusebius of the fourth century: *Ecclesiastical History* 3:5:3-5. Also see Eusebius's contemporary, Epiphanius, in his works: *De Mensuris* 15 and *Heresies* 29:7.

symbol would be confusing in its blatant anachronism. The temple is required to be standing for the symbolical action of the vision to have any meaning.

A Great City?

It might be thought that the phrase "the great city" (Rev. 11:8) indicates Rome, which actually authorized and performed the crucifixion of Christ. Such a designation of Jerusalem may seem much too grandiose. But it will not, however, excite wonder among those who are aware of either the covenantal-redemptive significance of Jerusalem, or its historical fame. Historically, even Roman historians spoke of its magnificence: Tacitus called it "a famous city."[12] He noted that Jerusalem housed a temple which "was famous beyond all other works of men."[13] Pliny the Elder said of Jerusalem that it was "by far the most famous city of the ancient Orient."[14] Appian, a Roman lawyer and writer (*ca.* A.D. 160) called it "the great city Jerusalem."[15] Truly, then, Jerusalem was one of the most famous cities of the civilized world at that time.[16]

More important, however, is the *covenantal* significance of Jerusalem. The obvious role of Jerusalem in the history of the covenant should merit it such greatness. The intense Jewish love of Jerusalem pictured it as of great stature among the famous cities of the nations.

The Fifth Book of the *Sibylline Oracles* is a Jewish oracle written from Egypt in the A.D. 90s. In this oracle Jerusalem is spoken of thus: "He seized the divinely built Temple and burned the citizens and peoples who went into it, men whom I rightly praised. For on his appearance the whole creation was shaken and kings per-

---

12. *Histories* 5:2.

13. *Fragments of the Histories* 1.

14. *Natural History* 5:14:70.

15. *The Syrian Wars* 50.

16. David Ben-Gurion, *The Jews in Their Land,* trans. Mordechai Nurock and Misha Louvish (Garden City, NY: Doubleday, 1966), p. 152.

ished, and those in whom sovereignty remained destroyed a *great city* and righteous people."[17] About three hundred lines later we read: "But now a certain insignificant and impious king has gone up, cast it down, and left it in ruins with a great horde and illustrious men. He himself perished at immortal hands when he left the land, and no such sign has yet been performed among men that others should think to sack a *great city*."[18]

Josephus sadly extols Jerusalem's lost glory after its destruction: "This was the end which Jerusalem came to by the madness of those that were for innovations; a city otherwise of *great magnificence, and of mighty fame* among all mankind."[19] A few paragraphs later we read: "And where is not that *great city*, the metropolis of the Jewish nation, which was fortified by so many walls round about, which had so many fortresses and large towers to defend it, which could hardly contain the instruments prepared for the war, and which had so many ten thousands of men to fight for it? Where is this city that was believed to have God himself inhabiting therein? It is now demolished to the very foundations."[20]

Clement of Rome

A number of evangelical scholars argue that the first-century writer Clement of Rome spoke of the temple as still standing, even though he (allegedly) wrote around A.D. 90+. Clement's relevant statement is: "Not in every place, brethren, are the continual daily sacrifices offered, or the freewill offerings, or the sin offerings and the trespass offerings, but in Jerusalem alone. And even there the offering is not made in every place, but before the sanctuary in the court of the altar; and this too through the high-priest and the aforesaid ministers, after that the victim to be offered hath been inspected for blemishes."[21]

---

17. *Sibylline Oracles* 5:150-154. Emphasis added.

18. *Ibid.* 5:408-413. Emphasis added.

19. Josephus, *The Wars of the Jews* 7:1:1. Emphasis added.

20. *Wars* 7:8:7. Emphasis added.

21. *1 Clement* 41.

This language in *1 Clement*, however, opens the whole question of the actual date of *1 Clement* itself. Unfortunately, there is almost as serious a question over the dating of Clement's letter as there is over the dating of Revelation. One of Clement's translators, A. Cleveland Coxe, who himself opted for an A.D. 97 date for the letter, was quite cautious: "I have reluctantly adopted that his Epistle was written near the close of his life, and not just after the persecution of Nero."[22] Though J. B. Lightfoot accepted the late date of *1 Clement*, he recognized some unusual factors of the letter (which we will consider below) that are quite curious if the letter is to be dated late.[23] Three noteworthy scholars who have opted for an early (A.D. 69 or 70) date for Clement are historians Arthur S. Barnes and George Edmundson and theologian John A. T. Robinson.[24] A brief summary of several of the leading early date evidences for *1 Clement* should easily demonstrate the early date of Clement.

The first line of evidence regards a matter of *silence*. If the letter were written after A.D. 90 — when Clement was appointed the bishop of Rome — then we must somehow account for an unusual ecclesiastical silence in the letter. Lightfoot was somewhat perplexed by this silence: There is absolutely no hint of a bishop at Rome in the letter.[25]

Robinson felt absolutely persuaded by the silence. He notes that there is no appeal to episcopal authority in the letter and that the offices of bishop and elder are synonymous (42:4ff; 44:1ff; 54:2; 57:1), as in New Testament times. If that was the case, it is

---

22. A. Cleveland Coxe, "Clement," in Alexander Roberts and James Donaldson, *The Ante-Nicene Fathers*, 10 vols. (Grand Rapids: Eerdmans, [1885] rep. 1985) 1:1.

23. J. B. Lightfoot, *The Apostolic Fathers, Part I: S. Clement of Rome* (London: Macmillan, 1889), p. 352.

24. Arthur S. Barnes, *Christianity at Rome in the Apostolic Age* (Westport, CT: Greenwood Press, [1938] 1971), pp. 209ff.; George Edmundson, *The Church in Rome in the First Century* (London: Longman's, Green, and Co., 1913), pp. 189ff.; and John A. T. Robinson, *Redating the New Testament* (Philadelphia: Westminster Press, 1976), pp. 328ff.

25. Lightfoot, p. 352.

remarkable that such a radical transition could occur within a period of only two decades. The letters of Ignatius twenty years later clearly indicate a bishopric distinct from the eldership.[26]

Robinson's point is well-taken. The evidence, such as it is, is more suggestive of a pre-bishopric era than for a later era.

Second, it would seem that in Clement's letter the internal evidence is suggestive of a more primitive Christian era. For instance, Edmundson noted that reference to Christ as the "child of God," the primitive form of Scripture quotations, the reference to the phoenix (which had been exhibited in Rome under Claudius, who reigned A.D. 41-54), and other such matters, lend themselves to the earlier period more readily.[27] Barnes added to these the reference to one Fortunatus (a friend of Paul in 54, cf. 1 Cor. 16:17), the selection of Claudius and Valerius (who were of the household of Claudius the Emperor, according to Lightfoot) as messengers, and other such indications.[28]

Third, the fact that he mentions the deaths of "the good Apostles" in "our generation" suggests a very recent occurrence which is quite compatible with a date around A.D. 69 or 70. In *1 Clement* 5:1 we read: "But to pass from the examples of ancient days, let us come to those champions who lived nearest our times. Let us set before us the noble examples which belong to our generation. By reason of jealously and envy the greatest and most righteous pillars of the church were persecuted, and contended even unto death. Let us set before our eyes the good Apostles." Clement thereupon mentions the deaths of Peter and Paul, which indisputably indicates that he is referring to the Neronic persecution.

Furthermore, it is more than a little interesting that Clement names some of those who died in the Neronian persecution. In *1 Clement* 5 he names Peter and Paul, but also in *1 Clement* 6 we

---

26. Robinson, p. 328.
27. Edmundson, pp. 194ff.
28. Barnes, pp. 213ff.

read of the names of a couple of other martyrs now virtually unknown, Danaids and Dircae. It is quite remarkable that he cites names of those involved in the Neronian persecution which allegedly occurred about thirty years previous to his own day, but that he is strangely silent about the names of those who died in the Domitianic persecution – even though they were supposed to be prominent members of his own congregation! In both sections five and six of his letter, Clement gives many sentences to explication of these Neronian woes. But it is quite curious, on the supposition of a Domitianic date, that in *1 Clement* 1 he uses only ten words (in the Greek) that supposedly refer to the Domitianic persecution, the persecution through which he and many of his friends were allegedly going! That reference reads: "by reason of the sudden and successive troubles and calamities which have befallen us."

If, however, the letter were written sometime approaching, or in, early A.D. 70, then the first, fifth, and sixth sections would *all* speak of the Neronian persecution. In the course of its long history the city of Rome had never witnessed so many "sudden and successive troubles and calamities" among its population generally, and for the Christians particularly, than in Nero's rule. His era eventually issued forth in the chaotic and destructive Year of the Four Emperors.

Tacitus introduces Rome's history after the death of Nero thus:

> The history on which I am entering is that of a period rich in disasters, terrible with battles, torn by civil struggles, horrible even in peace. Four emperors failed by the sword; there were three civil wars, more foreign wars and often both at the same time. There was success in the East, misfortune in the West. Illyricum was disturbed, the Gallic provinces wavering, Britain subdued and immediately let go. The Sarmatae and Suebi rose against us; the Dacians won fame by defeats inflicted and suffered; even the Parthians were almost roused to arms through the trickery of a pretended Nero. Moreover, Italy was distressed by disasters unknown before or returning after the lapse of ages. Cities of the rich fertile shores of Campania were swallowed up or overwhelmed;

Rome was devastated by conflagrations, in which her most ancient shrines were consumed and the very Capitol fired by citizens' hands. Sacred rites were defiled; there were adulteries in high places. The sea was filled with exiles, its cliffs made foul with the bodies of the dead. In Rome there was more awful cruelty. . . . Besides the manifold misfortunes that befell mankind, there were prodigies in the sky and on the earth, warnings given by thunderbolts, and prophecies of the future, both joyful and gloomy, uncertain and clear. For never was it more fully proved by awful disasters of the Roman people or by indubitable signs that gods care not for our safety, but for our punishment.[29]

Schaff commented on this period that "there is scarcely another period in history so full of vice, corruption, and disaster as the six years between the Neronian persecution and the destruction of Jerusalem."[30] Nothing approaching this chaos or even hinting at this level of upheaval was remotely associated with Domitian's death. Combining the Neronian persecution begun in A.D. 64 with the Roman Civil War in A.D. 68-69, all becomes very clear.

Finally, there is the very temple reference in question in *1 Clement* 41 (cited above). All things considered, the reference to the temple services as if they were still being conducted is best construed as demanding a pre-August, A.D. 70 dating. Edmundson insists that "it is difficult to see how the evidential value of c. xli. can be explained away."[31]

It would seem that, at the very least, reference to the statement in *1 Clement* 41 cannot discount the possibility of our approach to Revelation 11, in that the date of *1 Clement* is in question. And as is probably the case, Clement did write his epistle prior to the temple's destruction.

---

29. Tacitus, *Histories* 1:2-3.

30. Philip Schaff, *History of the Christian Church*, 3rd ed. (Grand Rapids: Eerdmans, 1910) 1:391.

31. Edmundson, p. 193.

Conclusion

The temple in Revelation is clearly the famous Herodian Temple of Jerusalem to which Christ and the apostles could point. This temple is standing when Revelation was written (Rev. 11:1). The evidence is multiple and varied in this direction: (1) The temple is located in historical Jerusalem (Rev. 11:2, 8). (2) The judgments on the temple and the city of Jerusalem are justified by reference to Christ's crucifixion (Rev. 11:8), which occurred in the first century. (3) The theme of Revelation directs the bulk of the judgment against the first-century Jews, "the tribes of the Land," who "pierced" Christ (Rev. 1:7). (4) John's account parallels Luke's account in Luke 21, which definitely speaks of the A.D. 70 destruction of the physical temple to which the disciples actually pointed. (5) There is no mention in Revelation of an already destroyed temple being rebuilt.

The appearance of the Jewish temple in this first century writing is impossible to account for if Revelation were written a quarter of a century after its destruction. Attempts to reduce its significance for dating fail in their purpose. But on the recognition of an A.D. 60s date for Revelation, the temple's presence in Revelation is not only accounted for but even expected.

12

THE ECCLESIASTICAL EVIDENCE

Behold, I will cause those of the synagogue of Satan, who say that they are Jews, and are not, but lie — behold, I will make them to come and bow down at your feet, and to know that I have loved you (Rev. 3:9).

The final evidence taken from within Revelation that we will consider is that of the primitive nature of Christianity in Revelation. There are strong indications that the stage of development of the Church is indicative of a pre-A.D. 70 era. But first, some brief background.

Early Christianity's Development

Regarding the origin of the Christian Church, New Testament scholars are in virtual agreement that "from the very beginning of the story in Acts this Christian group is marked as *Jewish* in its origins and background."[1] It is quite evident that Christianity gradually developed through several stages of self-awareness and missionary outreach in the first-century of its existence.

Christianity's earliest stage in Christ's ministry was almost wholly focused on racial Israel and religious Judaism. The Lord Himself ministered first to "the lost sheep of Israel" (see Matt. 10:6ff.; 15:21ff.; John 1:11; cp. Rom. 1:16). What careful reader of Scripture can deny this phenomenon? Somewhat later, in the

---

1. Joseph A. Fitzmeyer, *Essays on the Semitic Background of the New Testament* (London: Chapman, 1971), p. 274.

second stage, toward the end of Christ's ministry, the Great Commission (Matt. 20:28ff.; Acts 1:8) commanded a worldwide outreach to all nations. This was, however, only dimly understood by the early original (Jewish) Christians. The difficulty they faced in accepting the full implications of the Great Commission is witnessed in Acts 10, 11, and 15. Even in this early post-commission Christianity, the ministry continued to gravitate toward the Jews.

Furthermore, the earliest Christians even engaged in Jewish worship observances,[2] while focusing on and radiating their ministry from Jerusalem.[3] Not only so but they frequented the temple,[4] attended the synagogues,[5] and designated themselves as the true heirs of Judaism.[6] One modern writer discusses the matter of Jewish Christians worshiping as Jews and as Christians: "[Jesus'] disciples, however, were faithful at first in their observance of both, as Acts unobtrusively recounts . . . , so that their special teaching and customs offered no occasion for them not to be considered Jews. Indeed, they had not separated themselves publicly nearly as much as had the Essenes. Only after A.D. 70 did the requirements for membership in Judaism become more stringent."[7]

We can expect, then, that the earlier the date of a Christian book, the more Jewish it might appear. The question then arises as to whether or not Revelation has a strongly Jewish air to it. If it does, this may be supportive evidence for the pre-A.D. 70 date, as opposed to an A.D. 95 date.

The Jewish Character of Christianity in Revelation

As a matter of fact, in Revelation there is overwhelming evi-

---

2. Acts 2:1ff; 21:26; 24:11.

3. Acts 2-5.

4. Acts 2:46; 3:1ff.; 4:1; 5:21ff.; 21:26; 26:21.

5. Acts 13:5, 14; 14:1; 15:21; 17:1ff.; 18:4, 7, 19, 26; 19:8; 22:19; 24:12; 26:11.

6. Gal. 3:27-29; 6:16; Phil. 3:3.

7. Leonhard Goppelt, *Apostolic and Post-Apostolic Times*, trans. Robert A. Guelich (London: Adam and Charles Black, 1970), p. 26.

dence that the era in which John wrote was one in which Christianity was still largely affected by and strongly attached to the Jewish community. Let us survey a few aspects of Revelation that indicate this.

Revelation 2 and 3

In Revelation 2:9 and 3:9 we discover some interesting evidence in this direction:

> I know your tribulation and your poverty (but you are rich), and the blasphemy by those who say they are Jews and are not, but are a synagogue of Satan (Rev. 2:9).

> Behold, I will cause those of the synagogue of Satan, who say that they are Jews, and are not, but lie — behold, I will make them to come and bow down at your feet, and to know that I have loved you (Rev. 3:9).

In these two passages John indicates that at least two of the seven churches (Smyrna and Philadelphia) are plagued by "those who say they are Jews."

That those who plagued them were *racial Jews* and undoubtedly of the Jewish faith may be fairly assumed. This is so because the Jews wore a distinctive cultic mark: circumcision. In one of his debates with a Jew, early church father Justin Martyr (A.D. 100-165) mentions the distinctiveness of the Jew in this regard: "For the circumcision according to the flesh, which is from Abraham, was given for a sign; that you may be separated from other nations, and from us; . . . For you are not recognised among the rest of men by any other mark than your fleshly circumcision."[8] Pagan Roman historian Tacitus (A.D. 56-117) wrote of the Jews: "They adopted circumcision to distinguish themselves from other peoples by this difference."[9]

Now the question naturally arises: Who would array them-

---

8. *Dialogue with Trypho the Jew* 16.
9. *Histories* 5:5.

selves against the Church, posing as racial Jews, who were not racial Jews?[10] The Jews were universally recognized as a distinctive race. The Roman historians even spoke contemptuously of the Jews as a "second race" of men, quite distinguished from the rest of the Roman empire.[11]

Obviously, then, these two churches in Revelation were being persecuted by *Jews* in these two cities, as Christianity was very often persecuted in the first-century (cf. Acts 13:50; 14:2, 5, 19; 17:5). In fact, "down to A.D. 64 danger threatened the Christian Church from the Jews and the Jews alone."[12] Of the particular situation at Smyrna (Rev. 2:9), we should note that "Jews at Smyrna were both numerous and aggressively hostile."[13] Thus, in writing to these churches, John derides these persecuting Jews as not really being Jews *in the true, spiritual sense of the word.* As another late-date advocate puts it: "Members of the local synagogue may claim to be Jews, but the very claim constitutes them liars."[14] Here, then, John follows the pattern of Paul's reproach in Romans 2:17-29, by distinguishing between the "true Jew" (the Christian who is a "Jew" inwardly and spiritually) and the "false Jew" (one who is a Jew racially and religiously, but not spiritually). These racial Jews had forsaken the truth of historic, God-given Judaism by not following after the Messiah and subscribing to the Christian faith.

Thus, John attributes a spiritual significance of the highest order to being a "Jew," *i.e.* in the true sense of the word: a Christian. In defiance to persecuting Judaism, the Christians *at*

---

10. Interestingly for our thesis, in the two verses under consideration John uses the Hebrew word for the devil (*satanos*), rather than the more common New Testament Greek term (*diabolos*).

11. See Tertullian, *To the Nations* 1:8.

12. W. H. C. Frend, *The Early Church* (Philadelphia: Fortress Press, 1982), p. 29.

13. Henry B. Swete, *Commentary on Revelation* (Grand Rapids: Kregel, [1911] 1977), p. 31.

14. Robert Mounce, *The Book of Revelation* (Grand Rapids: Eerdmans, 1977), p. 119.

this stage were argumentatively presenting themselves as the true Jews.[15] This must be at an early stage of Christian development when Christianity still understood and presented itself as true Judaism.

Revelation 7

This primitive conception of Christianity is strongly reaffirmed later in Revelation. John speaks of Christians as the true Jews, the fullness of the Twelve Tribes of Israel (Rev. 7:4-8; 14:1ff.; 21:12). Revelation 7:4-8 is particularly instructive:

> And I heard the number of those who were sealed, one hundred and forty-four thousand sealed from every tribe of the sons of Israel: from the tribe of Judah, twelve thousand were sealed, from the tribe of Reuben twelve thousand, from the tribe of Gad twelve thousand, from the tribe of Asher twelve thousand, from the tribe of Naphthali twelve thousand, from the tribe of Manasseh twelve thousand, from the tribe of Simeon twelve thousand, from the tribe of Levi twelve thousand, from the tribe of Issachar twelve thousand, from the tribe of Zebulun twelve thousand, from the tribe of Joseph twelve thousand, from the tribe of Benjamin, twelve thousand were sealed.

It is true that an element of symbolism is involved here. If nothing else, the perfect rounding of numbers along with the exact and identical count in each of the tribes speak of a symbolic representation. Furthermore, the number "1000" is frequently used in Scripture as an indefinite, yet significantly large, number (Pss. 90:4; Dan. 7:10; 2 Pet. 3:8; Heb. 12:22).

Despite the obvious symbolism, however, the symbols must be founded upon some historical designation. And, of course, the "twelve tribes of Israel" is the long-standing historical configuration of the Jewish race.[16] In light of this, it would seem that two possible interpretations easily lend themselves to consideration:

---

15. Cp. Matt. 19:28; Luke 22:30; Gal. 6:16; James 1:1; 1 Pet. 2:9.

16. See Gen. 35:22ff.; 46:8ff.; 49; Ex. 1:1ff.; Num. 1; 2; 13:4ff.; 26; 34; Deut. 27:11ff.; 33:6ff.; Josh. 13-22; Judges 5; 1 Chron. 2-8; 12:24ff.; 27:16ff.; Ezek. 48; Acts 26:7.

Either this body of 144,000 people represents the totality of the Christian Church as the fulfillment of the Jewish hope. Or it represents the Christians of Jewish lineage. In either case the appearance of these 144,000 suggest the early date of Revelation. This is evidently due to the fact that the Christianity of John's era was at a stage in which either the Church at large was called by Jewish names or when the bulk of Christians were Jewish.

The Language of Revelation

Another indicator of the primitive Jewish stage of Christianity in Revelation has to do with the style of language John uses. A remarkable fact that has not escaped the notice of Greek scholars is that the language of Revelation is extremely Hebraic. Moses Stuart notes that "no book in all the New Testament is so Hebraistic as the Revelation."[17] R. H. Charles even developed a special grammar of the language of Revelation, based on its extremely Hebraic character.[18] C. C. Torrey has gone so far as to suggest that an Aramaic original was the forerunner of Revelation.[19]

In addition, some words in Revelation are even translated into Hebrew. In Revelation 9:11 the "angel of the abyss" is given both Greek and Hebrew names. In Revelation 16:16 the place of a great battle is called by its Hebrew name: "the place which in Hebrew is called Har-Magedon."

Elsewhere, the Church is pictured under a symbol strongly expressive of a Judaistic Christianity. It is portrayed as a woman with a crown of twelve stars on her head (Rev. 12:1ff.). Christians are represented as worshiping in the temple and ministering in Jerusalem (Rev. 11:1-8).

---

17. Moses Stuart, *Commentary on the Apocalypse*, 2 vols. (Andover: Allen, Morrill, and Wardwell, 1845) 1:229.

18. R. H. Charles, *A Critical and Exegetical Commentary on the Revelation of St. John*, 2 vols. (Edinburgh: T. and T. Clark, 1920) 1:cxvii ff.

19. Charles C. Torrey, *The Apocalypse of John* (New Haven: Yale University Press, 1958), p. x. Also see my discussion on p. 38 *infra*.

Interpreting the Evidence

We cannot help but conclude that Revelation belongs to the period in which Jews and Christians, even if uncomfortably so, still lived together. Yet it should be evident that the cataclysmic events of A.D. 70 played a dramatic role in the life of both the Church and of Judaism in terms of their inter-relationships.

Unfortunately, the significance of the destruction of Jerusalem and the temple is too often overlooked by many. But was not Christianity born in Jerusalem (Acts 2) in obedience to Christ's commands (Luke 24:44-53; Acts 1)? Was it not headquartered there in its earliest period (Acts 8:1; 11:2; 15:2; Gal. 1:17, 18; 2:1, 2)? However, when the dust settles after the Fall of Jerusalem, we no longer find any Christian focus on Jerusalem. In fact, we no longer find a dominant church community operating out of Jerusalem. Indeed, in A.D. 80 Jewish Rabbi Gamaliel II caused the Jewish daily prayer to include a curse on the Christians: "Let the Nazarene [*sc.* Christian] and the Menim perish utterly."[20]

In *Barnabas*, a letter written by an early Christian after the fall of Jerusalem (*ca.* A.D. 100), there is evidence of this division. This epistle indicates a radical "us/them" distinction between Christians and Jews: "Let us see if this people [*i.e.*, Christians] is the heir, or the former [*i.e.*, the Jews], and if the covenant belongs to us or to them" (*Epistle of Barnabas* 13:1). Apostolic church father Ignatius also provides us early evidence in this direction. He writes (A.D. 107): "It is absurd to speak of Jesus Christ with the tongue, and to cherish in the mind a Judaism which has now come to an end. For where there is Christianity there cannot be Judaism" (*Epistle to the Magnesians* 10). Both of these statements are in keeping with later, post-temple Christian practice.

Certainly the breach did not come overnight. Since its inception Christianity had been persecuted almost exclusively by the Jews. This persecution continued throughout the early period of Christianity, which is recorded in Acts. Yet many converts were

---

20. See *Ibid.*, p. 82. Cp. Tertullian, *Dialogue with Trypho*, p. 96.

being won from Judaism (Acts 2:41; 4:4; 18:8; 21:20-22; 28:23-24). The Christians were, in fact, found operating in Jewish circles. The non-Christian Jews realized, of course, that Judaism and Christianity were not one, for they zealously persecuted the Christians as heretics.

Up until the era of the mid-A.D. 60s (but not after A.D. 70) the Romans were prone to identify Christianity as a sect of Judaism, intimately and necessarily bound up with it.[21] This was obviously due to: its object of worship (Christ, a Jew); its origin (Judea), leadership (Jewish apostles), and the bulk of its membership (predominantly Jewish). In addition, its self-designation ("the Israel of God" [Gal. 6:15], "seed of Abraham" [Gal. 3:29], "the circumcision" [Phil. 3:3] etc.); its message ("to the Jew first," Rom. 1:16); and its constant involvement in the religious life of the Jews, added to the difficulty for the Romans.

Church father Sulpicius Severus (A.D. 360-420) reported that Titus's war council conducted before the siege of the temple debated whether or not to destroy the temple:

> Titus is said, after calling a council, to have first deliberated whether he should destroy the temple, a structure of such extraordinary work. . . . Titus himself thought that the temple ought specially to be overthrown in order that the religion of the Jews and of the Christians might more thoroughly be subverted; for that these religions, although contrary to each other, had nevertheless proceeded from the same authors; that the Christians had sprung up from among the Jews; and that, if the root were extirpated, the offshoot would speedily perish.[22]

Clearly the idea here involved the belief in the dependence of Christianity upon the temple.

The early Christians were earnest in their concern to win Israel, even attempting to operate within the temple-synagogue

---

21. Tacitus, *Annals* 15:44; Sulpicius Severus, *Sacred History* 2:30.

22. *Sacred History* 2:30. The importance of this statement lies in the fact that Severus had access to documents no longer available to us.

structure of Judaism. Nevertheless, regarding the gradual cleavage between the Jew and Christianity, it should be noted that "the breach was no doubt clinched by political circumstance. In the disastrous war of A.D. 66-70, the 'Nazarenes' (a term by then applied to the Jewish Christians) refused to participate in the Jewish resistance movement, the Zealot insurrection. . . . [T]he crisis of A.D. 66 decisively separated Jew from Christian."[23]

Conclusion

The matter is clear enough: When John wrote Revelation, Christianity's situation was one in which it was still operating within Jewish circles and institutions to a very large extent. Historically we know that this simply was not the case in the post-temple era beyond A.D. 70. The cleavage between Judaism and Christianity was too radical from that time forth. Hence, this factor of the situation of the Christianity of Revelation is indicative of a pre-70 date for Revelation.

---

23. C. F. D. Moule, *The Birth of the New Testament*, 3rd. ed (New York: Harper and Row, 1982), p. 59.

13

THE HISTORICAL EVIDENCE (1)

Give praise to our God, all you His bond-servants, you who fear Him, the small and the great (Rev. 19:5).

At this juncture we turn to a consideration of the evidence generally called "external evidence." This material is "external" in that it comes from church tradition, rather than from Revelation itself. I will start with a consideration of those indications from tradition that support my contention for an early date for Revelation. In the next chapter I will consider the witnesses that are generally deemed to support the late date.

As I begin, the reader should be aware of the insistence by the late-date camp that the evidence from tradition is virtually unanimously supportive of the late date. For instance, J. P. M. Sweet comments: "To sum up, the earlier date *may* be right, but the internal evidence is not sufficient to outweigh the firm tradition stemming from Irenaeus."[1] Similarly, Andre Feuillet writes: "The *traditional* setting of the Apocalypse in the reign of Domitian is too solidly established to be brought into question."[2] Henry B. Swete, one of the leading orthodox commentators on Revelation, insists that "early Christian tradition is almost unanimous in assigning the Apocalypse to the last years of Domitian."[3] In his monumental

---

1. J. P. M. Sweet, *Revelation* (Philadelphia: Westminster Press, 1979) p. 27.

2. Andre Feuillet, *The Apocalypse* (Staten Island: Alba House, 1965), p. 92.

3. Henry B. Swete, *Commentary on Revelation* (Grand Rapids: Kregel, [1911] 1977), pp. xcix ff.

two-volume commentary on Revelation, R. H. Charles introduces the evidence from tradition as follows: "This evidence almost unanimously assigns [Revelation] to the last years of Domitian."[4]

These grandiose statements simply do not fit the facts, as I will show. Some of the evidences to be used below are *directly* helpful to the debate, in that they speak rather clearly to the matter. Other pieces of the evidence are provided as merely *suggestive* possibilities, in that they are not as forthright. We will consider them chronologically.

The Shepherd of Hermas

A work little known among laymen today was once very important in early Christianity. That work is known as *The Shepherd*, or *The Shepherd of Hermas*. This work contains three parts: *Vision*, *Mandates*, and *Similitudes*. It is indirectly suggestive of an early date for Revelation. Cautious employment of *The Shepherd* is demanded in light of both the nature of its usefulness (as indirect, circumstantial evidence) and the difficulty of its dating.

The Usefulness of the Shepherd

The Shepherd of Hermas may be strong evidence for discerning the date of Revelation, if it was written in the first century. Many competent scholars detect evidence of Hermas's knowledge of Revelation. Among older scholars we could name Moses Stuart, B. F. Westcott, H. B. Swete, and R. H. Charles. In the classic series entitled *The Ante-Nicene Fathers*, it is stated boldly that Revelation "is quoted in *Hermas* freely."[5] In more recent times noted critics have concurred in this assessment; we mention but a few. Patristics scholar Edgar J. Goodspeed states confidently that Hermas is "clearly acquainted with the Revelation of John."[6] John

---

4. R. H. Charles, *A Critical and Exegetical Commentary on the Revelation of St. John*, 2 vols. (Edinburgh: T. & T. Clark, 1920), 1:xci.

5. A. Cleveland Coxe, in Alexander Roberts and James Donaldson, eds., *The Ante-Nicene Fathers*, 10 vols. (Grand Rapids: Eerdmans, n.d. [rep. 1975]), 5:600.

6. Edgar J. Goodspeed, *The Apostolic Fathers* (New York: Harper, 1950), p. 97.

Lawson agrees.[7] Even late-date advocates Donald B. Guthrie and Robert H. Mounce lean in this direction. Guthrie writes that "there are many common images in the two writers which are most naturally explained if Hermas knew our Apocalypse."[8]

But now: When was it written?

The Date of the Shepherd

Unfortunately, there is a problem with ascertaining the date of the composition of *The Shepherd* due to the question of its authorship. J. B. Lightfoot's analysis of the matter will guide our thinking.[9] Was it written by (1) the Hermas greeted by Paul in Romans 16:14, as Origen suggests? Or by (2) the brother of Pius I (A.D. 140-150), as the ancient Muratorian Canon teaches? Or by (3) some unknown Hermas who lived in the time of the bishopric of Clement of Rome (A.D. 90-100), as a number of modern scholars propose? An assured conclusion on the matter may never be reached. Even Lightfoot, who prefers a date in the era of A.D. 140-150, acknowledges that the internal evidence strongly suggests a date in the span of A.D. 90-100.[10]

Church historian Philip Schaff is decisively supportive of an earlier date for *The Shepherd*, arguing that it was written by the very Hermas mentioned in Romans 16:14. He notes that the earlier date is suggested by its authoritative usage in the writings of Irenaeus, Clement of Alexandria, Origen, Eusebius, and Jerome.[11] We can add that early in his career, Tertullian seems to

---

7. John Lawson, *A Theological and Historical Introduction to the Apostolic Fathers* (New York: Macmillan, 1961), p. 220.

8. Donald B. Guthrie, *New Testament Introduction*, 3rd ed. (Downers Grove, IL: Inter-Varsity Press, 1970) pp. 931-932. Compare Robert Mounce, *The Book of Revelation* (Grand Rapids: Eerdmans, 1977), pp. 36-37.

9. J. B. Lightfoot and J. R. Harmer, *The Apostolic Fathers* (Grand Rapids: Baker, [1891] 1984), pp. 293-294.

10. *Ibid.*, p. 294.

11. Philip Schaff, *History of the Christian Church*, 3rd. ed., 7 vols. (Grand Rapids: Eerdmans, 1910) 1:687ff.

have agreed, although later he changed his opinion.[12] Because of its assumed early date and apostolic connection, *The Shepherd* tended to be used as if it were an inspired book. Interestingly, it is found in one of the earliest, complete Greek manuscripts of the Bible, the Codex Sinaiticus. This seems to demonstrate *The Shepherd's* early and widespread respect as high authority, and even as Scripture by some.

Moreover, there are those who argue for a date prior to A.D. 85. Arthur S. Barnes and John A. T. Robinson argue most vigorously for this time-frame.[13] And the evidences they suggest are quite reasonable. Let us summarize them:

First, since the book is deemed at least quasi-scriptural by Irenaeus, Clement of Alexandria, Origen, (the early) Tertullian, Eusebius, and Jerome, we should expect a very early date. For a work to be deemed inspired it likely would had to have been written by an associate of the apostles, and probably very early, perhaps pre-A.D. 80.

Second, Irenaeus lived in Rome for awhile and just 20 years after Pius's death. It is highly unlikely that he would have viewed *The Shepherd* as "Scripture" if written in his own era and location.

Third, after initially accepting it as scriptural, Tertullian (A.D. 160-220) later discredited the book. It seems likely he would have mentioned its recent authorship in his arguments against it had it been written in the era A.D. 140-150. But he does not.

Fourth, the Muratorian Canon's view (A.D. 170-200) cannot be right, for several reasons. (1) It identifies Hermas as the brother of bishop Pius of Rome. But as a foster child sold into slavery in Rome (*Vision* 1:1:1), it is remarkable that *Hermas never mentions his alleged brother Pius, bishop of Rome.* (2) Nowhere in *The Shepherd* is there any indication that there exists a monarchical episcopate. Hermas speaks, instead, of "the elders that preside over the

---

12. Tertullian, *Orations* 16.

13. Arthur S. Barnes, *Christianity at Rome in the Apostolic Age* (Westport, CT: Greenwood, [1938] 1971), pp. 212ff.; and John A. T. Robinson, *Redating the New Testament* (Philadelphia: Westminster Press, 1976), pp. 319-320.

church" (*Vision* 2:4:3). (3) In *Vision* 2:4:2ff. Hermas is told in his vision to write two books and to send one of them to Clement, who in turn "was to send it to foreign cities, for this is his duty." This implies Clement's role as a subordinate secretarial figure. Yet, in about A.D. 90 Clement was appointed Bishop of Rome.

Where Does This Leave Us?

If *The Shepherd* was written somewhere around A.D. 85 consider the following: Certain allusions in it show its awareness of Revelation. Thus, Revelation influenced the writing of *The Shepherd* in the late A.D. 80s! Furthermore, *The Shepherd* was certainly written somewhere around Rome, for it mentions Clement of Rome (*Vision* 2:4).

For John's Revelation to have been written, to have been copied (laboriously by hand), to have made its way to Rome by the 80s, and to have influenced the writing of *The Shepherd*, would be strong evidence that Revelation existed a good deal of time before A.D. 85 +. It would, thus, be evidence against a date of *ca.* A.D. 95 and compatible with a pre-A.D. 70 date.

Papias of Hierapolis

Papias, Bishop of Hierapolis (A.D. 60-130), is reputed to have been a disciple of the Apostle John and a friend of Polycarp. As such he would be an extremely early and valuable witness to historical matters of the sort with which we are dealing. Unfortunately, none of his books is in existence today. There is, however, an important piece of evidence purportedly from Papias that is quite revealing. Late-date advocate H. B. Swete deals with this evidence in his treatment of the Apostle John's extreme longevity. Swete notes that two ancient manuscripts, one from the seventh century and one from the ninth, cite a statement by Papias which says John the Apostle and his brother, James, were martyred by the Jews. Of this statement Swete observes: "With this testimony before us it is not easy to doubt that Papias made some such statement. . . . But if Papias made it, the question remains whether he made it under some misapprehension, or merely by way of expressing his conviction that the prophecy of Mc. x. 39 had found a literal fulfillment. Neither explanation is very probable in view of the early date of Papias. He does not, however, affirm that the brothers suffered at the same time: the martyrdom of John at the hand of the Jews might have taken place at any date before the last days of Jerusalem."[14]

If these two pieces of data are in fact from Papias (as Swete, Lightfoot, and other competent scholars are inclined to believe), they provide interesting evidence. For those who hold that John wrote Revelation this would be strong external evidence for its pre-A.D. 70 composition.

The Muratorian Canon

Sometime between A.D. 170 and 200 someone drew up a list of canonical books. This list, known as the Muratorian Canon, is "the oldest Latin church document of Rome, and of very great importance for the history of the canon."[15] The witness of this manuscript, which is from the very era of Irenaeus and just prior to Clement of Alexandria, virtually demands the early date for Revelation. The relevant portion of the document states that "the blessed Apostle Paul, following the rule of his predecessor John, writes to no more than seven churches by name" and "John too, indeed, in the Apocalypse, although he writes to only seven churches, yet addresses all."[16]

The writer of the Canon clearly teaches that John *preceded* Paul in writing letters to seven churches. Yet, church historians are agreed that Paul died before A.D. 70, either in A.D. 67 or 68.[17] This is clearly taught by Clement of Rome (di. A.D. 100) in *1*

---

14. Swete, *Revelation*, pp. clxxix-clxxx.

15. Schaff, *History* 1:776.

16. The seven churches addressed by Paul would be Rome, Corinth, Galatia, Ephesus, Philippi, Colossae, and Thessalonica.

17. A. T. Robertson, "Paul, the Apostle" in James Orr, ed. *The International Standard Bible Encyclopedia* (Grand Rapids: Eerdmans, [1929] 1956), 3:2287; Richard Longenecker, *The Ministry and Message of Paul* (Grand Rapids: Zondervan, 1971), p. 86.

Clement, Section 5. Whatever dates the writer of the Canon assigned to Paul's epistles, he could not have made them later than Paul's death! This is a most important piece of early evidence with which to reckon. It clearly teaches, then, that John wrote his seven letters in Revelation prior to A.D. 68.

Tertullian

Tertullian lived from A.D. 160-220. His era overlaps Irenaeus's era briefly. We have many of Tertullian's writings still today. In his *Exclusion of Heretics* he makes a statement that is of significance to our inquiry. Tertullian implies that John's banishment occurred at the same time Peter and Paul suffered martyrdom (about A.D. 67-68): "But if thou art near to Italy, thou hast Rome, where we also have an authority close at hand. What an happy Church is that! on which the Apostles poured out all their doctrine, with their blood: where Peter had a like Passion with the Lord; where Paul hath for his crown the same death with John;[18] where the Apostle John was plunged into boiling oil, and suffered nothing, and was afterwards banished to an island."[19] In Jerome's *Against Jovinianum*, Jerome certainly understood Tertullian to state that John was banished by Nero.[20] In addition, when Tertullian speaks of Domitian's evil in the fifth chapter of his *Apology*, he does not mention anything about John's suffering under him! Such is quite strange if John actually suffered under Domitian.

It would seem that Tertullian's reference to an attempted oil martyrdom of John is quite plausible historically. This is due to the very nature of the Neronic persecution of Christians in A.D. 64. Roman historian Tacitus informs us that Christians were "fastened to crosses to be set on fire, that when the darkness fell they might be burned to illuminate the night."[21]

---

18. That is, John the Baptist.

19. Tertullian, *Exclusion of Heretics*, 36.

20. Jerome, *Against Jovinianum* 1:26.

21. Tacitus, *Annals* 15:44.

Such a spectacle doubtless could have involved the dipping of the victims in oil to provide a lasting illumination of fire. As Schaff observed: "If there is some foundation for the early tradition of the oil-martyrdom of John at Rome, or at Ephesus, it would naturally point to the Neronian persecution, in which Christians were covered with inflammable material and burned as torches."[22]

Epiphanius of Salamis

Epiphanius (A.D. 315-403) was elected the bishop of Salamis, Cyprus, in about A.D. 367, and was an intimate friend of Jerome. He is noted for his unique witness to the banishment of John: He states twice that it was during the emperorship of Claudius.[23] He writes that John "prophesied in the time of Claudius . . . the prophetic word according to the Apocalypse being disclosed."

A number of scholars see Epiphanius's statement not so much as an extravagant tradition, as a rare designation of Nero. Some have suggested that Epiphanius may have used another of Nero's names, rather than his more common one. Nero is often called by his adoptive name "Claudius" on inscriptions. For instance, he is called "Nero Claudius" and "Nero Claudius Caesar" in certain places. Even late-date advocates Donald Guthrie, Robert Mounce, and James Moffatt recognize that this was probably what was intended by Epiphanius.[24]

It is clearly the case that Epiphanius stands solidly in the early date tradition. It is extremely doubtful that he simply created his "evidence" out of the blue.

---

22. Schaff, *History* 1:428.

23. *Heresies* 51:12, 33.

24. Among these we may list late date advocates Guthrie, *Introduction*, p. 957; Mounce, *Revelation*, p. 31; and James Moffatt, *The Revelation of St. John the Divine*, in W. Robertson Nicoll, ed., *The Expositor's Greek Testament*, vol. 5 (Grand Rapids: Eerdmans, rep. 1980), p. 505; as well as early date advocates F. J. A. Hort, *The Apocalypse of St. John, I-III* (London: Macmillan and Co., 1908), p. xviii, and Robinson, *Redating*, p. 224.

The Syriac Tradition

The ancient Syriac tradition is uniformly early date in its orientation. The Syriac work entitled *History of John, the Son of Zebedee* makes reference to John's banishment under Nero: "After these things, when the Gospel was increasing by the hands of the Apostles, Nero, the unclean and impure and wicked king, heard all that had happened at Ephesus. And he sent [and] took all that the procurator had, and imprisoned him; and laid hold of S. John and drove him into exile; and passed sentence on the city that it should be laid waste."[25]

In addition, late-date scholar A. S. Peake noted that "[b]oth of the Syriac Versions of the Revelation give in the title the statement that John was banished by Nero."[26] Their titles read: "written in Patmos, whither John was sent by Nero Caesar."[27]

Arethas

According to A. R. Fausset, Arethas, who wrote a commentary on Revelation in the sixth century, "applies the sixth seal to the destruction of Jerusalem (70 A.D.), adding that the Apocalypse was written before that event."[28] On Revelation 6:12 Arethas writes: "Some refer this to the siege of Jerusalem by Vespasian." On Revelation 7:1 he notes: "Here, then, were manifestly shown to the Evangelist what things were to befall the Jews in their war against the Romans, in the way of avenging the sufferings inflicted upon Christ." Of Revelation 7:4 we read: "When the Evangelist received these oracles, the destruction in which the Jews were

---

25. William Wright, *Apocryphal Acts of the Apostles* (Amsterdam: Philo, [1871] 1968) 2:55-57.

26. Arthur S. Peake, *The Revelation of St. John* (London: Joseph Johnson, 1919), pp. 76-77.

27. Moses Stuart, *Commentary on the Apocalypse*, 2 vols. (Andover: Allen, Morrill, and Wardwell, 1845) 1:267.

28. A. R. Fausset, in Robert Jamieson, A. R. Fausset, and David Brown, *A Commentary Critical and Explanatory on the Old and New Testaments*, 2 vols. (Hartford: Scranton, n.d.) 2:548.

involved was not yet inflicted by the Romans."[29]

In his comments on Revelation 1:9, Arethas says: "John was banished to the isle of Patmos under Domitian, Eusebius alleges in his Chronicon."[30] Clearly Arethas is not satisfied with what Eusebius "alleges." This is all the more evident in his comments on various passages in Revelation.

Theophylact

A much later witness is Theophylact of Bulgaria, a noted Byzantine exegete (d. 1107). He also gives evidence of a dual tradition on John's banishment. A. S. Peake observed in this regard: "Theophylact also puts it [*i.e.*, Revelation] under Trajan, but elsewhere gives a date which would bring it into the time of Nero."[31] In his *Preface to Commentary on the Gospel of John*, Theophylact puts the banishment of John under Nero when he says John was banished thirty-two years after the ascension of Christ. In his commentary on Matthew 20:22 he mentions John's banishment under Trajan, the second emperor after Domitian!

Conclusion

The above survey shows that early church tradition was not uniformly set against the early date of Revelation, as some have implied. Indeed, when carefully scrutinized, the evidence even tilts in the opposite direction. Thus, Guthrie's statement does not appear to be well founded: "It would be strange, if the book really was produced at the end of Nero's reign, that so strong a tradition arose associating it with Domitian's."[32]

There are some early witnesses that strongly hint at a pre-A.D. 70 dating for Revelation, such as *The Shepherd of Hermas* and Papias. Other sources are even more suggestive of a Neronic banishment:

---

29. Cited in P. S. Desprez, *The Apocalypse Fulfilled*, 2nd ed. (London: Longman, Brown, Green, Longmans, 1855), p. 7.

30. Stuart, *Apocalypse* 1:268.

31. Peake, *Revelation*, p. 77.

32. Guthrie, *Introduction*, p. 957.

the Muratorian Canon, and Tertullian. These at least suggest either an early competition between theories, or a double banishment of John, once under Nero and later under Domitian. Undeniably supportive of a Neronic date are Epiphanius, Arethas, the Syriac *History of John*, and the Syriac versions of Revelation.

14

THE HISTORICAL EVIDENCE (2)

And I, John, am the one who heard and saw these things (Rev. 22:8a).

I have shown that, contrary to sweeping assertions made by late-date advocates, there are external evidences which are supportive of an early date for Revelation. Let us now turn to an analysis of the purported late-date witnesses from church history.

The statements confidently cited by late-date scholars almost invariably are from the following church fathers: Irenaeus of Lyons (A.D. 130-202), Clement of Alexandria (A.D. 150-215), Origen (A.D. 185-254), Victorinus of Pettau (di. A.D. 304), Eusebius of Caesarea (A.D. 260-340), and Jerome (A.D. 340-420). Without a doubt these names represent the mainstays of the late-date position. For example, the following biblical scholars list all or most of these church fathers as the leading witnesses from church tradition. Among conservatives we find: Henry B. Swete, Robert H. Mounce, Albert Barnes, B. B. Warfield, Henry C. Thiessen, Donald B. Guthrie, John F. Walvoord, and Merrill C. Tenney, to name but a few.[1] From among liberal commentators we note R. H.

---

1. Henry B. Swete, *Commentary on Revelation* (Grand Rapids: Kregel, [1911] 1977), p. c; Robert Mounce, *The Book of Revelation* (Grand Rapids: Eerdmans, 1977), p. 32; Albert Barnes, *Barnes' Notes on the New Testament*, 1 vol. ed. (Grand Rapids: Kregel, rep. 1962), pp. 1531ff.; B. B. Warfield, "Revelation, Book of", in Philip Schaff, ed., *A Religious Encyclopaedia: Or Dictionary of Biblical, Historical, Doctrinal, and Practical Theology* (New York: Funk and Wagnalls, 1883), 3:2035; Henry C. Thiessen, *Introduction to the*

Charles and James Moffatt.[2] Let us survey the evidence.

Irenaeus

As we begin consideration of the historical evidence for the date of Revelation, the obvious starting point is with Irenaeus, Bishop of Lyons. Beyond any shadow of doubt, Irenaeus is the key witness for the late date of Revelation. Some scholars cite only Irenaeus in alluding to the external evidence.[3] Irenaeus's famous statement is found in Book 5 of his work entitled *Against Heresies*.

Irenaeus is an important witness and deserves initial consideration for several reasons: (1) He seems to speak directly to the issue at hand. (2) He wrote the very work in question at a rather early date, between A.D. 180 and 190.[4] (3) He claims to have known Polycarp, who in turn may have known the Apostle John.[5]

New Testament (Grand Rapids: Eerdmans, 1943), pp. 317ff.; Donald B. Guthrie, *New Testament Introduction*, 3rd ed. (Downers Grove, IL.: Inter-Varsity Press, 1970), pp. 956-957; John F. Walvoord, *The Revelation of Jesus Christ* (Chicago: Moody Press, 1966), pp. 13ff.; Merrill C. Tenney, "Revelation, Book of," in Merrill C. Tenney, ed., *The Zondervan Pictorial Bible Dictionary* (Grand Rapids: Zondervan, 1967), p. 721; A. T. Robertson, *Word Pictures in the New Testament*, 6 vols. (Nashville: Broadman, 1933) 6:275.

2. R. H. Charles, *A Critical and Exegetical Commentary on the Revelation of St. John*, 2 vols. (Edinburgh: T. & T. Clark, 1920) 1:xciii; James Moffatt, *The Revelation of St. John the Divine*, vol. 5 in W. Robertson Nicoll, ed., *The Expositor's Greek Testament* (Grand Rapids: Eerdmans, rep. 1980), p. 320.

3. Leon Morris, *The Revelation of St. John* (Grand Rapids: Eerdmans, 1969), p. 34, n. 5; J. P. M. Sweet, *Commentary on Revelation* (Philadelphia: Westminster Press, 1979), p. 21; Charles C. Ryrie, *Revelation* (Chicago: Moody Press, 1968), p. 8; Alan F. Johnson, *Revelation* (Grand Rapids: Zondervan, 1983), p. 12; Werner Georg Kümmel, *Introduction to the New Testament*, trans. Howard Clark Kee, 17th ed. (Nashville: Abingdon, 1973), p. 446; William Hendriksen, *More Than Conquerors* (Grand Rapids: Baker, 1967), p. 20; George Eldon Ladd, *A Commentary on the Revelation of John* (Grand Rapids: Eerdmans, 1972), p. 8, n. 1; G. R. Beasley-Murray, *The Book of Revelation* (Grand Rapids: Eerdmans, 1978), p. 37; Marvin R. Vincent, *Word Studies in the New Testament*, vol. 2 (Grand Rapids: Eerdmans, [1887] rep. 1985), p. 3.

4. A. Cleveland Coxe, in Alexander Roberts and James Donaldson, eds., *The Ante-Nicene Fathers*, 10 vols. (Grand Rapids: Eerdmans, rep. 1975) 1:312; W. H. C. Frend, *The Rise of Christianity* (Philadelphia: Fortress Press, 1984), p. 921.

5. Irenaeus, *Against Heresies* 3:3:4.

Thus, the long-standing tendency to rely heavily on Irenaeus is not unreasonable. The strength of the reliance on Irenaeus is clearly indicated in A. S. Peake's commentary: "In deference to our earliest evidence, the statement of Irenaeus, the Book was generally considered to belong to the close of Domitian's reign."[6] More recent scholarship tends to rely heavily upon Irenaeus as well.[7]

Irenaeus's Statement

The evidence from Irenaeus is found in Book 5, Chapter 30, Paragraph 3 of his *Against Heresies*. Although originally composed in Greek, today this work exists in its entirety only in Latin translation. Thankfully, however, the particular statement in question is preserved for us in the original Greek twice in Eusebius's *Ecclesiastical History*, at 3:18:3 and 5:8:6.

Irenaeus's crucial statement occurs at the end of a section dealing with the identification of "666," which he applies to the Antichrist, in Revelation 13. That statement is generally translated into English as follows: "We will not, however, incur the risk of pronouncing positively as to the name of Antichrist; for if it were necessary that his name should be distinctly revealed in this present time, it would have been announced by him who beheld the apocalyptic vision. For that was seen no very long time since, but almost in our day, towards the end of Domitian's reign."[8] The late-date advocate argues that this serves as compelling evidence that John "saw" the Revelation "at the end of the reign of Domitian."

How shall early date advocacy deal with such strong and forthright testimony by this noteworthy ancient church father? As a matter of fact, there are several problems that arise which tend

---

6. Arthur S. Peake, *The Revelation of John* (London: Joseph Johnson, 1919), p. 70.

7. Mounce, *Revelation*, p. 32; Sweet, *Revelation*, p. 21; Guthrie, *New Testament Introduction*, pp. 956-957; Kummel, *Introduction to the New Testament*, pp. 466-467; Hendriksen, *More Than Conquerors*, pp. 19-20.

8. Coxe, in *Ante-Nicene Fathers* 1:559-560.

to reduce the usefulness of Irenaeus for late-date advocacy. Three of these will be brought forward.[9]

First, the translational problem. The most important matter facing us is the proper translation of Irenaeus's statement. The phrase "that was seen" or "it was seen" (as it is often translated) is the crucial matter in this statement. This statement is commonly considered to refer back to the immediately preceding noun from the preceding sentence, which means either: "apocalyptic vision" or "Revelation." But as John A. T. Robinson has observed regarding the commonly accepted translation: "This translation has been disputed by a number of scholars."[10] Compounding this problem are several contextual matters and a certain internal confusion in Irenaeus regarding the incompatibility of his statements on Revelation.

Second, the subject of *heorathe*. Indisputably, the most serious potential objection to the common translation has to do with the understanding of the Greek verb *heorathe*, "was seen." What is the subject of this verb? Is it "he who saw the Revelation" (*i.e.*, John) or "Revelation" itself? Either one will work grammatically because Greek is an inflected language that has no need of separate pronouns (although it does have them). The verb endings often serve in lieu of a pronoun and with an implied subject. The verb before us is found in the third person singular form. Considered alone and divorced from its context, it may be translated either "it was seen" or "he was seen." Hence the reason for our inquiry. Which of the two antecedents — "he who saw" (*i.e.*, John) or "Revelation" — "was seen" almost in Irenaeus's time and near the end of the reign of Domitian?

Let us paraphrase the possible translations of this statement in order to clarify our question. Did Irenaeus mean: "the *Revelation* was seen in a vision by John almost in our own generation"? This

---

9. Other problems are discussed in my *Before Jerusalem Fell: Dating the Book of Revelation* (Tyler, TX: Institute for Christian Economics, 1989).

10. John A. T. Robinson, *Redating the New Testament* (Philadelphia: Westminster Press, 1976), p. 221.

is the commonly accepted view. Or was he saying "*John*, who saw the Revelation, was seen alive almost in our own generation"? This is a grammatically possible view – one which I hold to be preferable.

Such questions are all the more significant when we consider the observations of the editor of the first English translation of Irenaeus. A. Cleveland Coxe has noted that "Irenaeus, even in the original Greek, is often a very obscure writer. At times he expresses himself with remarkable clearness and terseness; but, upon the whole, his style is very involved and prolix."[11] In an obscure writer such as Irenaeus, questions of translation of unclear grammatical usage become quite important.

Third, the syntactical structure. Moving beyond the grammatical ambiguity of the verb, we must consider the structural flow of the passage cited. We have to explain properly the conjunction "for" (Greek: *gar*) in Irenaeus's statement. This conjunction is grammatically difficult to account for if we accept the common translation. If, however, it introduces a statement which makes reference back to the *main* idea of the preceding statement, then all becomes simple.

But what is the main idea? The main idea Irenaeus is presenting may be illustrated in a paraphrase of his point: "It is not important for us to know the name of the Beast (or Antichrist), which was hidden in the number 666. Were it important, why did John not tell us? After all, he lived almost to our own era, and spoke with some men that I have known." The main idea involves John himself. *Irenaeus is speaking of John and his knowledge of the name of the Beast.* It seems quite clear that he is exhorting the reader to not worry about the name of the Beast. We should not trouble ourselves with the matter because even John, who lived a long time after writing Revelation, did not tell anyone the identity.

Fourth, the context. But there is still more to the translational argument. In his *Ecclesiastical History* (5:8:5, 6) Eusebius again cited

---

11. Coxe, in *Ante-Nicene Fathers* 1:312, 313.

Irenaeus's statement, this time with more of the context:

> These things were said by the writer [*i.e.*, Irenaeus] referred to in
> the third book of his treatise which has been quoted before, and in
> the fifth book he discourses thus about the Apocalypse of John and
> the number of the name of the Antichrist. "Now since this is so,
> and since this number is found in all the good and ancient copies,
> and since those who have seen John face to face testify, and reason
> teaches us that the number of the name of the beast appears
> according to the numeration of the Greeks by the letters in it. . . .
> [*Heresies* 5:30:1]" And going on later [*Heresies* 5:30:3] he says
> concerning the same point, "We therefore will not take the risk of
> making any positive statement concerning the name of the Anti-
> christ. For if it had been necessary for his name to have been
> announced clearly at the present time, it would have been spoken
> by him who also saw the Revelation; for it was not even seen a
> long time ago, but almost in our own generation towards the end
> of the reign of Domitian."[12]

Notice should be made of the *personal* knowledge which is
emphasized by Irenaeus. It seems clear that the verb "was seen"
is but the dim reflection of his preceding statement's more expan-
sive and precise statement: "those who have seen John face to face
testify." In fact, the very same Greek verb (*heorathe*, "seen") is used
in both statements! Surely it speaks of John in both instances.

Fifth, the intent of Irenaeus. Still further, the proposed re-
interpretation of Irenaeus is characteristic of Irenaeus's thought.
By this I mean that *Irenaeus constantly emphasizes the organic and living
unity of the Church's life.* According to church historian Philip Schaff,
Irenaeus's work sought to demonstrate that "the same gospel
which was first orally preached and transmitted was subsequently
committed to writing and faithfully preserved in all the apostolic
churches through the regular succession of the bishops and elders."[13] This being the case, the most natural interpretation of

---

12. Translation by Lake.

13. Philip Schaff, *History of the Christian Church*, 3rd ed., 7 vols. (Grand Rapids:
Eerdmans, [1910] rep. 1950) 2:753.

Irenaeus's statement would be that he was referring to John's being alive to communicate the number of Beast-Antichrist to his hearers.

Sixth, the incompatibility of Irenaeus's Revelation statements. Another difficulty with accepting the commonly received translation arises from another of Irenaeus's statements in the context. At *Against Heresies* 5:30:1 Irenaeus writes: "Such, then, being the state of the case, and this number [666] being found in all the most approved and ancient copies [of the apocalypse], and those men who saw John face to face bearing their testimony [to it]." As Guthrie notes: "Since he [Irenaeus] also mentioned ancient copies of the book, it is clear that he knew of its circulation at a much earlier time."[14]

Irenaeus's mention of "ancient copies" of Revelation may be suggestive as to the date. This reference to "ancient copies" definitely indicates that the original manuscript of Revelation is ancient. Surely "ancient *copies*" demand a *more ancient* original! It would seem that the "ancient" character of the "copies" would suggest something more ancient than the "end of Domitian's reign" which Irenaeus speaks of as "almost in our own generation" — does he consider himself "ancient"? If Revelation was written pre-A.D. 68, then its date would be about three decades older still.

Seventh, Irenaeus's use of eyewitnesses. In *Against Heresies* we read a very unusual historical statement:

> [Christ] came to Baptism as one Who had not yet fulfilled thirty years, but was beginning to be about thirty years old. . . . But the age of 30 years is the first of a young man's mind, and that it reaches even to the fortieth year, everyone will allow: but after the fortieth and fiftieth year, it begins to verge towards elder age: which our Lord was of when He taught, as the Gospel and all the Elders witness, who in Asia conferred with John the Lord's disciple, to the effect that John had delivered these things unto them: for he abode with them until the times of Trajan. And some of them saw not

---

14. Guthrie, *Introduction*, p. 933.

only John, but others also of the Apostles, and had this same account from them, and witness to the aforesaid relation.[15]

The careful detail he meticulously recounts in his argument, and the reference to the eyewitness accounts, should be noted. Yet, no respected New Testament scholar asserts that the biblical record allows for a fifteen year or more ministry for Christ, or His having attained the age of fifty. With Schaff we must heartily agree that Irenaeus was "strangely mistaken about the age of Jesus."[16] If this "eyewitness" account of Christ's age and length of ministry could be so woefully in error, why not his "eyewitness" sources for John's banishment?

Conclusion

A careful scrutiny of the Irenaean evidence for a late date for Revelation tends to render any confident employment of him suspect. The proper translation of Irenaeus's statement is the leading obstacle to confident use of him in the debate. He may not have even meant that Revelation was seen by John during Domitian's reign. He may have meant to press the point that *John* was seen alive in Domitian's reign.

Origen

Origen of Alexandria lived from A.D. 185-254. He was a disciple of Clement of Alexandria and wrote a great number of works, many of which we still have. As noted earlier, Origen is usually cited as among the leading external witnesses to a late date for Revelation. The "evidence" from Origen's *Commentary on Matthew* (at Matthew 16:6ff.) reads as follows: "The King of the Romans, as tradition teaches, condemned John, who bore testimony, on account of the word of truth, to the isle of Patmos. John, moreover, teaches us things respecting his testimony [*i.e.*, martyrdom], without saying who condemned him when he utters these

---

15. Irenaeus, *Against Heresies* 2:22:5.

16. Schaff, *History* 2:751.

things in the Apocalypse. He seems also to have seen the Apocalypse . . . in the island."

Needless to say, early date advocates find the use of Origen questionable, in that it is not at all clear that he had in mind Domitian as "the King of the Romans." Indeed, many late-date advocates even admit that this "leading evidence" is based on *presumption*! R. H. Charles, for instance, writes: "Neither in Clement nor Origen is Domitian's name given, but it may be *presumed* that it was in the mind of these writers."[17] H. B. Swete and Mounce agree.[18]

Thus we come again upon a widely acclaimed late-date witness which is wholly unconvincing. Additional arguments against the reading of Origen as a late-date witness may be garnered from the following material on Clement of Alexandria. This is due to the fact that Clement was not only the precursor and teacher of Origen, but is equally nondescript.

Clement of Alexandria

As we continue our survey of the evidence from tradition, we come to Clement of Alexandria (A.D. 150-215). Clement was a learned scholar of much prominence in early Christianity. The evidence from Clement almost universally is cited by late-date advocates as supportive of their view. Clement's statement is found in his *Who is the Rich Man that shall be Saved?*, Section 42: "Hear a story that is no mere story, but a true account of John the apostle that has been handed down and preserved in memory. When after the death of the tyrant he removed from the island of Patmos to Ephesus, he used to journey by request to the neighboring districts of the Gentiles, in some places to appoint bishops, in others to regulate whole churches, in others to set among the clergy some one man, it may be, of those indicated by the Spirit." The critical phrase here is "after the death of the tyrant he [John] removed

---

17. Charles, *Revelation*, p. xciii. Emphasis added.

18. Swete, *Revelation*, p. xcix, n. 2; Mounce, *Revelation*, p. 32.

from the island of Patmos to Ephesus."

Despite widespread employment of Clement's statement, a close consideration of it destroys its usefulness in the debate. Furthermore, some quite logical considerations actually tilt the evidence from Clement in an early date direction!

Read the text for yourself. John is said to return from Patmos after the death of "*the tyrant.*" It is painfully obvious that the required name, "Domitian," is absent, just as in the case with his disciple, Origen. Yet H. B. Swete calls Clement one of "the chief authorities" from tradition for the late date![19] But who was this "tyrant"? Can we confidently cite Clement's nebulous statement as evidence for a Domitianic date for John's banishment? These questions are all the more relevant when we realize that *Nero* above all other emperors best meets up to the billing of a notorious tyrant. Let us see why.

The Universal Fear of Nero

First, even outside Christian circles Nero's infamous evil was greatly feared. As I noted in Chapter 4, Roman writers such as historians Tacitus[20] and Suetonius,[21] naturalist Pliny the Elder,[22] satirist Juvenal,[23] and philosopher Philostratus wrote of Nero's tyranny. Philostratus (*fl.* 210-220) wrote that in his day Nero was "commonly called a Tyrant."[24] This is a most fascinating observation, in that Philostratus wrote during the time of Clement of Alexandria — he died just two years after Clement.

Nero scholar Miriam T. Griffin analyzes the presentation of Nero in the ancient tragedy *The Octavia* (second century), noting: "Nero is, in fact, the proverbial tyrant, robbed of any personal characteristics, a mere incarnation of the will to evil, unaffected

---

19. Swete, *Revelation*, p. xcix.
20. *Histories* 4:7; 4:8.
21. Suetonius, *Nero* 7:1; 27:1.
22. Pliny, *Natural History*, 7:45; 22:92.
23. *Satire* 7:225; 10:306ff.
24. Philostratus, *Life of Apollinius* 4:38.

by advice or influence."[25] Nero's memory long stained the memory of the empire. Surely this is why Clement could write merely "the tyrant" when he made reference to the emperor of the banishment!

The Dread of Nero's Return

Second, Nero was so dreaded by many that soon after his death there began circulating haunting rumors of his destructive return, either from the grave or from his place of hiding. This *Nero-redivivus* myth can be found in the writings of Tacitus, Suetonius, Dio Cassius, Zonaras, Dion Chrysostom, Augustine, and other ancient writers.[26] In the ancient writings known as the *Sibylline Oracles* (Second to Seventh Centuries A.D.) Nero appears as a constant threat to the world. Sibylline scholar J. J. Collins has noted in this regard that "there is the prominence of Nero as an eschatological adversary throughout the Sibylline corpus."[27]

Nero: Paradigm of Terror

Third, as noted earlier, Christians particularly detested Nero as the Arch Tyrant and enemy of God. Many of the early church fathers remembered Nero with loathing. Let us cite just a few.

Eusebius speaks of Nero's "depravity," "the perversity of his degenerate madness, which made him compass the unreasonable destruction of so many thousands," and his being "the first of the emperors to be pointed at as a foe of divine religion."[28] Lactantius (A.D. 240-320) observes that Nero was a tyrant: "He it was who first persecuted the servants of God . . . and therefore this tyrant, bereaved of authority, and precipitated from the height of empire,

---

25. Miriam T. Griffin, *Nero: The End of a Dynasty* (New Haven: Yale University Press, 1984), p. 100.

26. Tacitus, *Histories* 1:78; 2:8; Suetonius, *Nero* 57; Dio Cassius, *Xiphilinus* 65:9; Zonaras, *Annals* 11:15-18; Dion Chrysostom, *Orations* 21; Augustine, *The City of God* 20:19:3.

27. J. J. Collins, "Sibylline Oracles," in *Apocalyptic Literature and Testaments*, vol. 1 of James H. Charlesworth, ed., *Old Testament Pseudepigrapha* (Garden City, NY: Doubleday, 1983), p. 360.

28. Eusebius, *Ecclesiastical History* 2:25:2, 3.

suddenly disappeared."[29] Sulpicius Severus (A.D. 360-420) writes
that Nero was "the basest of all men, and even of wild beasts,"
that "he showed himself in every way most abominable and cruel,"
and that "he first attempted to abolish the name of Christian."[30]

Nero vs. Domitian

Fourth, the traditions about Domitian's alleged persecution
warranted his being called a "Nero" by many, Christian and
non-Christian alike. That Domitian was known as a "Nero,"
indicates Nero's name was paradigmatic of anti-Christian tyranny,
not Domitian's. Tertullian (a contemporary with Clement of Alexandria and early Christendom's greatest apologist) spoke of Domitian as not only "somewhat of a Nero in cruelty,"[31] but a "*sub-
Nero*."[32] He speaks of Domitian much more favorably than of
Nero: "Domitian too, who was somewhat of a Nero in cruelty, had
tried it [*i.e.*, persecution], but forasmuch as he was also a human
being, he speedily stopped the undertaking, even restoring those
whom he had banished."[33]

In his *Sacred History* Sulpicius Severus reserves two chapters
to a consideration of Nero's reign, and only three sentences to
Domitian's. Severus extols the sainted life of Martin of Tours by
noting that he would have gladly suffered for the Faith, even under
the two worst persecutors of the Church: "But if he had been
permitted, in the times of Nero and of Decius [A.D. 249-251], to
take part in the struggle which then went on, I take to witness the
God of heaven and earth that he would freely have submitted."[34]

Is Nero not a prime candidate for Clement's designation "the
tyrant"? Where is Domitian as scathingly treated as Nero? Ask
anyone on the street who Nero and Domitian were. You will

---

29. *On the Death of the Persecutors* 2.
30. Sulpicius Severus, *Sacred History* 2:28.
31. *Apology* 5.
32. *On the Mantle* 4.
33. Tertullian, *Apology* 5.
34. Sulpicius Severus, *Letters* 3 (To Deacon Aurelius).

discover Nero's name is known even today, whereas Domitian's is forgotten. Go to your local library and try to check out some books on Domitian. Probably you will not find any. But you very likely will find several on Nero. Nero gained himself great fame as a tyrant burned into the memory of history.

But there is more!

The Contextual Difficulty

To further compound the problem for late-date employment of Clement there is the difficulty which surfaces in the context of his famous statement. The context following the critical statement is more easily believable if John were about thirty years younger, as he would have been in A.D. 65-66 as opposed to A.D. 95-96. Let us consider it and see if you agree.

In connection with his returning from banishment under the "tyrant," Clement informs us of John's activities, which are wholly incredible if by a man in his 90s. I will cite the passage again: "When after the death of the tyrant he removed from the island of Patmos to Ephesus, he used to journey by request to the neighboring districts of the Gentiles, in some places to appoint bishops, in others to regulate whole churches, in others to set among the clergy some one man."[35] In further illustration of his activities, Clement immediately added to the account a story in which John, disturbed by a young church leader's forsaking of the faith, chased him on horseback: "But when he recognised John as he advanced, he turned, ashamed, to flight. The other followed with all his might, forgetting his age, crying, 'Why, my son, dost thou flee from me, thy father, unarmed, old? Son, pity me.'"[36]

This is quite strenuous missionary activity for a man who by that time had to be in his 90s! And the fact that he is said to have forgotten his "age" does not indicate he may have been ninety. Paul calls himself "the aged" while nowhere near that old (Philem.

---

35. Clement of Alexandria, *Who Is the Rich Man that Shall be Saved?* 42.

36. *Ibid.*

9). The whole episode is much more believable if speaking of a man much younger than in his 90s, perhaps in his 60s.

The Cessation of Revelation

What we have seen thus far should give us pause when we hear it asserted that Clement supports a Domitianic date for John's banishment. But if not, then the implications of the statement of Clement now to be given should totally reverse his usefulness in the debate.

In *Miscellanies*, Book 7, Clement deals with the perversion of truth by heretics. Their error is that "they do not make a right but a perverse use of the divine words." In his debate with them, he states that *apostolic revelation has ceased*: "For the teaching of our Lord at His advent, beginning with Augustus and Tiberius, was completed in the middle of the times of Tiberius. And that of the apostles, embracing the ministry of Paul, *ends with Nero*."[37]

Beyond all doubt, Clement considers the Apostle John to have written the book of Revelation. This may be seen in two of his writings: *Who is the Rich Man?* (Sec. 42) and *Miscellanies* (6:13). Yet here at *Miscellanies* 7:17 it is equally plain that he also holds that revelation through the apostles ceased under Nero. How could he have made this statement if John's Revelation had been written about 30 years *after* Nero?

Conclusion

When all the Clementine evidence is considered together, it is evident that Clement may be discounted as a late-date witness: The crucial statement by Clement lacks (1) specificity (it does not mention Domitian) and (2) credibility (if, in fact, it did refer to a Domitianic banishment we would be left with a record of incredible feats by a 90-year-old John).

Not only so, but Clement even serves as a positive external witness to the early date composition of Revelation, for the follow-

---

37. Clement of Alexandria, *Miscellanies* 7:17.

ing reasons: (1) The non-specific statement is more easily applied to Nero than Domitian (Nero is the classic and paradigmatic tyrant in ecclesiastical history) and (2) Clement teaches that divine revelation ceased with Paul under Nero (yet Clement accepts Revelation as having been written by John).

This evidence is from a church father not far removed in time from Irenaeus — and one much closer to the region where John labored.

Victorinus

Victorinus (d. A.D. 304), bishop of Pettau, is another of the mainstays of the late-date argument from tradition. Victorinus's relevant statement is found in his *Commentary on the Apocalypse* at Revelation 10:11: "When John said these things he was in the island of Patmos, condemned to the labour of the mines by Caesar Domitian. Therefore, he saw the Apocalypse; and when grown old, he thought he should at length receive his quittance by suffering, Domitian being killed, all his judgments were discharged. And John being dismissed from the mines, thus subsequently delivered the same Apocalypse which he had received from God."[38] It is abundantly clear that Victorinus taught that John was banished by Domitian.

What is striking about this traditional evidence, however, is that *John, who was doubtless well into his 90s, could be condemned to the mines and live!* This difficulty is similar to that expressed above regarding Clement of Alexandria. Such difficulties tax to the very limit the credibility of the reference.

Eusebius Pamphili

Eusebius (A.D. 260-340), Bishop of Caesarea in Palestine, is known as "the Father of Church History." In his *Ecclesiastical History* he writes:

Domitian . . . finally showed himself the successor of Nero's cam-

---

38. Victorinus, *Revelation* 10:1.

paign of hostility to God. He was the second to promote persecution against us, though his father, Vespasian, had planned no evil against us.

At this time, the story goes, the Apostle and Evangelist John was still alive, and was condemned to live in the island of Patmos for his witness to the divine word. At any rate Irenaeus, writing about the number of the name ascribed to the anti-Christ in the so-called Apocalypse of John, states this about John in so many words in the fifth book against Heresies.[39]

As we analyze the weight of this evidence, we must bear in mind that *Eusebius clearly declares his dependence upon Irenaeus* in this matter. Whatever difficulties there may be with Irenaeus (see previous discussion), such must necessarily apply to Eusebius. Furthermore, there are some perplexing difficulties in Eusebius's writings, even apart from his founding his view on Irenaeus. Let us briefly survey these problems.

Inconsistent Usage of Irenaeus

In the first place, despite Eusebius's express dependence upon Irenaeus in this area, Eusebius disagrees with Irenaeus on an extremely important and intimately related question. Eusebius denies what Irenaeus clearly affirms: that John the Apostle wrote Revelation.[40] This poses a problem. In another place in his book, Eusebius establishes the Apostle John's longevity based on Irenaeus's confident statement that John lived through Domitian's persecution.[41] But he disagrees with Irenaeus's teaching that John wrote Revelation, even though both ideas are found in the same place in Irenaeus. If Eusebius believed the one report, why not the other? The two issues — (1) that the Apostle John wrote Revelation (2) during Domitian's reign — are bound up together in Irenaeus. To doubt one would seem necessarily to entail the doubting of the other.

---

39. Eusebius, *Ecclesiastical History* 3:17-18.
40. *Ecclesiastical History* 3:29:1, 2, 5, 6.
41. *Ibid.*, 3:18:1-3; 5:8:5.

Contradictory Assertions

In the second place, Eusebius contradicts himself in his writings on the banishment of John. It is clear in his *Ecclesiastical History* that he believes John was banished under Domitian. But in *Evangelical Demonstrations* 3:5, he speaks of the execution of Peter and Paul in the same sentence with the banishment of John. This clearly implies the events happened together. Thus, it indicates that when he wrote *Evangelical Demonstrations*, he was convinced of a Neronic banishment of John.

Thus, again we discover that one of the leading witnesses from tradition for the late date of Revelation is not all that solid a piece of evidence.

Jerome

As a number of late-date proponents argue, Jerome seems to regard John as having been banished by Domitian.[42] Due to its context, however, this evidence may not be as strongly supportive as many think. The context tends to confuse the matter by giving evidence of Jerome's confounding of two traditions. In his *Against Jovinianum* we read that John was "a prophet, for he saw in the island of Patmos, to which he had been banished by the Emperor Domitian as a martyr of the Lord, an Apocalypse containing boundless mysteries with the future. Tertullian, moreover, relates that he was sent to Rome, and that having been plunged into a jar of boiling oil he came out fresher and more active than when he went in."[43]

As shown above, the reference from Tertullian strongly suggests a Neronic date. Thus, Jerome's evidence seems confused and is indicative of two competing traditions regarding the date of John's banishment, and, hence, the date of Revelation.

Conclusion

I cannot see how the external evidence can be used with much

---

42. See Swete, Charles, Mounce, Moffatt, Warfield, and Tenney.
43. Jerome, *Against Jovinianum* 1:26.

credence by late-date advocates. Irenaeus's statement, the major evidence by far, is grammatically ambiguous and easily susceptible to a most reasonable re-interpretation, which would eliminate him as a late-date witness. The evidence from Origen and Clement of Alexandria, the second and third most significant witnesses to the Domitianic date, are more in the mind of the modern reader than in the script of the ancient text. The important references from both of these two fathers wholly lack the name "Domitian." Victorinus is a sure witness for the late date, but his requires incredible implications. Eusebius and Jerome provide us with conflicting testimony.

15

OBJECTIONS TO THE EARLY DATE

He who has an ear, let him hear what the Spirit says to the churches (Rev. 2:16).

Despite the wealth of evidence from within Revelation as to its early date, since the early 1900s late-date advocacy has persisted among the majority of both liberal and conservative scholars. In the nineteenth century the evidence cited in defense of a late date for Revelation was derived almost exclusively from church tradition. Milton S. Terry, author of a much used text on the principles of biblical interpretation, wrote in 1898: "[N]o critic of any note has ever claimed that the later date is required by any internal evidence."[1] This is no longer true today.

Though depending mostly on evidence from tradition, current late-date literature does attempt to build a case from Revelation's self-witness. In order to better secure the early date argument in terms of the self-witness evidence, I will address the major contrary arguments put forward by late-date advocates.

The modern case for the late date of Revelation tends to concentrate its focus upon four basic arguments. These have been ably summarized by noted evangelical scholar and late-date advocate Leon Morris. We choose to investigate Morris's approach for two basic reasons. He has rightfully earned an international repu-

---

1. Milton Terry, *Biblical Hermeneutics* (Grand Rapids: Zondervan, undated reprint), p. 240.

tation among both evangelical and liberal scholars, and he has a demonstrated competence in the field of New Testament studies, having even produced an excellent commentary on Revelation itself. The order of our listing of these evidences will follow Morris's, which is based on his scholarly estimation of their priority.

Emperor Worship

First, Morris begins with what he calls "the principal reason for dating the book during" Domitian's reign, which is: Revelation "contains a number of indications that emperor-worship was practised, and this is thought to have become widespread in Domitian's day."[2] James Moffatt insisted that the role of emperor worship in Revelation was virtually conclusive: "When the motive of the Apocalypse is thus found in the pressure upon the Christian conscience exerted by Domitian's emphasis on the imperial cultus, especially as that was felt in Asia Minor, any earlier date for the book becomes almost impossible."[3] This argument is also held by Robert H. Mounce, R. H. Charles, H. B. Swete, Donald B. Guthrie, W. G. Kümmel, and William Barclay. References in Revelation which seem to reflect emperor worship are found in scattered places: Revelation 13:4, 8, 12, 15; 14:9, 11; 16:2; 19:20; 20:4. The most noteworthy passage is found in Revelation 13, where worship of the "beast" is compelled.

In effect, this objection has already been met in Chapter 6 above. There I showed that the worship of the emperor dates back to Julius Caesar and that Nero endorsed it. The emperor cult had a prominent role in the political and social life of the Roman empire well before Domitian, and even before Nero, although it is true that historical development continued to introduce new features and requirements into the practice. As even late-date advo-

---

2. Leon Morris, *The Revelation of St. John* (Grand Rapids: Eerdmans, 1969), p. 35.

3. James Moffatt, *The Revelation of St. John the Divine*, vol. 5 in W. Robertson Nicoll, ed., *The Expositor's Greek Testament* (Grand Rapids: Eerdmans, rep. 1980), p. 317.

cate James Moffatt wrote: "The blasphemous title of *divus*, assumed by the emperors since Octavian (Augustus = *sebastos*) as a semi-sacred title, implied superhuman claims which shocked the pious feelings of Jews and Christians alike. So did *theos* [god] and *theou huios* [son of god] which, as the inscriptions prove, were freely applied to the emperors, from Augustus onwards."[4]

The appearance of emperor worship in Revelation is held by many late-date theorists as the strongest evidence for a date during the last year of the reign of Domitian (A.D. 81-96). It is true that Domitian required people to address him as "Lord and God." Certainly the emperor cult was prominent in his reign. Yet when the historical evidence is scrutinized, there is abundant testimony to emperor worship at various stages of development well before both Domitian and Nero. Indeed, there are such clear statements of so many aspects of the emperor cult that it is surprising that this argument is used against the early date. That it is deemed "the principal reason" (Morris) that makes it "almost impossible" (Moffatt) for the early date view to stand is wholly incredible.

Persecution in Revelation

Second, Morris discovers "indications that Revelation was written in a time of persecution." This evidence is felt to accord "much better with Domitian."[5] W. G. Kümmel is quite confident that "the picture of the time which the Apocalypse sketches coincides with no epoch of the primitive history so well as with the period of Domitian's persecution."[6] Morris, Kümmel, and a number of other scholars list this as among their leading arguments for the A.D. 95-96 date.

Again, in effect, I have already spoken to this matter in Chapter 5. I agree that it seems clear enough that in Revelation

---

4. *Ibid.*, p. 429.

5. Morris, *Revelation*, p. 36.

6. W. G. Kummel, *Introduction to the New Testament*, trans. Howard Clark Kee, 17th ed. (Nashville: Abingdon, 1973), p. 328.

imperial persecution against the faith has begun. But I believe the evidence is heavily in favor of a Neronic (A.D. 64-68) persecution rather than a Domitianic (A.D. 95-96) one.

As noted in Chapter 5, it is extremely difficult to even prove a Domitianic persecution – secular history is totally silent on the possibility. Surprisingly, when we turn to Morris's own presentation, we are frustrated as we seek sure conviction: "While later Christians sometimes speak of a persecution under Domitian the evidence is not easy to find."[7] Many scholars understand Domitian's violent conduct in A.D. 95 as a paranoid outburst. It seemed to concentrate on "selected individuals whom he suspected of undermining his authority."[8] The problem with the evidence for this "persecution" is that it proceeds solely from Christian sources – sources somewhat later than the events. A Domitianic persecution is not mentioned by any secular historian of the era.

Though the historicity of a Domitianic persecution of Christianity is questioned, such cannot be the case with the persecution under Nero. Although many scholars argue that the Neronic persecution was confined to Rome and its environs, the indisputable fact remains: Nero cruelly persecuted Christianity, taking even the lives of its foremost leaders, Peter and Paul. The evidence for the Neronic persecution is overwhelming and is documentable from heathen, as well as Christian, sources.

In Chapter 5 above I showed clear evidence of a Neronic persecution from the writings of several pagan and Christian writers of the era. To that list let me now add Tertullian (A.D. 150-220), who was a lawyer who wrote in Latin, the legal language of the Roman Empire. In defending Christianity, he challenged men to search the archives of Rome for the proof that Nero persecuted the Church: "And if a heretic wishes his confidence to rest upon a public record, the archives of the empire will speak,

---

7. Morris, *Revelation*, p. 36. Other like references can be found in Chapter 5.

8. Glenn W. Barker, William L. Lane, and J. Ramsey Michaels, *The New Testament Speaks* (New York: Harper and Row, 1969), p. 368.

as would the stones of Jerusalem. We read the lives of the Caesars: At Rome Nero was the first who stained with blood the rising faith."[9] Surely he would not issue a challenge to search the archives of Rome, which could easily be taken and just as easily refuted, were his statement untrue.

It is indisputably evident that the sheer magnitude, the extreme cruelty, and the initial role of Nero's persecution of Christianity fit well the role required in Revelation. Thus, we are led again to repeat: The Domitianic evidence is doubtful and, if accepted at all, his persecution pales in comparison to Nero's. Interestingly, late-date advocate Robert Mounce, like so many others, admits that "the evidence for widespread persecution under Domitian is not especially strong." Yet, he goes on rather boldly to add that "there is no other period in the first century in which it would be more likely"![10] No other period?

The late-date use of the persecution theme in Revelation can neither establish the late date for Revelation, nor compete with the early date evidences.

The Nero Redivivus Myth

Third, a most unusual phenomenon seems to appear in Revelation, according to Morris. His third argument is very popular among many late-date theorists. This evidence has to do with the very unusual and ancient legend known as the *Nero Redivivus* myth. Morris briefly explains the myth and confidently employs it: "Again, it is urged that the book shows evidence of knowledge of the Nero *redivivus* myth (e.g. xvii. 8, 11). After Nero's death it was thought in some circles that he would return. At first this appears to have been a refusal to believe that he was actually dead. Later it took the form of a belief that he would come to life again. This took time to develop and Domitian's reign is about as early as we can expect it."[11]

---

9. Tertullian, *Scorpion's Sting* 15.

10. Robert Mounce, *The Book of Revelation* (Grand Rapids: Eerdmans, 1977), p. 34.

11. Morris, *Revelation*, p. 36.

James Moffatt[12] boldly asserts that "the phase of the Nero-redivivus myth which is represented in the Apocalypse cannot be earlier than the latter part of Vespasian's reign."[13] In his commentary on Revelation 17 he speaks strongly of the role of the myth in interpreting the passage, when he noted that "the latter trait is unmistakably due to the legend of Nero redivivus, apart from which the oracle is unintelligible."[14]

Nero so fearfully impressed the world in his era that pagan, Jewish, and Christian legends quickly began to grow up around his death. These legends asserted themselves among the general populace throughout the far-flung reaches of the empire. In the pagan literature references to the expectation of Nero's return after his fall from power may be found in the writings of Tacitus, Suetonius, Dio Cassius, Xiphilinus, Zonaras, and Dion Chrysostom.[15] Among the Jews the myth surfaces in the Talmud. In Christian circles it is mentioned in books by Lactantius, Sulpicius Severus, Jerome, and Augustine.[16] Several *Sibylline Oracles* of various origins – Christian, Jewish, and pagan – use the myth as well.[17]

---

12. Moffatt is of the liberal school of biblical interpretation. He denies the reality of predictive prophecy, deeming prophecy to be mere religiously based calculations. He also considers Revelation to be the work of several editors who employ "allusions to coeval hopes and superstitions, grotesque fantasies and glowing creations of an oriental imagination, the employment of current ideas about antichrist, calculations of the immediate future, and the use of a religious or semi-mythical terminology" (Moffatt, *Revelation*, p. 298). Consequently his use of the *Nero Redivivus* myth is of a wholly different character from that of orthodox commentators, such as Morris and Swete. Moffatt asserts that John was caught up in first-century mythical speculations and actually adopted the myth. Morris and Swete assert that John merely employed the myth as a relevant, well-known cultural phenomenon to get a point across.

13. Moffatt, *Revelation*, p. 317.

14. *Ibid.*, p. 450.

15. Tacitus, *Histories* 1:2; 2:8, 9; Suetonius, *Nero* 40, 57, *Domitian* 6; Dio Cassius, *Roman History* 63:9:3; 66:19:3; Xiphilinus 64:9; Zonaras, *Annals* 11:151-8; and Dion Chrysostom, *Orations* 21.

16. Lactantius, *On the Death of the Persecutors* 2; Sulpicius Severus, *Sacred History* 2:28; Jerome, *Daniel* 11:28; and Augustine, *The City of God* 20:19:3.

17. Sibylline Oracles 3:63ff.; 4:115ff.; 5:33ff.; 8:68ff.; 12:78; 13:89ff.

Interestingly, the myth was not simply a "wives' tale" of little significance. It had a measurable impact even on political affairs. Pretenders to the imperial throne, claiming to be Nero, are recorded to have attempted to use the myth in quests for power.[18]

Clearly the existence, spread, and influence of the *Nero Redivivus* myth cannot be disputed. It is one of the most fascinating and best-known legends in all of political history. But the questions with which we must deal are: Does the myth appear in Revelation? And if so, does this necessitate a late date for the composition of Revelation?

Despite the confidence with which some late-date advocates employ the *Nero Redivivus* myth, two intriguing facts arise in regard to its use by Biblical scholars.

First, not all late-date proponents allow the argument as helpful to the question of the dating of Revelation. We will cite just one example. Donald B. Guthrie, a most able late-date adherent, carefully considers the merits of the *Nero Redivivus* argument, but discourages its endorsement in the debate: "If then an allusion to the Nero myth is still maintained as underlying the language of Revelation xiii and xvii, it must be regarded as extremely inconclusive for a Domitianic date. The most that can be said is that it may possibly point to this."[19]

Second, a number of *early date* advocates believe the myth appears in Revelation, but still maintain the Neronic dating position! John A. T. Robinson is a case in point: "As virtually all agree, there must be a reference to Nero *redivivus* in the beast that 'once was alive and is alive no longer but has yet to ascend out of the abyss before going to perdition.'"[20]

It is most interesting to find proponents of *both* dating positions

---

18. Tacitus, *Histories* 1:78; 2:8; Suetonius, *Nero* 57.

19. Donald B. Guthrie, *New Testament Introduction*, 3rd ed. (Downers Grove, IL: Inter-Varsity Press, 1970), pp. 953-954.

20. John A. T. Robinson, *Redating the New Testament* (Philadelphia: Westminster Press, 1976), p. 245. Moses Stuart and J. Stuart Russell are orthodox, early-date scholars who have allowed that the myth appears in Revelation.

able to admit the presence of an element which the late-date school proffers as a leading proof for its position! Beyond these two initial problems, however, there are significant and reasonable possibilities available to hand which wholly undermine the *Nero Redivivus* argument for a late date.

Despite the intriguing correspondences between the *Nero Redivivus* myth and some of Revelation prophecies, the two are not related. An extremely strong case can be made for an interpretation of the relevant passages that has nothing whatsoever to do with the *Nero Redivivus* myth. In addition, this interpretation is more appropriate, not only in regard to one of the major events of the first century, but also to the theme of Revelation. The interpretation of which I speak is given in Chapter 7 above, on the revival of the Beast. What John is speaking about is not a myth, but the historical phenomena associated with the death of Nero, the near demise of Rome, and its reestablishment under Vespasian.

Late-date proponent James Moffatt is particularly interesting at this point. He attempts to hold to the best of both worlds: (1) He vigorously asserts that the *Nero Redivivus* myth appears in Revelation 13 and 17. He urges that its appearance is helpful for establishing the late date for Revelation, in that its highly developed form is not possible until Domitian's reign (A.D. 81-96).[21] (2) But then he also adopts the interpretation of Revelation 13 and 17 that we suggest! That is, that the death wound and revival of the beast make reference to the Roman Civil Wars of A.D. 68-69. Notice his comments on Revelation 13:3: "The allusion is . . . to the terrible convulsions which in 69 A.D. shook the empire to its foundations (Tac. *Hist.* i.11). Nero's death with the bloody interregnum after it, was a wound to the State, from which it only recovered under Vespasian. It fulfilled the tradition of the wounded head. . . . The vitality of the pagan empire, shown in this power of righting itself after the revolution, only added to its prestige."[22]

---

21. Moffatt, *Revelation*, p. 317.
22. *Ibid.*, p. 430.

Here a vigorous late-date advocate and *Nero Redivivus* enthusiast admits that the references allude to the Roman Civil Wars and Rome's revival under Vespasian! This is a telling admission.[23] If the references in question can be applied to the Roman Civil Wars of A.D. 68-69, how can these same references point to *Nero Redivivus* and demand an A.D. 96 date for the book?

If the verses in Revelation can properly be understood as making reference to the earth-shaking historical events of the era, why would any commentator be driven to employ a myth to make sense of the passages? And this being the case, how can the myth be used as a major chronology datum from the internal evidence?

From our observations, it is obvious that the *Nero Redivivus* myth cannot be used with any degree of success to establish a late date for Revelation. There is good reason to doubt that it even appears in Revelation! The doubt is so strong that some late-date advocates refuse to employ it.[24] The presumed evidence based on this myth cannot undermine the facts derived from the documented historical matters by which we have established its early date.

The Condition of the Seven Churches

Fourth, the historical situations of the seven churches, to which Revelation is addressed (Rev. 1:4; 2; 3), seem to suggest a late date. Since these are historical churches to which John wrote, the letters may be expected to contain historical allusions which would be helpful in dating. As Morris states it, the "indication is that the churches of Asia Minor seem to have a period of development behind them. This would scarcely have been possible at the time of the Neronic persecution, the only serious competitor in date to

---

23. Interestingly, Mounce does the same thing: On page 34 of his work, he employs the myth to demonstrate a late date for Revelation, but in his commentary at Revelation 13 and 17 he opts for the revival-of-the-Empire interpretation (*Revelation*, pp. 216, 253).

24. For example, Guthrie, *Introduction*, pp. 953-954.

the Domitianic period."[25] Mounce, Swete, Kümmel, and Guthrie employ the same argument.

Let us, then, turn our attention to a point-by-point consideration of the substance of these arguments. I have not previously touched upon this evidence, so it deserves a little lengthier treatment. I will consider the four strongest arguments from this perspective, following the order found in Morris's work on Revelation.

The Wealth of Laodicea (Rev. 3:17)

The first evidence Morris offers in this regard is found in Revelation 3:17: "Because you say, 'I am rich, and have become wealthy, and have need of nothing,' and you do not know that you are wretched and miserable and poor and blind and naked." Morris notes that in this letter the Laodicean church is spoken of as "rich," but "as the city was destroyed by an earthquake in AD 60/61 this must have been considerably later."[26] Virtually all late-date advocates follow Morris's approach.

According to Tacitus, it is true that Laodicea was destroyed by an earthquake about this time.[27] The idea behind the argument is that such a devastating event as an earthquake necessarily must have severe and long-term economic repercussions on the community. And in such a community, the minority Christians could be expected to have suffered, perhaps even disproportionately. If Revelation were written prior to A.D. 70, it is argued, the time frame would be insufficient to allow for the enrichment of the church at Laodicea. But by the time of Domitian a few decades later, such would not be difficult to imagine.

Despite the initial plausibility of this argument, it is not as strong as it appears. In the first place, who is to say that the reference to "riches" mentioned by John is not a reference to *spiritual* riches? After all, such language is used in Scripture of those

---

25. Morris, *Revelation*, p. 38.
26. *Ibid.*, p. 38.
27. Tacitus, *Annals* 14:27.

who glory in their presumed *spiritual* riches: Luke 12:21; 16:15; 18:11, 12; 1 Corinthians 1:5; 13:12; 2 Corinthians 8:9. In fact, this language is used in a way very similar to Revelation in 1 Corinthians 4:8 and Hosea 12:8. If the spiritual riches view is valid, then the entire force of the late-date argument would be dispelled. Surprisingly, this is even the view of late-date advocate Robert Mounce: "The 'wealth' claimed by the Laodicean church, however, was not material but spiritual." And this despite the fact he uses the wealth of Laodicea as a late-date evidence![28]

Second, there is fascinating historical evidence which undermines the whole foundation of the late-date point, even if material riches are in view. It is a documented fact that Laodicea had an effortless, unaided, and rapid recovery from the earthquake. Tacitus reports that the city did not even find it necessary to apply for an imperial subsidy to help them rebuild, even though such was customary for cities in Asia Minor.[29] Thus, despite the earthquake, economic resources were so readily available within Laodicea that the city easily recovered itself from the damage.

Third, who is to say that the Christian community was necessarily overwhelmed by the quake in that city? In Revelation 3:17 the *church* is in view, not the city. Even the horribly destructive earthquakes in Mexico City on September 19 and 20 of 1985 did not destroy *every* sector of the city. Perhaps, by the grace of God, the Christians were in areas less affected by the quake, as Israel was in an area of Egypt unaffected by the plagues (Ex. 8:22; 9:4, 6, 24; 10:23; 11:27). If the Laodicean church had been spared the effects of the quake, would this token of God's providence lead the Laodiceans to a too proud confidence in their standing, as in Revelation 3:17? Perhaps a roughly analogous situation is found with the situation at Corinth, which Paul set about to correct (1 Cor. 4:6-8). Such boastful pride is ever a danger to those blessed of God (Deut. 8:18, cp. vv. 11-17).

---

28. Mounce, *Revelation*, p. 126, cp. p. 177.
29. Tacitus, *Annals* 14:27.

The Existence of the Church in Smyrna

Morris's second argument is that "the church at Smyrna seems not to have been in existence in the days of Paul."[30] Obviously, if the church mentioned in Revelation 2:8-11 did not exist until after Paul's death it could not have been founded before Paul's martyrdom, which occurred in A.D. 67. Thus Revelation's date could not precede A.D. 67. (It would not necessarily affect, however, a date after A.D. 67 and before A.D. 70!)

This late-date objection is based on a statement by Polycarp in a letter written to the church at Philippi: "But I have neither perceived nor heard any such thing among you [*i.e.*, the church at Philippi], among whom the blessed Paul laboured, who are praised in the beginning of his Epistle. For concerning you he boasts in all the churches who then alone had known the Lord, for we had not yet known him."[31] Polycarp (*ca.* A.D. 69-155), was the bishop of the church at Smyrna and is thought to have been the disciple of John. He seems to refer here to the Smyrnaean church when he writes "we had not yet known him." By this statement he may mean his church at Smyrna was not yet founded while Paul was alive. Several late-date advocates consider this among their strongest arguments. Nevertheless, there are strong objections to its usefulness.

First, it is not at all necessary that Polycarp's statement be interpreted in the manner demanded by Morris and others, *i.e.*, as indicating that the church was founded after Paul died. Re-read the statement for yourself. Does it demand that Paul was dead before the church at Smyrna was founded? Or could it easily be interpreted to mean that Paul *praised* the church at Philippi in his letter before the church at Smyrna was founded? It is much easier to understand Polycarp to be merely stating that Paul praised the Philippians for their conversion, which praise occurred before the Smyrnaeans were even converted. Polycarp would not then be

---

30. Morris, *Revelation*, p. 37.
31. Polycarp, *Letter to the Philippians* 11:3.

saying that the Smyrnaean church was founded after Paul died.

In the second place, most probably Smyrna was evangelized soon after Ephesus. We say this in light of the statements in Acts 19:10, 26. The Acts account emphasizes in conjunction with Paul's labors in Ephesus, that "all who lived in Asia heard the word of the Lord Jesus" and that "in almost all of Asia" Paul was making progress in the promotion of the Gospel. Smyrna is one of the cities of Asia (Rev. 1:4, 11). If Smyrna was evangelized soon after Ephesus, then this would put the date of the founding of the church at Smyrna *before* the year 60. There really seems to be no necessity for presupposing a late date for Revelation based on John's letter to Smyrna and Polycarp's letter to the Philippians.

The Spiritual Decline in Ephesus, Sardis, and Laodicea

The most familiar of the evidences from the Seven Letters is that which is derived from warnings of spiritual decline at Ephesus, Sardis, and Laodicea. Obvious spiritual decline is noted in Revelation 2:4, 5; 3:1-2, 15-18. Morris states the late-date position thus: "All the churches in chapters ii and iii appear to have had a period of history. Especially is this the case with those of whom things could be said like 'thou hast left thy first love' (ii. 4)."[32]

Late-date theorists insist that the spiritual decline manifested in the churches demands a period of time more readily available if John wrote during Domitian's reign. It seems a reasonable expectation that the early fervency of a newfound faith would wane only after the passing of various perils encountered over an extended period of time.

Despite all the vigorous assertions advanced toward the establishment of this argument, however, a major objection destroys this view. Granting that there is a marked deterioration in the churches, the whole question of the length of time necessary for such a waning of faith lies at the heart of the situation. How long does it take for faith to wane? Was not Paul surprised at the rapid

---

32. Morris, *Revelation*, p. 37.

decline among the Galatians? In Galatians 1:6 Paul writes: "I am amazed that you are so quickly deserting Him who called you by the grace of Christ, for a different gospel."

Consider also Paul's concern over the multitude of troubles within the church of Corinth. This church was founded in A.D. 49 and Paul wrote to it with heavy heart in A.D. 57. Indeed, Paul anticipated such problems to be experienced among churches virtually as soon as he left the scene, as he noted to the elders of the church at Ephesus (Acts 20:29ff.). Was not Timothy urged to remain at Ephesus because of the entry of false doctrine within Paul's lifetime (1 Tim. 1:6)?

Paul also experienced distressing defections from fidelity to him as a servant of Christ within his ministry (2 Tim. 4:10). Paul expresses concern over the labors of Archippus at Laodicea (one of the churches in question) when he warns him to "take heed to the ministry which you have received in the Lord, that you may fulfill it" (Col. 4:16-17).

How much more would such a problem of slackened zeal be aggravated by the political circumstances generated from the initiation of the Neronic persecution in A.D. 64! Did not Jesus' teaching anticipate such (Matt. 13:20, 21; 24:9, 10)? There is no compelling reason whatsoever to reject the early date of Revelation on the basis of the spiritual decline in certain of the Seven Churches.

Conclusion

A careful consideration of the merits of each of the major arguments from the Seven Letters demonstrates their inconclusive nature. Neither the arguments considered individually, nor all of them considered collectively, compels acceptance of the Domitianic date of Revelation. This is all the more obvious when their inconclusive nature is contrasted with the wealth of other internal considerations for an early date, as rehearsed heretofore in the present work.

In fact, the Seven Letters even have elements more suggestive of a period of time prior to the destruction of the temple: (1) The presence of strong Judaistic elements in the churches (Rev. 2:9; 3:9). This bespeaks an early period of Christian development prior to the cleavage between Jew and Christian in the A.D. 60s.[33] (2) John's exhortation to the churches in anticipation of the "judgment-coming" of Christ (Rev. 2:5, 16; 3:3, 10). There are no events that could be expected soon in Domitian's day that approached the magnitude and significance — both culturally and theologically — of the Neronic persecution of Christianity, the death of Nero, the destruction of Judaism's temple, and the near demise of Rome in the Civil Wars of A.D. 68-69.[34]

The early date stands, despite the presumed objections on the foregoing bases.

---

33. See Chapter 12.
34. See Chapter 9.

CONCLUSION

And he said to me, "Do not seal up the words of the prophecy of this book, for the time is near" (Rev. 22:10).

We have been considering two of the most interesting and debated questions regarding Revelation: Who is the Beast of Revelation? And when did John write Revelation? Our journey has been a long and arduous one. We have dug deeply into Revelation and we have traveled far and wide in Church history. We have now come to the end of the investigation. I hope our inquiry was both profitable and convincing. If so, perhaps it has helped to unseal the meaning of Revelation for us.

The Importance of the Questions

The proper identity of the Beast and the proper dating of the book of Revelation are not simply trivia questions. Large issues hang in the balance. If the views I have presented in this book are correct, then Revelation was written about a terrible Beast that would afflict the people of God *before* and *in anticipation* of the Fall of Jerusalem and the destruction of the temple in A.D. 70.

That being the case, then, we do not have the Beast and a "Great Tribulation" to look forward to in our future. The Beast — ancient Rome (generically) and Nero Caesar (specifically) — has already lived and the Tribulation has already occurred, as Scripture said it would, in the first century "birth pangs" of Christianity (Matt. 24:8, 21). Revelation, then, does not leave us with biblical warrant to view earth's future as a "blocked

182

future" of despair. The woes of Revelation have already occurred!

If these views are correct – and I am convinced beyond any doubt that they are – then Revelation was given as God's divinely inspired and inerrant pre-interpretive Word on the destruction of the temple order and the divorce of Israel as God's covenant wife. We have God's Word that this was brought about in the first century by the decree of the Lord Jesus Christ.

In Revelation we have a biblical explanation of the catastrophic events of the A.D. 60s. The important events of that era included: the outbreak of the first, precedent-setting imperial persecution of Christianity; the death of Christianity's first and most heinous Roman persecutor, Nero Caesar; the subsequent near collapse of Rome, followed by its revival under the non-persecuting emperors (Vespasian and Titus); the destruction of Jerusalem and the temple; and the hope for the increase throughout the earth of God's New Creational salvation.[1]

The Evidence for Our Answers

Our convictions regarding the identity of the Beast and the date of Revelation's composition have not been demanded merely by our theological perspective or sociological outlook. The relief we may experience regarding the vanished prospect of sending our children into such a dismal future is a happy *side-effect* of our inquiry. Now that we have looked rather carefully at the evidence for the date of Revelation, I believe we are compelled by historical and exegetical evidence to assert that Revelation was written in the A.D. 60s – not in the A.D. 90s.

It is my deep conviction that much of the decline of the influence of orthodox Christianity on our culture today is due to a pervasive, pessimistic eschatology. As dispensationalist R. A. Torrey loved to say at the turn of the century: "The darker the night gets, the lighter my heart gets."[2] If Christians refuse to be the light

---

1. Cp. Rev. 21-22 with 2 Cor. 5:17; Gal. 6:15; Matt. 13:31ff.; 2 Cor. 5:21ff.

2. Cited in Dwight Wilson, *Armageddon Now!* (Grand Rapids: Baker, 1977), p. 37.

of the world, no wonder the nights get so dark! And what is the point of attempting to scatter the darkness if the darkness is a sign of the Lord's soon return? As Hal Lindsey has told tens of millions of Christians in our era: "We should be living like persons who don't expect to be around much longer" because Jesus is coming soon to snatch us "out of the world as it plunges toward judgment."[3] Why should Christians engage themselves in slow, long-term cultural reconstruction if we are soon to vanish from the earth?

Too often pessimistic eschatology is demanded by a wrong approach to Revelation, which sees the Beast as looming in our future. And a wrong approach to Revelation is often encouraged by a misconception of Revelation's date. But Revelation is clear: Its prophecies were to occur soon after John wrote, not millennia later (Rev. 1:1, 3, 19; 3:10; 22:6ff). The events symbolized in Revelation were earth shaking, but they are now past events.

Summary of Evidence for the Beast

Perhaps the most important evidence that begins drawing the line to the Roman Empire (generically considered) and Nero Caesar (specifically considered) is that of the *relevancy* of the Beast. John clearly and emphatically expected the events of Revelation — a number of which were associated with the Beast — to begin coming to pass "soon" (Rev. 1:1, 3; 22:6ff).[4] Such an anticipation clears away 99.9% of the modern suggestions regarding the identity of the Beast, suggestions demanding hundreds and thousands of years for accomplishment.

But this evidence alone, of course, does not demand Nero Caesar as the specific reference, although it would strongly indicate the Roman Empire as the generic reference. When we calculate the *number 666* and discover that it adds up to the Jewish

---

3. Hal Lindsey, *The Late Great Planet Earth* (Grand Rapids: Zondervan, 1970), pp. 145, 186.

4. See Chapter 2.

spelling of Nero's name, however, we are getting somewhere.[5] And when the *character* of the Beast is matched to Nero's infamous conduct, we become more confident still.[6] Nero was clearly a beastly character possessed with a horrendously sinful will to evil and great power to unleash his base desires.

In addition we noted the remarkable correspondence between the *war* of the Beast with the persecution of Christians by Nero.[7] This correspondence involved even the detail of time equations: 42 months, according to Revelation; November, A.D. 64, to June, A.D. 68, according to history. Filling out the evil character of the Nero-Beast was Nero's encouragement of *emperor worship*, which John alluded to in Revelation 13.[8] And then to top it all off, one of the most unusual features of the Beast — his death and "resurrection" — finds remarkable fulfillment in the events of the A.D. 60s after the death of Nero. Rome was buckling to its knees, fainting to its death, with the demise of its sixth head, Nero, in the Civil Wars of A.D. 68-69. But the empire — the Beast generically considered — was revived under Vespasian, to the "wonder" of the world.[9]

The Beast is clearly the Roman Empire, particularly expressed in its most evil head, Nero Caesar. This Beast has lived and died, according to the infallible prophecy of Scripture. But, of course, all of this evidence for the identity of the Beast depends on the date of Revelation's composition. For if it were written almost 30 years after his death, the whole theory would fail. So, I presented the case for the early date of Revelation in the pre-A.D. 70 era.

Summary of Evidence for Revelation's Date

The evidences for Revelation's early-dating, during the reign of Nero Caesar, are multiple, varied, clear, and compelling. In

---

5. See Chapter 3.
6. See Chapter 4.
7. See Chapter 5.
8. See Chapter 6.
9. See Chapter 7.

addition to all the positive evidence for Nero Caesar as the Beast (which itself is indicative of a pre-A.D. 70 composition), there are additional compelling evidences.

The Evidence from Within Revelation

The thematic evidence in Revelation 1:7:[10] Revelation insists upon the soon coming of certain events that would indicate a judgment-coming of Christ. That judgment-coming necessarily involved the destruction of the temple and the punishment of the first-century Jews, the crucifiers of Christ. This had to be the final destruction of the temple in Jerusalem and the devastation that accompanied it in A.D. 67-70. Jesus clearly prophesied it (Matt. 24; Mark 13; Luke 21), and so did John (Revelation).

The political evidence:[11] There is a clear statement of Revelation that the sixth emperor of Rome was living at the very time John wrote (Rev. 17:9, 10). Historically, Nero was the sixth emperor of Rome, which corresponds perfectly with our interpretation of the Beast. In addition, he was followed by a seventh ruler who reigned but a short while: Galba (Rev. 17:11). These political statements regarding imperial Rome's rule are objectively datable.

The architectural evidence:[12] One of the great examples of architecture of the ancient world was still standing as John wrote – the temple in Jerusalem (Rev. 11:1, 2). The destruction of this structure is datable from both documentary and archaeological evidence. It was destroyed, never to built again, in August, A.D. 70, by General Titus of the Roman Empire.

The ecclesiastical evidence:[13] The Christianity in John's day was at an early stage of development. Christians were obviously still intermingling with the Jews and presenting themselves as "true Jews" (Rev. 2:9; 3:9). Christianity is portrayed as the fullness of the Twelve Tribes of Israel (Rev. 7:4). The language of Revela-

---

10. See Chapter 9.
11. See Chapter 10.
12. See Chapter 11.
13. See Chapter 12.

tion has a strongly Hebraic cast.

The Evidence from Church History

Despite much of current opinion, neither is the evidence from church tradition capable of overthrowing the self-witness evidence. The strongest witnesses for Revelation's late-dating are fraught with interpretive difficulties (Irenaeus) or are ambiguous (Clement of Alexandria and Origen). Or they are internally contradictory (Eusebius). Another involves improbable actions (Victorinus). Still another seems to confuse both traditions into one (Jerome).[14]

Although the early date view prefers Revelation's own self-witness, it easily discovers evidence from tradition, as well. One late-date witness even has an observation that demands all revelation ceased under Nero (Clement of Alexandria). The contradiction in one witness provides a statement supportive of the early date (Eusebius).

But beyond these we find clear statements demanding a pre-A.D. 70 date for Revelation in a number of early witnesses (*Muratorian Canon*, Epiphanius, Syriac writers, Arethas). In addition there are strong implications of an early date in still others (Papias, *Shepherd of Hermas*, Tertullian).[15]

A Plea for a Hearing of the Evidence

I do hope from this inquiry that thinking Christians will reconsider the issues. At the very least I trust that any hasty dismissal of the identity of the Beast and the early date for Revelation, which I have proposed, will be pre-empted. Discussion of the matter of Revelation's date should not be closed with a "thus saith current opinion!"

Not all scholars hold to the futuristic identity of the Beast or the Domitianic date of Revelation. Nor is there anything approaching a unanimity of opinion in ancient church history in

---

14. See Chapter 14.
15. See Chapter 13.

either direction. Nor may we dismiss the self-witness of Revelation as obscure or inconsequential.

Regarding the date of Revelation, when even liberals are turning to reconsider the fallacy of the late date (e.g., C. C. Torrey, John A. T. Robinson, Rudolf Bultmann) and opting for the early date, orthodox Christians should take notice. Revelation was written *after* the initial outbreak of the Tribulation, for John was already enmeshed in it (Rev. 1:9). The Tribulation began with the Beast's "war against the saints" (Rev. 13), which started with the Neronic persecution in November, A.D. 64. Revelation *anticipates* the destruction of the Temple (August, A.D. 70) in Chapter 11, the death of Nero (June, A.D. 68) in Chapter 13, *and* the formal imperial engagement of the Jewish War (Spring, A.D. 67) in Chapters 6-7. Hence, Revelation was written sometime between November, A.D. 64 and Spring, A.D. 67 – probably in A.D. 65.

The evidence is there. It has always been there. We have simply been letting the blind lead the blind, causing both to fall into the ditch. Or should we say they both fall into the same old rut? For much of late-date advocacy is simply a rehearsing of time-worn but unconvincing arguments.

SCRIPTURE INDEX
(Prepared by Robert S. Nance)

189

GENERAL INDEX

Abaddon, 38.

"Abomination of desolation," 96.

"About to," (*See also*: Revelation — expectation), 22, 23.

Abraham, 91, 131, 136.

Abyss, 134, 173.

Actor, 18, 66.

Adam, 11.

Aggripina, 15.

Ahenobarbus, 14.

Ahenobarbus, Lucius (*See*: Nero).

Alexandria, 38, 140, 141, 149, 156.

Alphabet(s), 29-30.

Altar(s), 51, 58, 59, 62, 64, 66, 111, 120, 121, 123.

Animal(s) (*See also:* Beasts), xv, 17, 40, 46.

Angel(s), xxxv, 21, 22, 98, 134.
    interpretation by, 12, 105-106.

Antichrist, xii, xix, xx, xxii, xxxiv, 11, 45, 151, 153, 154, 155, 164, 172n.

Apocalypse (*See*: Revelation).

Apollo, 63, 64, 66.

Apollonius, 42, 158n.

Apologetic(s), 160.

Apostle(s), xv, xxxii, xxxvi, 49, 77, 86, 100, 109, 125, 135, 136, 141, 143, 144, 146, 150, 154, 156, 157, 162, 164.

Appian, 122.

Arabia, 42.

Aramaic, 38-39, 134.

Archaeology, 13, 31, 34, 58, 60, 118, 186.

Arena, 40, 41, 46.

Arethas, 146-147, 148, 18.

Armageddon, 4, 38, 95, 134.

Artist, 19, 63.

Ascension of Isaiah, 42n.

Asia, 60, 61, 62, 156, 179.

Asia Minor, 13, 37, 48, 54, 109, 168, 175, 176.
    Jewish population in, 38.

Assassinate, 82.

Astrology, 15.

"At hand" (*See also*: Revelation — expectation), 10, 23.

Athens, 63.

Augustine, 159, 172.

Augustus (emperor), 51, 62, 64, 104, 106, 107, 108, 162.
    name used as oath, 60.
    Nero as, 63, 64, 66.
    worship of, 59-61, 62, 64, 169.

Banishment (*See*: John the Apostle — banishment).

Barnabas, 116, 135.

Beast of Revelation, (*See also*: Nero), xi, xvii-xix, xxxii, xxxiv, 4, 5, 11, 12, 46, 48, 75, 81, 106, 155, 168, 173, 186, 188.
    appearance, 5.
    authority, 40, 57.
    character, 10, 14, 33, 40-46, 185.
    death, 5, 68-69, 73-75, 77.
    dual nature, 11.
    generic referent, 11, 12-14, 19, 67,

197